Jane Gleeson-White has worked as a bookseller, writer, book editor and reviewer in Sydney and London since completing her degrees in English and Australian literature, and economics, at the University of Sydney in 1987. She also worked as a student at the Peggy Guggenheim Museum in Venice, where she studied Byzantine, early Renaissance and modern art. She currently lives in Sydney.

CLASSICS

62 GREAT BOOKS

from the *Iliad* to *Midnight's Children*

Jane Gleeson-White

VINTAGE BOOKS
Australia

A Vintage Book
Published by Random House Australia Pty Ltd
Level 3, 100 Pacific Highway, North Sydney, NSW 2060
www.randomhouse.com.au

Sydney   New York   Toronto
London   Auckland   Johannesburg

First published by Knopf in 2005

This Vintage edition first published in 2007

National Library of Australia
Cataloguing-in-Publication Entry

Gleeson-White, Jane.
Classics: 62 great books from the Iliad to Midnight's Children.

ISBN 978 1 74166 473 7.

1. Books and reading. 2. Literature – Stories, plots, etc.
3. Best books. I. Title.

011.73

Cover and internal design by Gayna Murphy, Greendot Design
Typeset in Kaatskill by Midland Typesetters, Australia
Printed and bound by The SOS Print + Media Group

10 9 8 7 6 5 4 3 2

For my parents, Judith and Michael Gleeson-White

In memory of my cousin Matthew Street, 1960–1980

'I THINK THAT IF WE LOSE A SENSE OF THE PAST, WE'VE LOST MUCH MORE THAN WE CAN EVER CALCULATE.'
Norman Mailer

'AS ALWAYS WITH THE GREATEST WORKS, THE NOVEL IS SO MANY-SIDED THAT OVER TIME IT MIRRORS BACK THE SHIFTING CONCERNS OF THOSE WHO READ IT, AND THAT IS THE DEFINITION OF A CLASSIC.'
Carl F. Hovde on Moby-Dick

CONTENTS

✧

Introduction

✍

Classic: *adj.* of the first class; of acknowledged excellence; remarkably typical; outstandingly important.
Oxford English Dictionary

Mark Twain defined a literary classic as 'something that everybody wants to have read and nobody wants to read', a definition that is probably as true today as it was in the nineteenth century. And yet in our uncertain modern times, not only do books that are considered classics fill the shelves of many bookshops, but these books still exert a powerful influence on contemporary culture. Some do so in obvious ways, such as the film and television adaptations of the works of Homer, Jane Austen, George Eliot, Charles Dickens and Henry James; others in less obvious ways, through their enduring impact on fellow writers, artists and musicians.

Until the end of the twentieth century, many of these books were taught in schools and universities as part of a commonly recognised list of great literature known as 'the canon'. This canon has quite rightly been challenged by postmodern critics, essentially because it excluded writers from beyond the prevailing culture, especially women and non-European writers, and it is no longer taught. Nonetheless, the books the canon once embraced, and other books now considered classics, are invaluable for their insights into the human heart and soul; for their wisdom and humour; for their worth as records of social, political and economic life in other times and places; and for their extraordinary mastery of language – so extraordinary, in fact, that each book serves as a storehouse of literary quality, of style, rhythm, vocabulary, and ingenuity of expression. These books are important because they are among the best books ever published, whether in our times or in their own – and it's worth remembering that many of these novels were the bestsellers of their day, particularly those published before the twentieth century, before technological advances made it economically feasible to print small quantities of books for specialised markets.

Classics reintroduces three epic poems that mark the beginning of the Western literary tradition – Homer's *Iliad* and *Odyssey*, and Virgil's *Aeneid* – and a number of classic novels once considered part of the canon, such as Cervantes' *Don Quixote* (usually thought of as the first novel), Charlotte Brontë's *Jane Eyre*, Tolstoy's *War and Peace*, Dickens's *Bleak House*, Melville's *Moby-Dick* and Flaubert's *Madame Bovary*; as well as some great novels that have more recently (post-canon) been deemed to be classics, such as Kate Chopin's *The Awakening*, Elizabeth Smart's *By Grand Central Station I Sat Down and Wept*, Mikhail Bulgakov's *The Master and Margarita*, Ralph Ellison's *Invisible Man* and Jack Kerouac's *On the Road*. And it covers books published in the last few decades that I believe might one day be considered classics – Günter Grass's *The Tin Drum*, for example, and Toni Morrison's *Beloved*, Cormac McCarthy's *Blood Meridian*, Don DeLillo's *Underworld*, J.M. Coetzee's *Waiting for the Barbarians* and Salman Rushdie's *Midnight's Children*.

Having grown up in a bookish family, where stories and books and book-talk were more important, almost, than anything else, I find books as familiar as friends, and I love them as passionately and as particularly, for their myriad strengths and weaknesses, as I do my friends. They are in my blood. My paternal grandmother, born May Annie Bloom in London, lived and breathed books and stories all her feisty ninety-seven years. Her endless tales about her epic romance with my grandfather, Eric Gleeson-White – a romance that began when they eloped during their lunch break from the Bank of England in London and celebrated with a cup of Bovril in Baker Street Station – were entwined with books. Eric, who came from a literary household (his father, Joseph Gleeson White, was the first editor of the fin-de-siècle art magazine *The Studio*), read Robert Browning to my grandmother during their courtship and engraved her wedding ring with words from one of Browning's poems. Later, when they were parents of young children and living outside London, he read her the complete works of Thomas Hardy while she ironed, folded clothes and darned socks. Still later, when they had sailed to a new world in Potts Point, Sydney, he read her the novels of Patrick White.

From this literary heritage I have learned to value each individual book, rather than theories about books, and for this reason *Classics* focuses on a number of individual texts rather than on authors or movements or a general overview of literary history. As far as possible, I want each author's words to speak clearly, to be revealed beneath the many readings that have been layered over them across the years, in some cases across the centuries. So my task has been like a literary excavation: I have aimed to strip away as much as possible our preconceptions about these books and the reputations that have grown up around them. These preconceptions and reputations are often daunting; and many have loomed large over our landscape, to an intimidating degree.

Because I think of books as living entities that change over time and as their readers change, and given that books are written by people in particular historic times, I have placed each book in the time of its birth, each author in their historic moment. I have included details of the author's life, their trials and tribulations and joys. One of the most striking things for me in this regard was to discover the enormity of each author's call to write and the extent of their struggle through poverty, loneliness, war, heartbreak, despair or alienation, sometimes madness, to continue to write. That alone was inspiring. Of Homer we know little, but from then on, since the beginning of written time, the vocation of writing seems to have called only lunatics willing to forego most of life's comforts in service to their art. I have also included details of the notable political, social and economic events of the writer's day, to provide the context in which they were working and in which their books were formed. In some cases, such as the succession of rulers of seventeenth-century England or nineteenth-century France, the history was too complex to include in the body of the text, so I have provided potted histories in boxed sections between the entries.

From among the vast number of possible classics, I have chosen those that I love, for one reason or another (for their characters, story, language, wisdom, humour), or that have remained with me, bothered me in some way. There can be no other criteria for selecting books to write about — one must be moved deeply in some way to be able to rise to the occasion. The number of classics chosen, sixty-two, derives from the total of epic poems and novels I considered it possible to re-read, engage with and write about in a year. It amounts to one book per week of that year, with a further ten thrown in for good measure. In making my selection I have also felt the need to include books from a range of countries. The one anomaly in the book as I see it is the inclusion of three Australian writers among the sixty-two, a choice that quite deliberately reflects my Australian bias — my desire that these three Australian voices should be heard more often — rather than my sense that these three books tower over others that might have been included in their place. And I have excluded the great literary traditions of Asia and the Middle East, about which I know too little.

The choosing was the most challenging part of the writing. There were some novels I felt had to be included — *Don Quixote*,

Jane Eyre, Wuthering Heights, Madame Bovary, War and Peace, The Great Gatsby, The Catcher in the Rye — because I thought readers would expect them. They are well known, widely accepted classics. And then I wanted to include some unexpected books by authors universally considered to be writers of classics. These books are often the author's less read works, but they are books that happen to have struck a chord with me, books that I prefer over the author's more widely known novels, even if they might be less finished, polished, or perfect. Among these are Jane Austen's *Persuasion*, George Eliot's *Daniel Deronda*, Fydor Dostoyevsky's *The Idiot*, Hermann Hesse's *Narcissus and Goldmund*, Henry Handel Richardson's *Maurice Guest*, Christina Stead's *For Love Alone* and Truman Capote's *The Grass Harp*.

And I have included some books by authors who might be unexpected by Australian readers, because they are not widely known here: Sigrid Undset's *Kristin Lavransdatter*, Ralph Ellison's *Invisible Man*, Christa Wolf's *The Quest for Christa T.* and Marie Cardinal's *The Words to Say It*. I have left out some great writers, including Marcel Proust, because, in his case, I have yet to read *Remembrance of Things Past* — or *In Search of Lost Time*, as Malcolm Knox, among others, refers to it. (This is the book I intend to read next.) Others, like Emile Zola, Saul Bellow and Thomas Pynchon, I have not included because at the time I read their books, perhaps when I was too young, they didn't seize my imagination and live with me in the way that other books have. I will read them again one day.

In order to provide some balance and to reflect my belief that greatness is a perception of individual readers, rather than something that can be objectively measured, I have invited distinguished writers and readers to contribute a list of up to ten of their favourite classic novels. Some responded with a note on one author or novel only, as the American writer Don DeLillo, singer-songwriter Paul Kelly and Australian writer Andrew McGahan all chose to do. Other respondents provided a list of titles – such as South African writer J.M. Coetzee, London-based biographer Brenda Maddox, New Zealand writer Elizabeth Knox, Australian writers Louis Nowra, Mandy Sayer and Tim Winton, and Professor Margaret Harris from the University of Sydney. And many others provided lists with passionate reasons for their choices, like director of the Art Gallery of New South Wales, Edmund Capon, and Australian writers Christos Tsiolkas, Luke Davies, Nikki Gemmell, Sophie Cunningham and Georgia Blain. Another local writer, James Bradley, provided a lucid contribution explaining why he was unable to contribute a list. The thoughts of all these people are included in boxed sections throughout *Classics*.

The enthusiasm with which these writers and readers responded to my request for their favourite classics, and the agony with which many of them deliberated over their lists, give the lie to Mark Twain's definition of a classic as being something that 'nobody wants to read'. In a typically thoughtful and elegant essay, 'Why Read the Classics?', Cuban-born Italian writer Italo Calvino gives fourteen definitions of a classic. Among his many luminous observations is one that strikes to the heart of this book: a classic book must establish a personal relationship with a reader and we must be drawn to it through love, not duty. We all have our own favourite classics, books about which we are passionate, that become 'our' books and help us to define who we are. This book is an introduction to some of my favourite classics, written in the hope that it will inspire you to seek out and discover your own classic books for life.

Jane Gleeson-White
Sydney, July 2005

1 . *Iliad*

by

HOMER

(EIGHTH CENTURY BCE)

⚬

HOMER IS AN OBVIOUS PLACE to start a discussion of classic literature because his two epic poems, the *Iliad* and the *Odyssey*, form the cornerstone of the almost 3000-year Western literary tradition. The ancient Greeks revered Homer. Even for them, in the fifth century BCE, Homer was legendary — widely known for his remarkable epics and yet a man already lost to history, for even the ancient Greeks knew nothing of his life. After the fall of Troy, which coincided with the fall of Mycenaean Greece between 1200 and 1100 BCE, there was a dark age in Greece about which we know almost nothing. Unfortunately for historians, Homer lived towards the end of this period, just before the dawning of Greece's golden age, so all we know of Homer is in the realm of probability: he probably lived in the eighth century BCE; he was probably an oral poet and master of improvisation; he may or may not have been the sole author of the *Iliad* and the *Odyssey*; he was probably literate and may have written down parts of the poems (writing came into use in the Greek world in the mid eighth century BCE).

Iliad means 'a poem about Ilium [Troy]', but the *Iliad* is about much more than Troy. It is one of the most devastating war stories of all time and centres on the god-like fury of the Greek warrior Achilles. The poem opens in the tenth and final year of the Greek siege of Troy, when Achilles has been slighted by Agamemnon, the commander of the Greek armies, and refuses to fight. The *Iliad* recounts the events that lead inexorably to the fatal clash between the two mightiest warriors – Achilles, son of the goddess Thetis, and Hector, eldest son of King Priam of Troy.

The *Iliad* has not only inspired Greek dramatists, Latin poets, Renaissance painters and twenty-first century Hollywood, its numerous translations by poets and scholars are in themselves great works of literature – for example, the eighteenth-century poet Alexander Pope's translation. The most recent translation of the *Iliad* to be published, in 1990, was by the Academy Award–winning American classics scholar Robert Fagles. Fagles's acclaimed verse translation brings Homer's narrative, his heroes and gods, irresistibly to life in modern English. His version is not only compelling, it is immensely readable.

'Rage – Goddess, sing the rage of Peleus' son Achilles, / murderous, doomed, that cost the Achaeans countless losses, / hurling down to the House of Death so many sturdy souls . . .' So begins Fagles's translation, and immediately we are plunged into Homer's energetic narrative. Greece's greatest warrior, Achilles, sits idly in his tent, too enraged by Agamemnon to put on his armour and fight the Trojans. Agamemnon has stolen one of Achilles's war trophies, the young girl Briseis. In furious defiance, Achilles refuses to join the battle and the Greek armies are being fought back across the battlefield by the Trojans, from outside the city of Troy to the beaches where their ships are moored. Agamemnon has led a coalition fleet of allied forces from Greece across the Aegean Sea to war against Troy, ostensibly to demand the return of his brother's wife, Helen, from the beautiful Trojan prince Paris, Hector's younger brother.

The interrelationships of the gods and mortals form a complex web in the *Iliad* and are the basis of its action. Many years before the *Iliad* opens, Helen was famously abducted by Paris and taken to Troy, an act which began the earthly war. But there is also a war being fought among the gods and goddesses on Olympus, sparked by the equally famous Judgement of Paris. When no god dared to judge which goddess – Zeus's wife, Hera; Athena, Goddess of Wisdom; or Aphrodite, Goddess of Love and Beauty – was the most beautiful, Paris was called to Olympus from Troy to decide. Paris chose Aphrodite, but only after she'd bribed him by promising to give him the most beautiful woman on earth, Helen. (Aphrodite completely disregarded the fact that Helen was already married, to the King of Sparta, Agamemnon's brother, Menelaus.) The two spurned goddesses, Hera and Athena, become the sworn enemies of Aphrodite's beloved Troy. They help the invading Greek warriors, flying down from Olympus to turn the course of the battle in favour of the Greeks. Aphrodite and her lover Ares, God of War, assisted by her father, Zeus, and his brother Poseidon, fight for the survival of Troy.

The story of the Trojan horse — the ruse designed by Odysseus to transport the Greek soldiers concealed in a wooden horse beyond the walls of Troy to destroy it — is well known, but Homer's *Iliad* ends before this fated moment, which is recalled in the *Odyssey*. The *Iliad* focuses on the clash of the Achaean and Trojan armies on the beaches and fields beyond the gates of Troy. This ancient city was long believed to be mythical, but in the nineteenth century a German schoolboy, Heinrich Schliemann, refused to believe the Trojan War could be a figment of Homer's imagination. Schliemann did eventually discover the site of ancient Troy in 1871, not far from Gallipoli, the scene of another memorable battle. Today, Schliemann is condemned in Turkey for having smuggled Trojan treasures out of the country and into Germany in 1873. When the Russian army invaded Berlin at the end of the Second World War, the treasure was uncovered and flown to Moscow in 1945. Sixty years later, the Turkish government is still trying to reclaim its treasure from the Pushkin Museum in Moscow.

Homer's Trojan epic is notable for its powerful dramatisation of character and its structure — it opens in the middle of the action and recaps the story of the Trojan War as it progresses. This technique has been widely adopted by writers, including the fifth-century Greek dramatist Sophocles in his tragedy *Antigone*, although David Benioff, the screenwriter for the film *Troy* (2004) based on the *Iliad*, decided to unravel the story to start at the beginning of the war, in order to give the film a more conventional Hollywood linear narrative.

In an age in which most people's experience of war is edited and viewed on a small screen, it is sobering to read Homer's vivid, hyper-real accounts of the battlefield, of the madness and terror of war, as well as its terrible beauty and the noble qualities, such as courage and honour in the face of death, it can call forth from the human spirit. The *Iliad* unsentimentally accepts violence as a permanent feature in our lives. In the words of French philosopher Simone Weil, written in 1939, 'those who can see that force, today as in the past, is at the center of all human history, find in the *Iliad* its most beautiful, its purest mirror.'

2. *Odyssey*

by

HOMER

(EIGHTH CENTURY BCE)

∞

THE TITLE 'THE *ODYSSEY*' is taken from the Greek word *Odusseia*, which means 'the story of Odysseus'. Odysseus is a Greek warrior famous for his diplomatic skills, silken tongue and cunning. It is Odysseus who conceives the idea of the Trojan horse, using ingenuity, not brute force, to storm the walls of Troy and conquer the city after ten long years. The *Odyssey* is the epic tale of Odysseus on his long voyage home from the Trojan War. It is also the story of his son, Telemachus, and his search for his lost father; and of his wife, Penelope, who waits faithfully for her husband to return to Ithaca.

The American poet Wallace Stevens observed that together the *Iliad* and the *Odyssey* demonstrate 'war's miracle begetting that of peace'. Yet, despite the fact that the *Odyssey* takes place after the war's end, much of the energy of its verse comes in scenes of violence: Odysseus recalling the closing moments of the Trojan War; meeting the war's heroes in the Land of the Dead; his battles to survive on his way home; the deaths of his men; and the 'blood wedding' that is the brutal final battle against Penelope's suitors. Although scholars have questioned whether the *Odyssey* was composed by the same poet as the *Iliad*, it is generally accepted that Homer produced the two poems and that the *Odyssey* was composed after the *Iliad*. Throughout the classical age of Greece, Homer's two epics formed the basis of Greek education. In the era of imperial Rome, however, the *Odyssey* was seen as threatening to the Roman autocracy and, in 35 CE, the Roman emperor Caligula tried to suppress it because of its Greek ideals of freedom.

Robert Fagles's beautiful translation of the *Odyssey* was published in 1996. It opens: 'Sing to me of the man, Muse, the man of twists and turns/driven time and again off course, once he had plundered/the hallowed heights of Troy.' But unlike the *Iliad*, where the poet requests his Muse to begin her song at the moment when Agamemnon and Achilles 'first broke and clashed', in the *Odyssey* the Muse is asked to 'start from where you will'. And so the Muse begins her tale with a meeting of the gods. We learn that all those Greeks who survived the Trojan War are safe at home, 'But one man alone . . ./his heart set on his wife and his return – Calypso,/the bewitching nymph, the lustrous goddess, held him back,/deep in her arching caverns, craving him for a husband.' The gods – all except for Poseidon, who is still raging against Odysseus because he blinded his son the Cyclops Polyphemus – have taken pity on Odysseus, entrapped by the goddess Calypso. But, fortunately for Odysseus, Poseidon is away visiting the

Ethiopians. After Zeus has complained about the shamelessness of mortals ('the way these mortals blame the gods') and tells the tragic story of Agamemnon's fate at the hands of his wife's lover, Athena takes advantage of Poseidon's absence to persuade Zeus to free Odysseus from Calypso's grasp. Hermes is sent to instruct Calypso to release Odysseus, while Athena flies off to rouse Telemachus, to 'inspire his heart with courage' to go in quest of his father.

And so Odysseus's tale is launched with the story of his son, Telemachus, who voyages out from Ithaca to learn news of his father from the warriors Nestor and Menelaus, both home from Troy and living peacefully. As Telemachus travels away from home, Odysseus, free at last from Calypso, embarks again on his long voyage home to Ithaca. Odysseus faces many trials, not only on his homeward journey but also on his return to Ithaca, where his son, Telemachus, and wife, Penelope, have all but given up hope for him after his twenty-year absence. The *Odyssey* is also the story of Telemachus's coming of age, the loyalty of Penelope, and her skill in managing and stalling the many suitors for her hand in marriage who have assembled in the halls of her palace after her husband's long absence and suspected death. It is the story of married love and loyalty, and the primacy of family.

The stories of Odysseus's adventures and the characters he meets along the way are well known: the enchanting goddess Calypso, the nymph Circe (who turns men into pigs), Odysseus's visit to the Land of the Dead, the Sirens with their haunting song, the land of lotus eaters, the Cyclops, and the monsters Charybdis and Scylla. The *Odyssey* also recalls fragments of the tale of the Trojan War, including the story of the Trojan horse, the rape of

Trojan princess Cassandra in Athena's temple (to which desecration Athena responds by scattering the Greek fleet following its victorious departure from Troy), the tales of the great Greek warriors Nestor and Menelaus, as well as the fates of their leader Agamemnon and mightiest warrior Achilles, both of whom now dwell in the Land of the Dead.

These stories have inspired centuries of poets, dramatists, novelists, artists and musicians, so that, like the *Iliad*, the energy of the *Odyssey* lives on not only in the original poem but in the work of others. The Greek dramatist Aeschylus used the story Zeus alludes to in his complaint to the gods about mortals (which opens the *Odyssey*) as the basis of one of his greatest tragic cycles, the *Oresteia*. These three plays tell the story of Agamemnon's return from Troy, his murder by his wife Clytemnestra and her lover, and Orestes's eventual return from exile to plot the murder of his mother (Clytemnestra) with his sister Electra, to avenge the murder of their father. In light of the male-dominated Western literary tradition, it is interesting to note that the goddess protector of Odysseus, Athena, later casts the deciding vote in the council organised by Apollo to judge the guilt of Orestes, following his murder of his mother. Athena finds in favour of Orestes, effectively dismissing the central role of mothers in relation to their children and sanctifying father right over mother right, saying: 'In heart, as birth, a father's child alone. Thus will I not too heinously regard a woman's death who did her husband slay.' Athena, the goddess born from the head of her father, Zeus, prevails.

Homer's structural technique in the *Odyssey* — that of opening his tale away from the centre of action, focusing on Telemachus before circling back to Odysseus, then cutting between Telemachus and Odysseus before son and father finally meet up on the shores of Ithaca — has been adopted by dramatists and writers from James Joyce (*Ulysses* opens with the 'son' Stephen Dedalus) to Quentin Tarantino (*Pulp Fiction*). One of the greatest novels of the twentieth century, Joyce's *Ulysses*, is famously based on the *Odyssey*, as is Christina Stead's novel *For Love Alone*. The Coen brothers' film *O Brother, Where Art Thou?* (2000) — starring George Clooney as Ulysses Everett McGill, who is divorced from his wife, Penny — also draws on the *Odyssey*. Homer's story of the wanderings of Odysseus so captures the essence of a long and tumultuous voyage that its title, *Odyssey*, now means 'a long series of wanderings, a long adventurous journey' (Oxford English Dictionary), and has been used by artists from Stanley Kubrick (*2001: A Space Odyssey* (1968)) to Australian musicians Powderfinger (*Odyssey Number Five* (2000)) to evoke such a momentous journey.

3 . *Aeneid*
by
VIRGIL
(7 0 – 1 9 B C E)

⁊

THE EARLIEST ROMAN LITERATURE was made up of Latin translations of Homer's *Odyssey*, and Latin writing continued to be modelled on Greek literature until Christian times. One of Rome's greatest and most loved poets was Publius Vergilius Maro, commonly known as Virgil, considered by many to be 'the father' of Western literature. Virgil's epic poem the *Aeneid* tells the story of Aeneas, a Trojan warrior mentioned in Homer's *Iliad*. Virgil recounts the travels of Aeneas following his escape with a band of Trojans from the burning walls of Troy, after its sack by the Greek armies, and, in so doing, tells the story of the founding of Rome. Virgil, born during an era of great political turmoil, wrote the *Aeneid* in the first years of the new empire of Rome and through his epic poem gave his beloved Rome a glorious history, connecting it to Homer's legendary city of Troy.

Born in 70 BCE, Virgil was a shy country boy who grew up on his parents' farm in the north of Italy, and at sixteen moved to Rome to study rhetoric and philosophy. Virgil lived through civil war and witnessed the transformation of republican Rome into the Roman Empire, a process begun by Julius Caesar and completed by his grand-nephew Octavian, who became Augustus Caesar. Virgil was in Rome when Julius Caesar crossed the Rubicon in 49 BCE — an act of treason — to march on the city with his army. Five years later, Caesar's assassination on the floor of the Senate exploded in civil war, which ended only when Octavian defeated Antony and Cleopatra off western Greece in 31 BCE. Octavian's victory marked the end of Rome's republican government and the beginning of the Roman Empire, and, in 27 BCE, Octavian became Augustus Caesar, the first emperor of Rome. Augustus skilfully adapted the great republican traditions of Rome and its constitutional forms to suit his own autocratic rule, bringing peace to the Mediterranean after a century of violent upheaval. Virgil's most famous poem, the *Aeneid*, celebrates the new age of Augustus and recalls the lost origins of Rome in ancient Troy.

This history of war and peace informs the *Aeneid*, to which Virgil devoted the last eleven years of his life. Following the publication of his first two works, the *Eclogues* (37 BCE) and *Georgics* (30 BCE), Virgil's growing fame brought him into contact with some of the most powerful men in Rome, including the patron Maecenas and Augustus himself. It was at the suggestion of Augustus — and inspired by his own love of Italy and sense of Rome's destiny as a ruler of nations — that Virgil spent his last years working on this patriotic poem about the founding of Rome.

Virgil died in 19 BCE before completing the *Aeneid*, but, against Virgil's express wishes, Augustus ordered it to be published. It is not hard to see why Augustus rushed the *Aeneid* into print, given that it associates Rome with the heroic age of Greece and draws on legends from Homer and from Greek tragedy.

In C. Day Lewis's translation, the *Aeneid* opens: 'Arms, and the man I sing, who forc'd by fate,/And haughty Juno's unrelenting hate,/Expell'd and exil'd, left the Trojan shore./Long labours, both by sea and land he bore.' This is the essence of Aeneas's story, and these long labours lead him to his fated founding of Rome. Following the destruction of Troy by the Greeks, Venus (the Roman Aphrodite) tells her son Aeneas to flee his native land with the surviving Trojans in order to fulfil his great destiny – to found a city in Italy greater than Troy. As with Odysseus's journey from Troy to Ithaca, Aeneas's journey from Troy to Italy is prolonged by the intervention of the gods and he has many adventures along the way. And as in Homer's epics, in the *Aeneid* another battle rages in the heavens, between Juno (the Roman Hera), wife of Jupiter (the Roman Zeus), and Venus, patroness of the Trojans. Because of her love for Dido, queen of Carthage, and her people, Juno tricks Aeneas into marrying Dido, hoping that he will stay in Africa and build his glorious empire in Carthage with Dido. Venus, determined that her son will fulfil his noble destiny in Italy not Carthage, undermines Juno's plot. The union of Dido and Aeneas ends tragically in the famous Book Four of the poem.

In this fourth book, Aeneas and his fleet of ships are swept to northern Africa by his enemy Juno, who plots to bring him to her beloved Carthage to meet and fall in love with one of her favourite mortals, Dido. The passionate affair of Dido and Aeneas is one of the most tragic love stories in all of literature. Aeneas, urged by his mother, Venus, is forced to betray the calling of his heart for an apparently greater duty, and abandons Dido to fulfil his fated destiny in Italy. Mad with grief, the devastated Dido commits suicide.

Like Odysseus, Aeneas must visit the underworld before he can complete his journey. Here, he meets his father, Anchises, who foretells the glorious future of Rome up to the age of Julius Caesar and Augustus (thereby allowing Virgil to celebrate in his poem the reign of Augustus, who Virgil was convinced would found another golden age equivalent to the legendary Golden Age of antiquity). Once on Italian soil, Aeneas must face the mighty Italian warrior Turnus, competing with him for the hand of the local princess, Livinia. Despite the omens and prophecies that have foretold the coming of the Trojans and the marriage of the great Trojan leader to a local Italian princess, the noble, loyal, impassioned warrior Turnus refuses to the death to give in to the invading newcomers and a bloody battle ensues.

Virgil's rural upbringing is apparent in the poignant metaphors of the *Aeneid*, taken from the natural world. When he describes the decapitation of a young Trojan, Virgil likens him to a flower:

> the blood ran down
> His beautiful limbs, and his neck dropped feebly onto
> one shoulder.
> So, when its stalk is cut by the ploughshare, a shining
> flower

Grows limp and dies, or poppies droop down their heads
  upon
The languid stems when the weight of the shower is too
  much for them.

He calls a funeral bier a 'country bed', and likens the lifeless body it cradles to 'a flower plucked by a girl's fingers — a gentle violet, perhaps, or a fainting hyacinth'. This delicacy of Virgil's imagery conveys a tenderness and sorrow that is rarely present in Homer, and it is perhaps for this reason that Virgil was so revered by many of the later Christian poets and writers. Virgil's influence on Christian Europe was most famously expressed by Dante, who chose Virgil as his guide through the *Inferno*, and the *Aeneid* as the model for his own epic poem, *Divine Comedy*.

Such was Virgil's renown throughout the Roman world that the *Aeneid* came to be seen as a source of wisdom and was even used as a prophetic tool. The Roman emperor Hadrian was said to have divined the future using the *Aeneid*. Known as *Sortes Vergilianae* (the lots of Virgil), the random consultation of the *Aeneid* for answers to a stated question became a popular method of divination for both pagans and Christians, in much the same way as yarrow sticks are thrown to consult the *I Ching*.

The English poet John Dryden translated the *Aeneid* in 1697 and in his introduction drew on the parallels between Virgil's story and England's 'moral and political' confusion following the experience of civil war and the revolution of 1688. Dryden's translation was the standard text of the *Aeneid* for many years. Among modern translations, David West's prose translation is excellent;

for those who prefer the rhythms of poetry, the 1956 verse translation by poet C. Day Lewis (father of actor Daniel Day-Lewis) is rich and engaging. A new translation of the *Aeneid* by Robert Fagles was published in 2006. Drawing on the poetic voices of W.B. Yeats, T.S. Eliot, Derek Walcott and Robert Frost, Fagles has rendered Virgil into modern English. His powerful translation of this epic tale of empire is energetic, vibrant and lyrical – and timely in an age of new empire building.

From Virgil to Cervantes

Volume I of Miguel de Cervantes' *Don Quixote* was published in Spain in 1605 – some 1600 years after the publication of Virgil's *Aeneid* in Rome. Cervantes' Mediterranean world was radically different from Virgil's, transformed in large part by two new monotheistic religions that arose alongside Judaism: Christianity and Islam. The Roman Empire (the birth of which, under Augustus, Virgil witnessed) became exclusively Christian in 392 CE. Nearly two-and-a-half centuries later, in September 622, Islam came into being when Muhammad arrived in Medina from Mecca and requested his followers to build a temple.

Such was the power and wealth of the caliphs who adopted Islam that their armies rapidly conquered lands throughout the Mediterranean. Islam spread until it formed a volatile border around the southern Mediterranean and eastern Europe, effectively shaping Europe as the new centre of Christendom. In 711, the Muslims invaded Spain, where they held ever-diminishing territory for the next seven hundred years. The competing territorial fortunes of Islam and Christianity underwent a massive shift in the fifteenth century: in the east, the last vestige of the Roman Empire was conquered by Islam in 1453, when Constantinople fell to the Ottoman Turks; in the west, Catholicism vanquished Islam in Europe when Grenada, the last Muslim kingdom in Spain, was defeated in 1492. That same year, Christopher Columbus happened to be in Spain and witnessed the fall of Grenada. In the euphoria following the Spanish victory, Columbus secured its monarchy's patronage for his famous voyage across the Atlantic. The newly invigorated Spain sparked an explosion in western European exploration and the conquest of new worlds.

In the sixteenth century, the wealth generated from this expansion fed into the continuing intellectual and cultural blossoming of Renaissance Europe. At the dawn of the sixteenth century, in 1504, Michelangelo's 'David' was completed in Florence. Some fifty years earlier, around 1450, the invention of the printing press had begun to transform learning and literature by enabling the reproduction of thousands of identical copies of an original text. In 1543, the dawn of the scientific age was heralded by the publication of two revolutionary science books that would change the way people thought about the world: Nicholas Copernicus's *On the Revolution of Celestial Bodies* and Andreas Vesalius's *On the Structure of the Human Body*. Writing in the vernacular became widespread, encouraged by humanist thinkers such as Erasmus of Rotterdam (also known as Desiderius), and, in Spain, Cervantes helped to establish this popular new form.

4. Don Quixote
by
MIGUEL DE CERVANTES
(1547–1616)

≈

DON QUIXOTE IS CONSIDERED TO BE the world's first modern novel. It is still the most published and translated book in the world, after the Bible, and is still a bestseller four hundred years after its publication. Its story of a deranged, aging man setting out on a scrawny nag for a life of adventure with his pleasure-loving companion and trusty squire, Sancho Panza, is one of the best-known stories in the world. Don Quixote, determined to live by the chivalric codes he's read about in books yet completely oblivious to the changing world around him, comes to the rescue of damsels who are not in distress and terrorises the countryside in pursuit of wrongs to right. Perhaps no novel since has risen to such sustained comic heights as Miguel de Cervantes' great original, although so rich is *Don Quixote* that there is also much tragedy mixed in with its comedy.

Cervantes was over fifty when he wrote *Don Quixote*, which he probably conceived while in prison for financial misdemeanours. The first of the two volumes of *The Ingenious Hidalgo Don Quixote of La Mancha* appeared in January 1605 and created an immediate sensation. The adventures of Don Quixote (known as 'the Knight of the Sorrowful Countenance'), Sancho Panza and Don Quixote's horse Rozinante so captured the public's imagination that from the moment they appeared in print they were impersonated in parades and festivals from South America to Germany. *Don Quixote* was widely translated and published in English in 1612. Its popularity became so widespread that a counterfeit second volume by one Alonso Fernandez de Avellaneda appeared in 1614, before Cervantes could publish his own second volume in 1615. In Cervantes' Volume II, Don Quixote is aware of his own renown throughout the real world:

> so that, by numberless exploits becoming a christian hero,
> I am now celebrated in print through almost all the nations
> of the habitable globe. Thirty thousand copies of my
> renowned history are already in the hands of the public.

Cervantes was born in 1547, about twenty miles from Madrid. His family moved from town to town for his father's work as a barber-surgeon. Not much is known about his education, except that he was a voracious reader and was introduced to the work of Erasmus. His life can be seen in two distinct parts: a decade of high adventure, followed by years of financial difficulty as he struggled to make a living from writing while working as a government administrator. Cervantes spent his early adulthood as a soldier, joining the Spanish infantry in Naples and taking part in his first military action at the victorious Battle of Lepanto against the Turks near Corinth in 1571. He fought courageously and received three gunshot wounds, one of which destroyed his left hand. On his return voyage to Spain four years later, his ship was captured by Barbary pirates and Cervantes was sold into slavery in Algiers, which was the centre of Muslim trade in Christian slaves. He was held captive for five years, until 1580, when his family paid the ransom for his release. Cervantes based several episodes of *Don Quixote* on his time soldiering in Europe's war against the Turks and his captivity in Muslim hands.

Back in Spain, Cervantes found work hard to find and life expensive (Europe experienced its first inflation in the sixteenth century). He had a daughter, Isabella, with a married woman, then in 1584 married a young woman from La Mancha. With his first published book, *La Galatea* (1585), he discovered he could not make a living from writing and was forced to take a series of administrative posts, including one with the Spanish Armada (which he lost, following its destruction in 1588) and one collecting taxes. He continued to write, mostly for the stage, but it was not until the publication of *Don Quixote* that he had his first major literary success.

In the brilliant English translation by the eighteenth-century novelist Tobias Smollett, *Don Quixote* remains an exuberant, funny story. Written as a spoof of the tales of chivalry, it is filled with as many tall tales of romance, chance and coincidence as the comedies of Shakespeare (it was published the same year as Shakespeare's

King Lear and *Macbeth*). As Cervantes writes in his preface, his 'sole aim' in writing was 'to invalidate the authority, and ridicule the absurdity of those books of chivalry, which have, as it were, fascinated the eyes and judgment of the world, and in particular of the vulgar'.

The see-saw relationship between Don Quixote and Sancho Panza is wildly funny. Their preposterous friendship, characterised by great affection and intense frustration, is echoed in the twentieth century in couples from Samuel Beckett's Vladimir and Estragon in *Waiting for Godot* to the friends played by Jim Carrey and Jeff Daniels in the Farrelly brothers' film *Dumb and Dumber* (1994). Their rambling conversations are the source of much of the book's humour. Don Quixote's hold on reality is famously slippery – Carlos Fuentes describes his failure in practical matters as 'the most gloriously ludicrous in recorded history (perhaps it is only paralleled by the great clowns of the silent screen)' – which appals the earthy Sancho, who never ceases to be astonished by the extent of his friend's madness, yet loves him dearly in spite of it. Where Don Quixote clearly sees a 'yonder knight who rides this way, upon a dappled steed, with a golden helmet on his head', Sancho sees 'no other than a man upon a grey ass, like my own, with something that glitters on his head'. The thing that glitters happens to be no golden helmet but an upturned barber's bowl.

Cervantes was a great literary experimenter and the fictional world he creates in *Don Quixote* is complex. The novel's purported genesis is multi-layered. *Don Quixote* presents itself as the work of an Arab historian, Cide Hamete Benengeli, that has been translated into Spanish by a Moor and then edited by

Cervantes. The lines of truth and fiction are further blurred by
Cervantes when he appears in his own novel — one of his characters, the curate, says: 'that same Cervantes has been an intimate
friend of mine, these many years, and is, to my certain knowledge, more conversant with misfortunes than with poetry . . .'
And, as Woody Allen did with Zelig in his film *Zelig* (1983), in
which he superimposed the eponymous character (played by
Allen himself) onto footage of key moments of the twentieth
century, Cervantes places Don Quixote in real historical
moments with real people of his time, such as the notorious
robber Roque Guinart. Cervantes even includes the counterfeit
second volume of *Don Quixote* (written by the historical
Avellaneda) in his own Volume II, allowing his Don Quixote to
change his plans in order to distinguish himself from Avellaneda's
Don Quixote, 'so eager was [Don Quixote] to fix the lye upon the
new historian by whom they said he was so scurvily treated'.

Don Quixote was originally seen as a comedy, but by the end of
the seventeenth century it was taken more seriously and viewed
as a mock epic in prose. Perhaps reflecting the intimate relationship between comedy and tragedy, the early German Romantics
saw the comic figure of Don Quixote as a tragic hero, and
Dostoyevsky called *Don Quixote* 'the saddest book of them all'.
In the Soviet Union, Don Quixote was seen as the ideal rebel
anti-capitalist hero; in Revolutionary France, as a doomed
visionary. This extraordinary novel has inspired countless artists,
including Picasso, and writers, like William Faulkner, who read
Don Quixote every year. Superstition says that all attempts to
adapt the novel to film are doomed to failure — Orson Welles

tried to make a film of it for twenty years and failed. Monty Python Terry Gilliam's attempt to film it, starring Johnny Depp, was so plagued by misfortune that it ended up as a documentary, *Lost in La Mancha* (2002). It has been made into a musical, *Man of la Mancha* (1965), and adapted by the BBC for television in *Donovan Quick* (1999), starring Colin Firth. Don Quixote, in his determined efforts to live by archaic codes of chivalry in a world where they no longer apply, still retains his power to move audiences to laughter and to tears four hundred years after his first appearance in print.

CHIVALRIC LITERATURE

The chivalric literature that Cervantes parodies in *Don Quixote* had its origins in medieval romances, which were shaped by two powerful forces — Christianity and knighthood. Historically, the age of chivalry was ushered in by Pope Urban II on 27 November 1095 when he called for Christians to liberate Jerusalem from Islam, thereby instituting the Crusades, or 'wars of the Cross'. Culturally, this new Christian movement led to what has been called 'the twelfth-century Renaissance' in Europe, which saw a rapid rise in the production of books, especially histories, Latin literature and tales of chivalry.

Geoffrey of Monmouth's *History of the Kings of Britain* (ca 1136) and its French translation introduced Arthurian legend to continental Europe and inspired a new literary genre, the

Arthurian romance. The romances of Chrétien de Troyes, particularly his Arthurian trilogy, were the most celebrated of the new genre. Monmouth himself had been inspired by Virgil — like Virgil, he sought to trace the origins of his people to the Trojan warrior Aeneas. According to the Celtic legend Monmouth records, Aeneas's great-grandson Brutus founded Britain with a group of Trojans around 1100 BCE.

In Spain, the chivalric romance *Amadis de Gaul* dominated the popular imagination. Based on Celtic romances and possibly originating in Portugal, the first known version appeared in 1508 and inspired a rush of bad imitations — which eventually drove Cervantes to write his great parody. Don Quixote's reference to himself as 'a christian hero' is a key to the success of these chivalric romances, for they introduced a new contemporary literary hero — the knight, or 'Christian hero' — to the medieval world, in place of the epic heroes of pagan Greece and Rome, like Achilles, Odysseus and Aeneas. As Don Quixote himself tells it, knighthood arose following the decline of the golden age of ancient times: 'when mischief grew to a greater head, the order of knight-errantry was first instituted to defend damsels, protect widows, and succour the needy and the fatherless . . .'

5 . *Robinson Crusoe*
by
DANIEL DEFOE
(1 6 6 0 – 1 7 3 1)

✣

DANIEL DEFOE WAS BORN IN LONDON in 1660, into a time of shifting
political and religious allegiances with which he was actively
engaged. The complex politics of his day had their seeds in two
conflicts — one between the Protestants and the Catholics; the
other between the King and Parliament. Two years before Defoe's
birth, the death of Oliver Cromwell had marked the end of the
brief British Commonwealth founded on the execution of Charles
I. The monarchy was restored the year of Defoe's birth when
Charles II was recalled from exile to the British throne. But Charles
left chaos in his wake when he named his overtly Catholic brother
James II as his successor to the Protestant throne: soon after James's
ascension in 1685, Charles's illegitimate son, the Duke of
Monmouth, led a rebellion against the King. Among Monmouth's
rebel soldiers was one Daniel Defoe, staunch Protestant. In an

intriguing confluence of public and private history, following the defeat of the rebel army, Defoe found refuge in a churchyard — and it was here that he happened to notice the name 'Robinson Crusoe' carved into a stone.

Thirty-four years later, Defoe published his first novel: *Robinson Crusoe*. The novel is well known as a thrilling tale of adventure, the story of a restless Englishman, Robinson Crusoe, who sails to the New World only to be shipwrecked and stranded on a deserted tropical island where he eventually befriends a native, Friday. But, at its core, *Robinson Crusoe* is predominantly the story of a man alone in the universe, a Puritan moral tale. The moral dimension of Defoe's story is Christian, but Crusoe's discovery that it is possible to calm his mental anguish through a connection with God is more broadly the story of the soul-quieting and beneficent effects of giving over one's self to a power beyond. Crusoe's tale is told in the first person, using diary entries, which gives the novel the feeling of real life and intimately connects us to the inner workings of Crusoe's mind. The universal dimension of Crusoe's particular experience is one reason *Robinson Crusoe* met immediate and abiding popularity. Another reason for its immense and long-lasting appeal lies in the character of its narrator, Crusoe, and its portrayal of an enduring human fantasy — being stranded alone on a desert island.

Its perceptive portrayal of solitude and what happens to a human mind, heart and soul without human company make compelling reading. Defoe beautifully teases out a profoundly human dilemma: the conflict between our craving for company and our need for solitude. We are social animals and yet when we're alone we are closer to our selves and our particular god or gods. Alone on the island, Crusoe is overcome by despair, melancholy and madness until one day he finds himself calling out: 'Why has God done this to me? What have I done to be thus used?' He then has a realisation of God as the creator and his conscience seems to speak to him 'like a voice'. He takes out his Bible and then 'I did what I never had done in all my life, I kneeled down and prayed to God.'

Among other things, *Robinson Crusoe* is a story of contemplation, a quasi-monastic tale of Crusoe's 'conversion' to Christianity, or his understanding of Christianity from first principles (in that he builds his apprehension of Christianity on one primary belief – his sudden realisation of the existence of God). Like those medieval monks for whom work in the fields, vineyards and orchards with the seasonal round became their path to God, contributing to their worship and knowledge of God, Crusoe becomes immersed in the rhythms of his daily life.

It might be truly said, that now I worked for my bread;
'tis a little wonderful, and what I believe few people have
thought much upon, viz. the strange multitude of little
things necessary in the providing, producing, curing,
dressing, making, and finishing this one article of bread.

Defoe himself was intended by his father for the Presbyterian ministry, and with that end in mind was given a strict Puritan education. But instead, fascinated all his life by economics, Defoe defied his father to become a merchant. His commercial life brought many twists of fortune, including bankruptcy, and his reputation was shadowy. His contemporary Jonathan Swift called him a rogue and it was rumoured he was a spy (he did work as an intelligence agent for William III). The son of a butcher and born plain Daniel Foe (he added the aristocratic 'De'), Defoe was not among the literary gentlemen of London, and the remarkable success of *Robinson Crusoe* was greeted by them with much disdain.

Before he turned to writing fiction late in life, Defoe was a well-known and successful political writer and journalist. He wrote a number of powerfully argued and influential pamphlets, including *The True-Born Englishman* (against racial prejudice), *The Shortest-Way with the Dissenters* (for which he was imprisoned in 1702) and *On the Education of Women* – 'I have often thought of it as one of the most barbarous customs in the world . . . that we deny the advantages of learning to women.'

As with *Don Quixote*, the success of *Robinson Crusoe* was so immense and so immediate that not only did Defoe write a sequel the same year of its publication to cash in on its success, but pirated versions, copies, translations and adaptations appeared like mushrooms after rain. By the end of the nineteenth century, *Robinson Crusoe* had been translated into over 180 languages, including Hebrew, Bengali, Persian and Eskimo.

Defoe's novel was written in an era when sea travel was an essential part of life. English Puritans were founding their colonies in America, and sea travel and trade were the daily news. Behind the novel is the history of conquest of South America by Spain and Portugal, and England's settlement of the

West Indies, and it is rich with references to trade routes and the traffic of slaves from Africa, sugar, tobacco, rum and molasses. Spain even extended its Inquisition to its American territories, and Crusoe fears the Inquisition in 'the Brasils' if he reveals he's a non-Papist (that is, a Protestant).

Robinson Crusoe is based on the true story of Alexander Selkirk, who was marooned on an uninhabited island off the coast of Chile in 1704 and not rescued until 1709. On his return to England, Selkirk's adventures caused a sensation. He was inter-viewed by Richard Steele, founder of *Tatler* and co-founder of *The Spectator*, who published an essay on him in *The Englishman* in 1713. Steele observed that Selkirk 'frequently bewailed his Return to the World, which could not, he said, with all its Enjoyments, restore him to the Tranquility of his Solitude'. The adventuring Selkirk found that 'he was a better Christian while in this solitude than ever he was before, or than, he was afraid, he should ever be again', adding that once he had conquered his melancholy through reason, reading the Scriptures, moderation and vigorous physical exercise, his life had become joyful, 'one continual Feast'.

Crusoe's practicality and adaptability make him an archetype of the ideal Western industrial-capitalist man. He believes in reason; through reason, anyone can become a 'mechanick', and reason consoles him in his despair. Like the best British shopkeeper, Crusoe keeps an account of his condition, recording the good versus the bad of his life in two columns according to the princi-ples of double-entry bookkeeping, remarking that 'by this experi-ment I was made master of my business'. And, like the best English colonist, Crusoe surveys his island, seeing 'the whole country was my own meer property . . .'

Robinson Crusoe has had such an enduring cultural influence that most people know its story of a sailor shipwrecked on a deserted island. The French nineteenth-century philosopher Jean Jacques Rousseau called it: 'The one book that teaches all that books can teach.' It became so popular in France during the Revolution that until the 1930s a large umbrella was called in French '*un Robinson*' (after the goatskin umbrella Crusoe made). *Robinson Crusoe* has inspired numerous other works, including R.L. Stevenson's *Treasure Island* (1883), Muriel Spark's *Robinson* (1958), J.M. Coetzee's *Foe* (1986) and Luis Buñuel's film *Las Aventuras de Robinson Crusoe* (1954). There are even echoes of Defoe's wolves in Cormac McCarthy's *The Crossing* (1994).

RULERS OF SEVENTEENTH-CENTURY ENGLAND

1603–1625: James I (son of Mary Queen of Scots)

1611: Authorized Version of the Bible published

1616: Death of William Shakespeare

1620: Pilgrim Fathers sail to America and found New England

1625–1649: Charles I (son of James I)

1642–1649: English Civil War

1649: Charles I executed outside Whitehall

1649–1660: Commonwealth under Oliver Cromwell

1658: Death of Oliver Cromwell

1660: Charles II invited to return from exile

1660–1685: Charles II (son of Charles I)

1665: Plague in London

1666: Great Fire of London

1685–1689: James II (second son of Charles II)

1685: Insurrection of James, Duke of Monmouth, illegitimate son of Charles II and staunch Protestant; led a failed rebellion against the Catholic King James II and is beheaded in July 1685

1688: Leading nobles and statesmen invite William of Orange (Dutch Protestant and husband of Mary – daughter of James II) to liberate England from James II; William of Orange lands at Torbay on 5 November 1688

1689–1702: William III and Mary II

1689: Bill of Rights passed

1694: The Bank of England established to enable the government to borrow money cheaply and easily to pay the expenses of war

1694: Death of Mary

1702–1714: Queen Anne (last of the Stuart sovereigns; second daughter of James II)

6. TOM JONES
by
HENRY FIELDING
(1707–1754)

CERVANTES WAS HENRY FIELDING's acknowledged literary master. In
Tom Jones (1749), Fielding takes Cervantes' comic prose epic and
turns it into a romance: the driving force of Fielding's novel is the
apparently hopeless love of a foundling for a neighbouring squire's
daughter. Fielding's love story, wrapped in a panoramic portrait of
English society encompassing town and country, rich and poor,
influenced the English novel until the end of the nineteenth
century. In chapter one, he declares:

> We shall represent Human Nature at first to the keen
> appetite of our reader, in that more plain and simple manner
> in which it is found in the country, and shall hereafter hash
> and ragout it with all the high French and Italian season-
> ings of affectation and vice which courts and cities afford.

Here Fielding sets out his vision for the novel — of a story rooted in local particularities and extending outwards to embrace every level of sophisticated urban life, told with irony and humour by an omniscient narrator — which would later be taken up by Charles Dickens, George Eliot and William Makepeace Thackeray.

Tom Jones opens with a country gentleman, Squire Allworthy, discovering a baby boy tucked between the sheets of his bed, whom he adopts and names Tom Jones. Tom grows into a dashing, hot-blooded young man who falls in love with Squire Western's beautiful daughter Sophia. But, because of the gaping chasm between their social stations, their love is doomed. When Tom is thrown out of home and Sophia flees her overbearing father, they both end up on the road. The story unfolds across the English countryside, in alehouses and inns, as Tom and Sophia alternately pursue and flee from each other on the way to London, where Tom eventually finds Sophia and discovers his true identity.

Popular Scottish writer Sir Walter Scott (1771–1832) called Fielding 'the father of the English novel' (and Fielding's influence can be clearly seen in the vast scope of Scott's own work, which developed the historical novel in English). While Scott's claim is debatable, *Tom Jones* was certainly one of the first novels in English — and Fielding was writing at a defining, formative moment in the history of this new literary form. A dramatist and lawyer, Fielding was turned to novel writing by his disgust at the sensational success of Samuel Richardson's novel *Pamela: Or, Virtue Rewarded*. Published in 1740, *Pamela* was the *Bridget Jones's Diary* of its day. Written in the form of letters and journal entries, it tells the story of a young servant girl whose refusal to succumb to her master's sexual advances is rewarded by her marriage to him. It sparked one of the fiercest literary debates ever in England, so dividing contemporary opinion that one commentator claimed it had split England in two — into 'Pamelaists' and 'Antipamelaists'.

Among the numerous imitations and parodies of *Pamela* that appeared was an anonymous spoof attributed to Fielding (but never claimed by him) — *Shamela*, published in 1741. The following year, Fielding published *Joseph Andrews* (about Pamela's brother) in which he directed his considerable wit and learning against what he believed to be *Pamela's* shallow, sentimental morality — and against the general political and religious corruption of his day. And, as he later did in *Tom Jones*, Fielding used *Joseph Andrews* to set out his alternate view of what a novel should be.

Handsome and intelligent, Fielding was born in Somerset into a family with aristocratic ancestry. His father was a dashing lieutenant-general and his mother was the daughter of a judge. Fielding was sent to Eton, where he developed the lifelong love of classical literature so evident in *Tom Jones*: 'The learned reader must have observed, that in the course of this mighty work, I have often translated passages out of the best antient authors, without quoting the original.' Four years after leaving school, following a failed elopement with an heiress and a stint in the theatre, Fielding continued his classical studies at the University of Leiden in the Netherlands, until a lack of money forced him home.

Back in London, Fielding became one of the leading playwrights of his day. Among his many successful satirical comedies was an adaptation of the folktale *Tom Thumb*, which was said to have made Jonathan Swift laugh for the second time in his life. But Fielding's theatrical career came to an abrupt end in 1737 when the Prime Minister, Sir Robert Walpole, instituted the Licensing Act which required the Lord Chamberlain's approval for all new plays. This was largely directed at Fielding, whose play *The Historical Register for the Year* 1736 had fiercely lampooned Walpole's government.

Thirty years old, Fielding now had a wife — another beautiful heiress, Charlotte Cradock, with whom he'd fallen madly in love and married in 1734 — and two daughters to support. To earn a living, Fielding studied law while writing a newspaper, *The Champion: or British Mercury*, from 1739 to 1741. But Fielding's world fell apart when his elder daughter died and, soon after, in 1744, his beloved wife died in his arms. Fielding then moved to the Strand with his surviving daughter and sister Sarah (also a successful writer and novelist), and in 1747 married Charlotte's maid Mary, who was pregnant at the time and with whom he had five children.

In 1748, Fielding was appointed justice of the peace for Westminster and Middlesex and, with his younger brother Sir John Fielding, established in 1750 London's first effective police force, the Bow Street Runners (named after the street in which Fielding's office was located). Fielding continued to write and it was in 1749 that he published his great comic novel *Tom Jones*, which contains in its heroine, Sophia Western, a tender and glowing portrait of his late wife Charlotte.

The labyrinthine plot of *Tom Jones* — considered by the poet

Samuel Taylor Coleridge (1772–1834) to be one of 'the three most perfect plots ever planned' – is deftly handled by Fielding, whose theatrical experience is evident in the novel's rich dialogue, rapid scene changes and numerous moments of brilliant characterisation. These gifts are well displayed in his portrait of Squire Western – a fox-hunting autocrat with an explosive temper and mercurial heart, who brings the novel violently to life, Basil Fawlty–style, whenever he enters a room.

The force of Fielding's satire is directed against the moral and political corruption of his day, and is particularly pointed at hypocrisy. His portraits of Tom's two tutors, the reverend Mr Thwackum and Mr Square, highlight the destructive potential of education and the comic possibilities of pretentious learning. Mr Square and Mr Thwackum 'scarce ever met without a disputation; for their tenets were indeed diametrically opposite to each other'. While the reverend Mr Thwackum finds the source of all his sophistry in the New Testament and Christian fathers, Mr Square draws on the works of Plato and Aristotle for his: 'In morals he was a profest Platonist, and in religion he inclined to be an Aristotelian.'

Although *Tom Jones* was an immediate success, selling ten thousand copies in its first year, it was criticised in some circles for its frank treatment of sex. The writer Samuel Johnson (1740–1795) was famously offended by it, calling it a 'vicious' book and contending 'I scarcely know a more corrupt work . . .' Fielding's portrayal of wanton sex would not be out of place in a novel today – if only he allowed Sophia the same sexual liberties as Tom. But, true to his times, Fielding's moral tolerance of sex-crazed boys is not extended to girls. In the twenty-first century, the novel's easy depiction of sexual desire is shocking only in comparison to other novels published in Fielding's eighteenth century and in the century that followed, in which treatment of sex in novels was notoriously veiled.

The spirited and open-hearted hero of *Tom Jones* reflects the great humanity and compassion of its author, Fielding. In his generous treatment of Tom's struggle to reconcile his hearty sexual urges (he finds most women utterly irresistible) with his heart's undying love for one woman, Fielding demonstrates a complex understanding of sexual dynamics, and the experience of his own wayward youth. Fielding knew from experience that sexual desire is enhanced by love 'to a degree scarce imaginable' to those who have only ever previously experienced the former.

As a journalist, Fielding was actively involved in the politics of his day, which were coloured by the last claims of the Stuarts to the British throne. The Jacobite rebellion of 1745 provides much of the political background to *Tom Jones* and prompted Fielding to produce two weekly papers which condemned the Catholic rebels. This rebellion had its roots in the succession of James II, which so preoccupied Defoe. James's heirs – his son James III ('the Old Pretender') and grandson 'Bonny Prince Charlie' ('the Young Pretender') – both attempted to seize the British throne. James III's aborted rebellion took place in 1715, against George I of Hanover, who in 1714 succeeded Queen Anne, James II's last surviving Protestant child. Following James III's failure, hopes for a Stuart monarch were turned to his son Charles. In 1745, the Young Pretender led a Scottish army in an attempt to seize the British throne. When France's promised backing of the Catholic heir did not materialise, the Young Pretender's rebellion failed in 1746. France's commitment to support the Young Pretender is the French invasion so feared in *Tom Jones*, and the motley troops of British soldiers that Tom and Sophia meet along the way are mobilising to crush it.

Tom Jones's panoramic canvas, biting social satire and cast of comic characters have influenced writers as diverse as Jane Austen, Charles Dickens and George Eliot. The following observation on marriage, made by Sophia's urbane aunt, could have come from the pen of Dickens or Oscar Wilde: 'I have not an acquaintance who would not rather be thought to dislike her husband, than to like him. The contrary is such out-of-fashion romantic nonsense, that the very imagination of it is shocking.'

The raunchy 1969 film of *Tom Jones*, with screenplay by English playwright John Osborne (of *Look Back in Anger* fame), starred Albert Finney and Susannah York. The film was a box-office success and won four Academy Awards, a testament to the enduring appeal of the novel's concerns with love, sex, class and English life, as well as its generous moral spirit and great humour.

In 1754, Fielding travelled to Portugal for the sun and died there two months later. The radiant energy of *Tom Jones* is reflected in Fielding's cousin Lady Mary Wortley Montagu's words on his death: 'It is a pity he was not immortal, he was so formed for happiness.'

Hanoverian kings of England

<u>1714–1727</u>: George I (son of Sophia, granddaughter of James I); aged fifty-four, German Protestant George I succeeds to the throne of England

1715: First Jacobite Revolution, by James III (son of James II), 'the Old Pretender'

1720: The South Sea Bubble (founded in 1711 for trading in 'the South Seas') bursts, ruining thousands of investors

<u>1727–1760</u>: George II (son of George I)

1745: Second Jacobite Revolution, by Bonnie Prince Charlie (grandson of James II)

<u>1760–1820</u>: George III (grandson of George II)

1776: Declaration of Independence of the United States of North America, 4 July

1776–1783: American Revolution

1782: Independence of the United States recognised

1783: George Washington becomes first president of the United States

1788: Convict colony established at Botany Bay, Australia

1789–1802: French Revolution

1811: George III declared insane; his son the Prince of Wales appointed as prince regent

1815: Wellington defeats Napoleon at the Battle of Waterloo

<u>1820–1830</u>: George IV (son of George III)

7 . *Persuasion*
by
J ANE   A USTEN
(1 7 7 5 – 1 8 1 7)

∽

T HERE IS NOTHING IN LITERATURE quite like the exquisite pleasure of a Jane Austen novel. But in the slow unfolding of her sixth and final novel, *Persuasion* (1817), Austen subjects her readers to something closer to exquisite agony. If *Pride and Prejudice* and *Emma* are the spring and summer of Austen's novels, then *Persuasion* is their autumn, pensive and wistful. Its heroine, Anne Elliot, not yet thirty years old, has arrived prematurely at the autumn of her life, her youthful hopes of love and happiness appear lost. Early in the novel, as she walks across autumn fields on a November day, Anne reflects on the 'apt analogy of the declining year, with declining happiness, and the images of youth and hope, and spring, all gone together'.

Jane Austen's favourite novel, Samuel Richardson's *Sir Charles Grandison*, contains the line: 'Persuaders know not what they make such a [soft, gentle] person suffer.' It is this suffering — of the soft, gentle Anne Elliot, at the hands of persuaders — that lies at the heart of *Persuasion*. When she was only nineteen, Anne refused an offer of marriage from Frederick Wentworth. Now, nearly eight years later, Wentworth is back home in Somersetshire, returned from the war against Napoleon — and Anne is still in love with him. At nineteen she'd been persuaded that Wentworth, without family connection or inheritance, would be a poor match for her beauty, intelligence and aristocratic breeding. But much has changed in the ensuing years: success in the illustrious British navy has brought Wentworth a fortune and the rank of captain; disappointment and regret have faded Anne's beauty and dampened her spirits. From this potent mix, Austen teases out an excruciating love story, complete with misunderstandings, rival lovers, painful awkwardness, and obstacles temperamental, social and geographic, that prevent Anne and Wentworth from speaking their feelings.

Austen's own life had reached its autumn when she wrote *Persuasion*. When she began writing it in 1815 — two years before her death at age forty-one — she was already suffering the debilitating illness, probably Addison's disease, that would take her life. Perhaps for this reason, there is an intensity of emotion in *Persuasion* that is not found in Austen's other novels. Despite being written with Austen's characteristic light touch, *Persuasion* is so filled with agonised longing and regret that it is hard not to feel Austen was pouring into her novel her own lifetime of unrealised passion. Austen's singleness of focus — almost exclusively on the inner life of her heroine, through whom the events of the novel are filtered

— brings an air of urgency and immediacy to *Persuasion* that makes us feel that in this, of all her novels, we come closest to Austen herself. Its ending, too, almost modern in its openness, is distinct among her novels.

Although Anne Elliot is characterised by reserve, she is nevertheless a passionate woman — a deeply intelligent, bright, bookish heroine, outspoken about women's powers of loving and their inequality of opportunity. When Anne exclaims near the end of the novel: 'Yes, yes, if you please, no reference to examples in books. Men have had every advantage of us in telling their own story. Education has been theirs in so much higher a degree; the pen has been in their hands', we feel that Austen is speaking from her own experience, as a writer and the anonymous author of four acclaimed novels. For not until after her death was Austen officially acknowledged as the author of her novels, when her brother Henry arranged for the publication of *Persuasion* and *Northanger Abbey*, with a 'Biographical Notice of the Author'.

Despite not having the educational advantages of a man of her social class, Austen was well educated, at home and for two years at school in Reading. Born in Hampshire in 1775, Austen was the seventh in a family of six boys and two girls. Her parents, Reverend George Austen and Cassandra Leigh-Austen, were keen readers. When their younger daughter, Jane, decided around the age of twelve to devote her spare time to writing, they encouraged her. By the time she moved with her family to Bath on her father's retirement in 1801, Austen had written drafts of most of her novels we know today. Following her father's death in 1804, Austen, her mother and sister struggled financially and had no permanent home until 1809, when Austen's brother Edward offered them a cottage on his estate in Chawton, Hampshire. Settled at last and in need of money, Austen returned to her writing with renewed vigour. In 1811, aged thirty-six, she published her first novel, *Sense and Sensibility* ('By a Lady'), at her own expense. It was an immediate success, with reviewers praising its morality and humour. With the publication of *Pride and Prejudice* in 1813 and *Mansfield Park* in 1814, Austen became an established author and her readers were desperate to know the identity of this wildly popular, new, anonymous novelist.

Although Austen never formally revealed her authorship in her lifetime, the secret was not well kept. Among those who discovered her identity was the Prince of Wales, who had become regent in 1811 when his father, mad King George III, was finally declared unfit to rule. The Prince Regent was a great admirer of Austen's novels, particularly *Mansfield Park*, and, through his librarian, he condescended to grant his royal permission for Austen to dedicate any further books to him. Although Austen thoroughly disapproved of the dissolute prince, she dutifully dedicated her next novel, *Emma*, to him when it was published in 1815.

That same year, the war against Napoleon came to an end. The war had dominated Europe since its outbreak in 1793 and was the most significant event of Austen's day. *Persuasion*, which opens in mid 1814 and closes in 1815, is Austen's only novel set during the time in which it was written. Although it does not engage directly with the events of the day, they are potently felt through their influence on the lives of the characters, particularly the men like Wentworth who have chosen a career in the navy. Austen was well versed in contemporary naval exploits from two of her brothers who were naval men. During Captain Wentworth's absence from provincial England, the British navy has prevented Napoleon from invading Britain and broken his blockade. The return from war of successful naval men like Wentworth contributed in England to a shift in power away from the landed gentry towards the professions, a shift that was already being felt at this early moment of the Industrial Revolution. *Persuasion* is true to the spirit of the times: Anne Elliot is Austen's only heroine who does not marry into the landed gentry; Wentworth her only hero who is a modern, self-made, professional man.

Through Anne's father Sir Walter Elliot, a vain and superficial baronet, Austen expresses the old-world attitudes to professional success. In a discussion of the navy, which has so recently been pivotal in Britain's victory over Napoleon, Sir Walter concedes that 'the profession has its utility' – but he nevertheless objects to it strongly: 'I have two strong grounds of objection to it. First, of being the means of bringing people of obscure birth into undue distinction.' And second? Because 'a sailor grows old sooner than any man'. For the unnaturally youthful Sir Walter, any appearance of aging is abhorrent.

Although Austen's novels famously focus on love and marriage, Austen herself never married. As far we know, the closest she came to marriage was a proposal from Harris Bigg-Wither, the heir of a Hampshire family, in 1802. If she accepted his proposal, she changed her mind immediately, for the following morning she fled his country estate with her sister, Cassandra. Austen also lived through the anguish of her sister's doomed love when Cassandra's long engagement ended tragically with the death of her fiancé in the West Indies before they could be married. So the two Austen sisters never achieved the social position and security that marriage alone could bring a woman in Regency England – and we can sense in *Persuasion*, through Anne Elliot's passionate outspokenness about men's opportunities, their education and the many books they've authored, in striking contrast to the confined nature of women's lives, that Austen was beginning to question this state of affairs. The place of women was an issue gaining momentum in Austen's day: Mary Wollstonecraft's *A Vindication of the Rights of Women* had been published in 1792 in the wake of the French Revolution, when Austen was seventeen. Wollstonecraft's polemic was a hastily written attack on British MP Edmund Burke's *Reflections on the Revolution in France* (1790), which was a defence of monarchy and hereditary title, and became part of a heated debate about government at the time.

In Austen's novels, we see for the first time, compellingly in English, the power of stories about everyday people in everyday life, an innovation that distinguished her novels from the romantic melodramas so popular in her day. Austen described her novels, in a letter to the Prince Regent's librarian, as 'pictures of domestic life in country villages'. Sir Walter Scott, in a journal entry in 1826, wrote that Austen had:

> a talent for describing the involvements and feelings and
> characters of ordinary life which is to me the most wonder-
> ful I have ever met with . . . the exquisite touch, which
> renders ordinary commonplace things and characters

interesting from the truth of the description and the
sentiment, is denied to me.

Austen was widely read in her lifetime, but it was not until after
the publication in 1870 of her nephew J.E. Austen-Leigh's affec-
tionate, glowing portrait of his aunt, *A Memoir of Jane Austen*, that
her life and remarkable achievements were brought to public
attention and she gained a cult following. The many screen adaptations of Austen's novels attest to the continuing power of
her storytelling and humour, and our abiding fascination with her
subject matter − love and courtship. In 1995, the BBC adapted
Persuasion for the small screen in a film that perfectly conveys the
subtlety and subdued drama of Austen's last novel. That same year,
Austen was the star of Hollywood's Academy Awards when *Sense
and Sensibility* was nominated for seven Oscars. In an interview, the
film's Taiwanese director, Ang Lee, spoke of Austen's universal
appeal: 'Austen tells us how much we have to suffer in order to find
real love and truth as well as the pain of growing up. These
conflicts, in one way or another, determine our lives. This is a
universal issue.'

Rulers of nineteenth-century France

1799–1804: Consulate of Napoleon

9 November 1799: Napoleon seizes power

1804–1815: Napoleonic Empire under Napoleon I

1814–1848: Bourbon Restoration (Bourbon royal family is restored to the throne and rules until 1848)

1814–1824: Louis XVIII

1824–1830: Charles X

1830: July Revolution forces the abdication of Charles X; Chamber of Deputies elects Louis-Philippe as 'Citizen-King'

1830–1848: July Monarchy of Louis-Philippe King of France

24 February 1848: Louis-Philippe forced to abdicate following economic crisis of 1847, which erupted in revolution on 23 February 1848

1848–1852: The Second Republic

10 December 1848: Louis-Napoleon Bonaparte (nephew of Napoleon I) elected president of the Second Republic

2 December 1852: Louis-Napoleon crowns himself Emperor Napoleon III

1852–1870: Napoleon III

1870–1940: The Third Republic

8. The Red and the Black: A Chronicle of 1830

by

STENDHAL
(1 7 8 3 – 1 8 4 2)

⚜

SOME FIFTEEN YEARS AFTER THE FALL from power of Napoleon Bonaparte, Stendhal's dazzling, fast-paced novel *The Red and the Black: A Chronicle of 1830* was published in France. Napoleon was Stendhal's lifelong hero and *The Red and the Black* is a fierce attack on France following Napoleon's demise, the story of a young man determined to find heroism in those vacuous days, and a lament for heroic times gone by: 'Since the fall of Napoleon, any appearance of gallantry has been strictly banned from provincial mores ... Boredom has become acute. The only pleasures are reading and agriculture.'

The hero of *The Red and the Black*, Julien Sorel, is a young man with a 'mad passion for Bonaparte'. Inspired by Napoleon, Julien dreams of rising to the glorious heights of French society from his meagre peasant origins. Handsome, proud and overly sensitive, driven by passion and ambition like Napoleon, Julien is convinced a great destiny awaits him. Unlike his older brothers who work in their father's sawmill, Julien learns to read and write. His prodigious memory and astonishing ability to quote entire passages from the New Testament in Latin secure him his first job as tutor to the sons of the Mayor of Verrières, an imaginary town in the foothills of the Jura Mountains where Julien grows up.

Julien soon realises that in post-Napoleonic France the surest path to success for a poor peasant boy is the priesthood, just as the military was in Napoleon's day: 'All right then! he said to himself, laughing like Mephistopheles, I've got more intelligence than they have; I can pick the right uniform for my century. And he felt a resurgence of ambition and attachment for the robes of the priesthood.' But the Church and its uniform are not the only weapons in Julien's arsenal for his assault on society. He uses another equally potent one: seduction. While struggling with the demands of the priesthood, including the hypocrisy it requires, Julien plans to advance by seducing beautiful, powerful women. Just as his heroes use their intelligence, looks, passion and energy as weapons, Julien intends to do the same.

Stendhal based *The Red and the Black* on two contemporary court cases he read about in one of his favourite journals, which recorded daily court proceedings. The journal's extraordinary tales of extreme crimes of passion among ordinary people convinced Stendhal that the energy, passion and imagination required for the future of France lay not in the hands of aristocrats and bourgeoisie, but in those of the workers and peasants like Julien Sorel.

At every turn on Julien's faltering path to success, he chooses imagination over bland materialism: 'Like Hercules he found himself with a choice — not between vice and virtue, but between the unrelieved mediocrity of guaranteed well-being, and all the heroic dreams of his youth.' At the same time, however, Julien wonders if he has what it takes for success, worries that his need to earn a living will exhaust him before he's achieved glory: 'I'm not made of the stuff of great men, since I'm afraid that eight years spent earning my living may drain me of the sublime energy which gets extraordinary feats accomplished.'

As well as being a sensitive portrayal of a new kind of hero, *The Red and the Black* is a brilliant satirical portrait of French society. Stendhal writes fiercely of his contemporary world, the post-Napoleonic reign of the reactionary Charles X. Stendhal lived in Paris from November 1821 to November 1830, and his novel is based on first-hand experience of the corruption, hypocrisy and self-interest that prevailed. In a scene that could come from *Yes, Prime Minister*, the counter-revolutionary French aristocrats plot the invasion of France:

> Foreign kings will only listen to you when you announce
> the presence of twenty thousand gentlemen ready to take
> up arms to open the gates of France to them. Guaranteeing
> this support is a burden, you'll tell me; gentlemen, our heads
> remain on our shoulders at this price.

And Stendhal's social commentary is astute. He understands the power of the priesthood and perhaps the dawning power of the press: 'Yet men like this [priests] are the only moral teachers available to the common people, and how would the latter fare without them? Will newspapers ever succeed in replacing priests?' He diagnoses the symptom of the increasingly influential new class, the bourgeoisie, that will so nauseate Flaubert: 'BRINGING IN MONEY: this is the key phrase which settles everything in Verrières.'

Balzac (1799–1850) commented that Stendhal's *The Charterhouse of Parma* (1839) 'often contains a whole book in a single page', and so it is with *The Red and the Black*. Stendhal writes with such urgency, cramming his pages with such remarkable, breathtakingly unexpected events, that his novel encompasses the length and breadth of a whole society. And his chatty narrator often breaks from the story to engage directly with the reader, discussing current fashions, politics, mores and modes of thought, which gives the novel a topical immediacy that was unheard of in Stendhal's day:

> in Paris, love is born of fiction. The young tutor and his shy
> mistress would have found three or four novels, and even
> couplets from the Théâtre de Madame, clarifying their
> situation. The novels would have outlined for them the
> roles they had to play, and given them a model to imitate.

Stendhal was born Marie-Henri Beyle in Grenoble in 1783. His beloved mother died when he was seven and he was left in the care of his domineering father, a barrister in Grenoble's high court of justice. As soon as he could, Stendhal left Grenoble for Paris to seek his fortune and escape his father, whom he resented. Stendhal arrived in Paris at a fateful moment – in 1799, the day after

Napoleon Bonaparte took power with the coup d'etat of 18 Brumaire. Napoleon was to be the shaping force not only of the age but of Stendhal's life and novels. Stendhal had shown an interest in literature and mathematics, and his father expected him to go to the Ecole Polytechnique in Paris. Instead, in Paris, Stendhal was taken up by his father's cousin Noel Daru and his sons Pierre and Martial, powerful members of Napoleon's bureaucracy. Pierre and Martial educated their provincial relative in the ways of a Parisian dandy and found him a position as a clerk in Napoleon's Ministry of War. When Napoleon decided to attack the Austrians in Italy, Stendhal was offered a commission and travelled through the Alps to join Napoleon's army in Italy. Here, especially in Milan, Stendhal discovered the pleasures of Italian culture, as well as the hardships of military life. His dreams of noble military life were dashed by the coarseness of military men. In 1802, aged nineteen, Stendhal returned to Paris and began to write.

In Paris, Stendhal was given one of the top government positions in the empire and mixed with the cream of Parisian society, including Napoleon's sisters, Prince Metternich, Mme de Staël, Mme Récamier and the painter Jacques-Louis David. He even had an audience with the Empress, Marie-Louise, before joining Napoleon's invasion of Russia, where he witnessed the burning of Moscow.

When Napoleon was defeated in 1814, Stendhal could not bring himself to live in Restoration France, so he settled in Milan. Here he published his first books on art, music and travel, under the pseudonym 'Alexandre César Bombet'. In the climate of fear and opportunism in Restoration France, spies and counterfeit activities were rife. Beyle himself adopted about two hundred different names, including 'William Crocodile', and finally settled with 'Stendhal' for his novels, a name that he used for the first time in 1817 when he published his travel book *Rome, Naples and Florence in 1817*. Stendhal, who never married, had many affairs and fell madly in love with Metilde Dembowski in Milan in 1818. His unrequited passion for her haunted him for the rest of his life.

Stendhal left Milan in 1821 and moved to Paris, where his sharp intellect and original wit were much celebrated in the salons. His first novel, *Armance*, was published in 1827. Three years later, aged forty-seven, he published *The Red and the Black*, dedicated 'To the Happy Few'. The 'happy few' were the small group of people who espoused the view of life Stendhal named 'beylism', those who believed in the value of passion, energy and originality, who constantly questioned the customs and codes of the day while appearing to conform to them, in order to be happy.

Following the July Revolution of 1830 and the ascendancy of 'the bourgeois monarch' Louis-Philippe, Stendhal was appointed French consul in the port of Civitavecchia in the Papal States. He eventually returned to Paris due to ill-health — probably due to syphilis — and in 1842, after dinner with the Minister of Foreign Affairs, Stendhal collapsed in the street and died soon after. His self-composed epitaph was: 'He lived, He wrote, He loved'.

Stendhal predicted that his work would not be appreciated for another fifty years. His novels, with their penetrating, ironic portraits of contemporary society, were shocking in his day and his genius was not widely appreciated until after his death. Many later writers of the nineteenth and twentieth centuries were influenced by his vision, including Nietzsche, Proust and Camus. In his novel *Vertigo* (published in English in 1999), the German writer W.G. Sebald draws on Beyle's recollections of his youthful military adventures in Napoleon's army. The opening section of Sebald's novel is titled 'Beyle, or Love is a Madness Most Discreet'.

The widely documented 'Stendhal syndrome' is named after Stendhal's ecstatic, hallucinatory response to Giotto's frescoes in a chapel of the church of Santa Croce in Florence, about which he wrote: 'Absorbed in the contemplation of sublime beauty ... I reached the point where one encounters celestial sensations ... Everything spoke so vividly to my soul.' From the early nineteenth century on, there have been many stories of people fainting before the beautiful art of Florence, but the syndrome was only named in 1979 by Italian psychiatrist Dr Graziella Magherini (at the time, chief of psychiatry at Florence's Santa Maria Nuova Hospital), who saw over one hundred cases of the syndrome, ranging from panic attacks to cases of madness that lasted days.

9 . *Père Goriot*
by
HONORÉ DE BALZAC
(1 7 9 9 – 1 8 5 0)

≫

EVERYTHING ABOUT HONORÉ DE BALZAC is on a grand scale, from his encyclopedic vision for the novel to his appetite for food and drink, from the enormity of his debts to his Herculean eighteen-hour writing sessions. He even aggrandised his name, changing it from the ordinary 'Balssa' to the aristocratic 'de Balzac'. His life's quest was to accomplish with the pen what Napoleon had achieved with the sword — and, although he died at fifty-one having only partly realised his vision for his novel cycle *La Comédie Humaine* (*The Human Comedy*), he had completed over ninety novels and novellas of the great work, including *Père Goriot* (*Old Goriot*), as well as numerous other essays, criticism and studies. The definitive edition of *La Comédie Humaine* was published in twenty-four volumes between 1869 and 1876, and includes an estimated 2472 named characters and 566 unnamed ones. For the massive embrace of his literary achievement and his supreme mastery of French, Balzac has been fittingly called 'the Shakespeare of the novel'.

Balzac lived to see wealth and power shift from the landed aristocracy to the moneyed commercial and industrial middle classes, and, following the example of the Comte de Buffon, who catalogued the natural world in his 44-volume bestselling *Histoire Naturelle (Natural History)* published from 1749 to 1804, Balzac set out to catalogue the entire social species of his day. His great overarching scheme was to include all his novels, written and unwritten, in one great portrait of contemporary society. As would be expected from the author who set out to write a comprehensive account of early-nineteenth-century France, a nation that was changing rapidly at the hand of a shocking series of violent revolutions and the rise and fall of Napoleon, Balzac was a man of superhuman energy. The task he set himself was Napoleonic in scale. Inspired by Homer, he introduced to his work characters who would reappear in different novels throughout the cycle. In 1840, Balzac named his cycle *The Human Comedy* after Dante's *Divine Comedy*, because it was to survey the only realm not included in Dante's epic – the earthly, human sphere.

One of the most powerful shaping forces of Balzac's human environment was money, and this becomes a pervasive theme of *La Comédie Humaine*. It is also central to *Père Goriot*. As Goriot says, 'Money is life itself, it's the mainspring of everything.' In the early nineteenth century, the seeds of post-industrial capitalism are sown.

Originally published in *Révue de Paris* in 1834 and in book form in 1835, *Père Goriot* opens in November 1819, about four years after the time in which Austen's *Persuasion* is set. But what was background in Austen's novel becomes the focus of Balzac's: the rise of the bourgeoisie and the increasing power of money. The three central characters in *Père Goriot* — the old man Goriot, the student Eugène de Rastignac and the mysterious Monsieur Vautrin — are all obsessed with money, all for apparently quite different reasons, but ultimately because they are each struggling to get ahead in the moral wilderness of post-Napoleonic Paris. As Vautrin explains: 'you have to dirty your hands if you want to live well. The only thing that matters is to know how to get them clean again; in that art lies the whole morality of our times.'

Although *Père Goriot* centres on the fortunes of the eponymous Goriot and his two beautiful daughters who have made successful society marriages, the story is told through the eyes of Rastignac, a classic Balzac character and one close to the author himself. Part of the genius of Balzac lies in his ability to draw rounded 'real' characters; his heroes are not wholly good, his villains not wholly bad. Like Vautrin, Rastignac is one of Balzac's most memorable creations, and reappears in other novels of *La Comédie Humaine*. A handsome young law student from the provinces, Rastignac is the only son of an impoverished noble family, determined to find social success in Paris. Endeavouring to navigate the labyrinth of Parisian society, Rastignac is assisted by his relative and mentor — the beautiful society hostess Mme de Beauseant — whose influential name guides him like Ariadne's thread and is his magic key to the heart of Paris, 'the space that lay between the column of the Place Vendôme and the dome of the Invalides; there lay the splendid world that he had wished to gain'. Balzac uses heroic metaphors of knights and chivalry for his non-heroic times. The knights of old accepted armour, swords and horses from their mistresses, and Rastignac accepts money and the trappings of a gentleman. As his mistress says to him: 'Well Eugène, the things I offer you are the weapons of the times, tools needed by a man who wants to make himself someone of consequence.'

Like Julien, Rastignac discovers that in Paris 'social success is everything, it is the key of power', and that social success comes through the patronage of a powerful woman, not through hard work in a profession. Once you have the patronage of a society hostess, 'You can then set your ambitions as high as you like, you will have the entry everywhere.' But Rastignac tries to balance his ambition and need for money with the needs of his soul: 'It is perhaps only those who believe in God who do good secretly, and Eugène believed in God.'

Balzac's grand ambitions for the novel arose during the 1820s and '30s, a time when the novel was still seen as a literary form inferior to drama and poetry. But Balzac's vision came to him gradually, and he had many false starts. Born in Tours, ten years after the 1789 Revolution, Balzac was the eldest of four children. His father was a civil servant, first under Louis XVI, then under Napoleon. Balzac's childhood was spent in the wake of the French Revolution, his early teens in the heroic days of Napoleon, and his adulthood during the restoration of the Bourbon monarchy (under Louis XVIII and Charles X) and the July Revolution of 1830, which established the constitutional monarchy of Louis-Philippe, 'the bourgeois king'.

After the fall of Napoleon, Balzac's family moved to Paris. Here, Balzac completed school and studied law, but, much to his parents' dismay, he abandoned his legal career to become a writer. In 1819 his play *Cromwell* was a failure. He turned to writing sensational novels under various pseudonyms, hoping to make his fortune. But, when a series of failed business ventures in publishing and printing nearly ended in bankruptcy, Balzac returned wholeheartedly to writing. Inspired by the historical novels of Sir Walter Scott, which were the talk of Paris, he decided to use an historical event – the story of a group of Breton peasants, the Chouans, who'd joined a royalist uprising in 1799 – as the basis of a novel, and in doing so was one of the first novelists to treat history as a serious subject for fiction. Having thought of the idea, with typical impatience Balzac immediately left Paris for Brittany to research his novel. *Les Chouans* (*The Chouans*) was published in 1828, his first novel to appear under his own name, and was an instant success. Balzac then embarked on a frenzy of creation; while continuing to frequent the aristocratic salons of Paris, he managed to write up to eighteen hours a day, working by candlelight, dressed in a white monkish gown with a golden belt. To keep himself awake, he drank endless cups of coffee. He wrote that with coffee 'everything leaps into action; thoughts and ideas rush pell-mell over one another, like battalions of the grand army on the field of battle . . .'

The publication in 1831 of *Le Peau de Chagrin* (*The Wild Ass's Skin*), a philosophical novel about the power of money admired by the elderly Goethe, brought Balzac fame across Europe, but he still struggled under insurmountable debt. Balzac's life, driven by a quest for love and fame (the two chivalric ideals of the lost heroic age he so admired), was irreversibly altered in 1832 when he received an anonymous letter from a female admirer. In the author of the letter (eventually revealed to be Mme Evelina Hanska, the wife of a wealthy, ailing Polish count), Balzac found the damsel who would inspire him to his mighty feats of writing. In 1833, Balzac met Evelina, the damsel, in Switzerland. Captivated by her physical and spiritual beauty, he fell in love with her. Following a passionate correspondence, they eventually married in March 1850, several years after her husband's death and just months before Balzac's own death. In order to clear his debts so they could marry, Balzac was spurred to even greater heights of productivity – between 1832 and 1835 alone he completed over twenty works, including *Père Goriot*.

Balzac was an extremely popular novelist in his day, famous throughout Europe and much admired by his contemporaries, including Victor Hugo, Gaultier, Dumas *père*, George Sand and Chopin. The social theorists Karl Marx and Frederick Engels also admired Balzac. In the revolutionary spirit of the times, their *Communist Manifesto*, published a decade after *Père Goriot* in 1848, proclaimed: 'The proletarians have nothing to lose but their chains … Working men of all countries, unite!' Many decades later, in 1973, the American writer and musician Ed Sanders (famous for *The Family*, his 1971 study of Charles Manson) read the entire works of Balzac. Inspired by his reading, he decided to write in minute detail about his life in SoHo in the 1960s (a time when the warehouse and factory lofts where he lived still had oil stains from machinery from fifty years earlier and it was illegal to live in them), noting in his novel *Fame and Love in New York* (1980) such things as the exact month in 1967 in which the word 'beatnik' was replaced by 'hippie'.

Balzac, with his dazzling wit and appetite for food, drink and the salons of Paris, was played, fittingly, by Gérard Depardieu in the 1999 French television film *Balzac: A Life of Passion*.

MALCOLM KNOX

I suppose if I said anything about this list, it would be that these books are not necessarily the ones I settled down to live with forever, but they're the books that set me off in the first place — youthful, fiery, sharp-toothed loves that I've never quite got over.

- *Gargantua and Pantagruel* by François Rabelais
- *The Red and the Black* by Stendhal
- *Emma* by Jane Austen
- *War and Peace* by Leo Tolstoy
- *In Search of Lost Time* by Marcel Proust
- *The Magic Mountain* by Thomas Mann
- *The Good Soldier* by Ford Madox Ford
- *Journey to the End of Night* by Louis-Ferdinand Céline
- *USA* by Dos Passos
- *Lolita* by Vladimir Nabokov

Malcolm Knox is the author of the acclaimed novels *Summerland* and *A Private Man*, and the former literary editor of *The Sydney Morning Herald*.

10. *Jane Eyre*

by

CHARLOTTE BRONTË

(1 8 1 6 – 1 8 5 4)

❧

CHARLOTTE BRONTË WAS JUST TWENTY years old when she wrote to the British poet laureate Robert Southey to ask his advice on her poetry. Remarkably, Southey replied to this young, unknown writer – but only to advise that 'Literature cannot be the business of a woman's life.' Brontë assured Southey that she had 'endeavoured not only attentively to observe all the duties a woman ought to fulfil, but to feel deeply interested in them. I don't always succeed, for sometimes when I'm teaching or sewing I would rather be reading or writing; but I try to deny myself.'

This complex mix of audacity, determination, longing, submissive restraint and forbearance revealed by Brontë in this episode is painfully evident in the pages of her greatest novel, *Jane Eyre*:

I could not help it: the restlessness was in my nature; it agitated me to pain sometimes. Then my sole relief was to . . . allow my mind's eye to dwell on whatever bright visions arose before it . . . a tale my imagination created, and narrated continuously; quickened with all of incident, life, fire, feeling, that I desired and had not in my actual existence.

Jane Eyre burns with the restless fire of contained desire. It opens with Jane, aged ten, seated by scarlet curtains, gazing out onto a wild and sombre winter's afternoon. There is something about Jane that unsettles her aunt and the three cousins with whom she lives; 'I was a discord in Gateshead Hall: I was like nobody there,' she confides to the Reader. On this fateful afternoon, her life is forever altered when, tormented by her cousin John, she fails in her habitual obedience. Soon after, she is sent from rural Gateshead Hall into the world, to boarding school, from where she eventually secures a post as governess at Thornfield Hall. The story of Jane's passionate love for the master of Thornfield Hall, Edward Rochester, is one of the great love stories of fiction.

Jane narrates her own story. She directly addresses 'the Reader', recalling her innermost thoughts and feelings as she struggles through her teenage years to honour both her sense of duty and her own wild nature — for Jane shares not a little of Catherine Earnshaw's moorland spirit. Brontë's novel is remarkable for its innovative approach to narrative — told retrospectively by an adult Jane from her point of view as a child — and the intimacy, energy and intelligence this brings to Jane's confessions.

Brontë's language is rich, compressed and dense, at times it is intimate and hushed, at others muscular and Gothic, rising to moments of vivid Biblical intensity worthy of Nick Cave: 'that blood-bleached robe with which Christianity covers human deformity'. Brontë's observations are filled with psychological astuteness and subtle discrimination, such as Jane's understanding of the potential ruthlessness of religious zeal: 'I felt how – if I were his wife, this good man, pure as the deep sunless source, could soon kill me, without drawing from my veins a single drop of blood, or receiving on his own crystal conscience the faintest stain of crime.'

Although Brontë had taken Southey's advice by attempting to curb her writing ambition and turning her energies to teaching, circumstances conspired to reveal her talent to the world. Having been educated briefly at two boarding schools, Charlotte worked as a teacher and governess. She then decided, with sisters Emily and Anne, to open a school in Haworth, Yorkshire. With this in mind, Charlotte and Emily went to Brussels in 1842, where they studied French, German and school management. Their teacher, Constantin Héger, recognised the sisters' literary talent – and in turn it seems that Charlotte fell in love with the brilliant Héger, for when she returned to Yorkshire in 1844 she wrote him a series of passionate letters. Héger responded by tearing each letter to pieces. (Miraculously the letters survive today, their fragments stitched together by Héger's suspicious wife.)

In 1844 the Brontë sisters advertised their school, but could attract no pupils to the distant village of Haworth. Then, by chance the following year, Charlotte discovered some poems written by Emily, which she thought remarkable. Soon after, Anne and Charlotte revealed their own secret writings. In 1846, the three Brontës published their poems as *Poems by Currer, Ellis and Acton Bell*, choosing male pseudonyms for secrecy and to avoid the special treatment they believed was given to women (although they did retain their initials, so Charlotte became 'Currer Bell'). Only two copies of *Poems* sold, but the experience opened up a new world to the sisters and they began to send their novels to publishers. Charlotte's first novel, *The Professor*, was rejected. She then sent her second manuscript, *Jane Eyre: An Autobiography*, to Smith, Elder & Co. The first reader praised it so effusively that the publisher, seeking a more levelheaded response, gave it to a sober Scotsman to read. But he was so gripped by Brontë's manuscript that he stayed up half the night to finish it – and less than eight weeks later, in October 1847, *Jane Eyre* was published.

The first edition of *Jane Eyre* sold out in two months. When the second edition appeared in January 1848, dedicated to Charlotte's hero William Makepeace Thackeray, controversy exploded on the streets of London. Little did Charlotte realise that, like Rochester's first wife in *Jane Eyre*, Thackeray's wife had gone mad and was kept in the attic. It was soon rumoured that 'Currer Bell' was once Thackeray's governess and lover, although Charlotte did not in fact meet Thackeray until after the third edition of *Jane Eyre* was published. More rumours circulated when Emily and Anne's publisher claimed Currer, Ellis and Acton Bell were one single author. To prove they were not, Charlotte and Anne travelled to London in July 1848, where they revealed to their astonished publishers their identity not as one man but three women.

Charlotte became a minor celebrity, but her fame and fortune were soon overshadowed by the death of her brother, Branwell, in September 1848, and her beloved sisters Emily and Anne within the next eight months. In 1854, Charlotte married her father's Irish curate, Arthur Bell Nicholls, having turned down his first proposal and three other offers of marriage. She was pregnant when she died the following year, aged thirty-eight.

Jane Eyre was written during a time of massive change — revolution in Europe and profound unrest in England — and women were beginning to challenge their social bounds. Jane's internal rebellion against the restrictions placed on her as a woman of no independent means, her sexual longing and her passionate claim to be equal to Rochester before God were highly contentious in Brontë's day. As Elizabeth Rigby chastised in her review of *Jane Eyre* in *Quarterly*, December 1848, 'the tone of mind and thought which has overthrown authority and violated every code human and divine abroad, and fostered Chartism and rebellion at home, is the same which has also written *Jane Eyre* . . .'

There have been some fifteen film versions of *Jane Eyre*, attesting to the enduring power and drama of its passionate story. The 1944 film starring Joan Fontaine as Jane, and Orson Welles as Rochester, was billed as 'A Love Story Every Woman Would Die a Thousand Deaths to Live'. An opera of *Jane Eyre* by English composer Michael Berkeley, with a libretto by Australian writer David Malouf, premiered in 2000.

SOPHIE CUNNINGHAM

What all the books on this list have is wonderfully intense atmosphere and sense of place, and, in most cases, a really interesting portrayal of human relationships. What I love about *Orlando* is its audacity with time. I think about these books as I do my own writing. They stay with me and inspire me.

- *Great Expectations* by Charles Dickens
- *Jane Eyre* by Charlotte Brontë
- *Wuthering Heights* by Emily Brontë
- *Orlando* by Virginia Woolf
- *Wide Sargasso Sea* by Jean Rhys
- *The Lover* by Marguerite Duras
- *Voss* by Patrick White
- *The Vivisector* by Patrick White
- *The English Patient* by Michael Ondaatje
- *A Child in Time* by Ian McEwan
- *Disgrace* by J.M. Coetzee

Sophie Cunningham is the author of *Geography* and writes the column 'Couch Life' for *The Age*. Before becoming a full-time writer, Cunningham had a successful career as a publisher, first for McPhee Gribble/Penguin and then for Allen & Unwin.

11. Wuthering Heights
by
EMILY BRONTË
(1 8 1 8 – 1 8 4 8)

॰ॐ॰

IN 1820, PATRICK BRONTË, an Irish clergyman, moved with his wife, five daughters and son to Haworth, a remote township high in the Yorkshire Pennines – and it was from this wild landscape that his daughter Emily would distil *Wuthering Heights*, one of the most extraordinary novels in English literature. The Brontë parsonage was on the edge of town, flanked by a moorland wilderness. Its desolation was heightened by the tolling of funeral bells and the mason's chisel cutting gravestones in the churchyard that surrounded the parsonage on three sides. Death was ever-present in Haworth – the average age of death was twenty-five years, due largely to the town's dismal sanitary conditions – and within five years of their arrival, the Brontë children had suffered the deaths of their mother and two eldest sisters (aged eleven and ten).

The remaining four children, Charlotte, Branwell, Emily and Anne, were cared for by their mother's sister, Aunt Branwell. They grew up in relative isolation, creating their own entertainment. From an early age, they invented stories set in an imaginary land, Angria, which they recorded in miniature books in tiny writing so their aunt and father couldn't read them. Emily and Anne broke away from the Angrian stories when Emily was about thirteen, and invented their own fantastic world – Gondal – which was dominated by powerful, capricious women. Emily's few surviving diary entries show her as much preoccupied with the imaginary world of Gondal as she was by the world around her. In 1845, she wrote:

> the Gondals still flourish bright as ever I am at present writing a work on the First Wars – Anne has been writing some articles on this and a book by Henry Sophona – We intend sticking firm by the rascals as long as they delight us which I am glad to say they do at present.

The three Brontë girls rarely walked in the village. As Charlotte's friend and biographer Elizabeth Gaskell noted, they 'never faced their kind voluntarily, and always preferred the solitude and freedom of the moors'. Emily was particularly attached to her moorland home, and would sink into melancholy and homesickness when parted from it. Her few absences from Haworth, to study or teach, were brief, mostly cut short. When Emily was six she spent several months at Clergy Daughters' School; aged seventeen, she went away to school for three months; in 1838, she became a teacher for six months. Her longest absence from home began in February 1842, when she went to Brussels with Charlotte to study at the Pension Héger. Here she studied French, German and advanced piano, and her musical talent was particularly praised by their teacher, Monsieur Héger. When Aunt Branwell died the following October, Emily returned home from Brussels to Haworth – and there she remained until her death six years later in December 1848.

Following the publication at the sisters' expense of *Poems by Currer, Ellis and Acton Bell* in 1846, Emily sent out the manuscript of her novel *Wuthering Heights* to publishers. It was accepted for publication the next year and was published in December 1847, two months after the publication of Charlotte's *Jane Eyre*. Unlike Charlotte, Emily did not base her novel on the events of her own life, and her vision was intense, focused laser-like on two houses, two families, and the moors, from which small range she spins a whole world. The principal narrator of *Wuthering Heights*, Mr Lockwood, remarks:

> I perceive that people in these regions acquire over people in towns the value that a spider in a dungeon does over a spider in a cottage, to their various occupants; and yet the deepened attraction is not entirely owing to the situation of the looker-on. They *do* live more in earnest, more in themselves, and less in surface change, and frivolous external things.

He could be describing Emily's own way of living – for what she might have lacked in breadth of experience, she made up for in depth.

In the opening pages of *Wuthering Heights*, Emily Brontë raises spectres, Lear's mad ravings on the moor, salivating dogs, dripping blood and an impassable snow storm, to evoke the atmospheric tumult — or 'wuthering' — that will haunt the pages of her only novel. One of the most striking features of Brontë's book is its tortured landscape, which manifests not only in the form of rocks and stunted trees and grey overarching skies, but is alive in its human inhabitants, most notably Catherine Earnshaw and Heathcliff. 'Tell her what Heathcliff is,' urges Catherine, '— an unreclaimed creature, without refinement, without cultivation; an arid wilderness of furze and whinstone.'

The desolation of the Yorkshire moors is exactly what the world-weary Mr Lockwood is seeking when he rents Thrushcross Grange from Mr Heathcliff as the novel opens. Lockwood notes with pleasure that 'In all England, I do not believe that I could have fixed on a situation so completely removed from the stir of society. A perfect misanthropist's heaven'; and his heart warms to the withdrawn and suspicious countenance of Heathcliff, his new landlord. But, despite his desire for isolation, Lockwood persuades Nelly Dean, the housekeeper, to keep him company while he shivers long evenings by the fire. Nelly then relates an extraordinary tale of wild love and hate, a tale of torment that begins with the arrival at Wuthering Heights of a ragged gypsy child named Heathcliff, 'dark almost as if it came from the devil'.

So immense was Brontë's genius that the names Catherine and Heathcliff now stand for passionate, demented love — and their fierce obsession remains one of the most disturbing and exhilarating of literature. 'Whatever our souls are made of, his and mine are the same,' declares Catherine. They love with a religious fervour, pitched at the extremes of life and death, on the edge of madness. 'Be with me always — take any form — drive me mad! only *do* not leave me in this abyss, where I cannot find you!' cries Heathcliff. 'Oh God! it is unutterable! I *cannot* live without my life! I *cannot* live without my soul!'

But it is the corrupt child of this love — Heathcliff's poisonous hatred nursed over years — that drives Brontë's novel, his bitter resentment that fills its pages. The relentlessness of Heathcliff's vengeance born of his love — wrought on Hareton Earnshaw, Catherine Linton, Linton Heathcliff — is chilling, its dark violence almost palpable. The power of Emily's creation was felt by her sister Charlotte, who wrote: 'Whether it is right or advisable to create things like Heathcliff, I do not know: I scarcely think it is.'

While *Wuthering Heights*, published under the pseudonym 'Ellis Bell', did not receive the acclaim of *Jane Eyre* on publication, contemporary critics found much in it to praise. A review in *Atlas* from 1848 observed of *Jane Eyre* and *Wuthering Heights* respectively: 'The work of Currer Bell is a great performance; that of Ellis Bell is only a promise, but it is a colossal one.' Charles Dickens's friend Wilkie Collins, whose bestselling novels *The Woman in White* and *Moonstone* appeared in the 1860s, was a great admirer of *Wuthering Heights*. Like others after him, including Joseph Conrad (*Heart of Darkness*) and F. Scott Fitzgerald (*The Great Gatsby*), Collins was influenced by the innovative and structurally complex double narrative of *Wuthering Heights*. Its story, told by two curious bystanders, is an early example of the use of multiple narrators. With the publication of A. Mary F. Robinson's biography of Emily

Brontë in 1883, the magnitude of her talent began to be more widely appreciated.

To date there have been thirteen film versions of *Wuthering Heights*, including a 1939 film directed by William Wyler (starring Laurence Olivier and Merle Oberon), French and Japanese versions, and an MTV musical. The Spanish surrealist filmmaker Luis Buñuel, who believed 'desire is the one true motor of the world', had long been haunted by the mad, untrammelled love unleashed in Brontë's novel when he came to make his 1954 adaptation, *Abismos de Pasión*, which he filmed in Mexico.

The English singer Kate Bush, who shares a birthday with Emily Brontë (30 July), based her hit song 'Wuthering Heights' on Brontë's novel. Written under a full moon, the song was released in 1978.

MARGARET HARRIS

- *Waverley* by Walter Scott
- *Pride and Prejudice* by Jane Austen
- *Jane Eyre* by Charlotte Brontë
- *Barchester Towers* by Anthony Trollope
- *Great Expectations* by Charles Dickens
- *Sylvia's Lovers* by Elizabeth Gaskell
- *Middlemarch* by George Eliot
- *Daniel Deronda* by George Eliot
- *The Egoist* by George Meredith
- *The Man Who Loved Children* by Christina Stead

Margaret Harris is professor in English literature at the University of Sydney, and has published extensively on Victorian fiction (especially the work of George Eliot and George Meredith). She considers herself bound to acknowledge that she is Christina Stead's literary executor.

1 2 . *D a n i e l   D e r o n d a*

by

G EORGE   E LIOT

(1 8 1 9 – 1 8 8 0)

⚹

DANIEL DERONDA, GEORGE ELIOT's extraordinary last novel, was published in eight monthly parts from February to September 1876. The reading public eagerly awaited each new instalment of a work that promised to be a love story between a dangerously beautiful girl and a handsome young man. The novel opens in a European casino with the question 'Was she beautiful or not beautiful?' 'She' is Gwendolen Harleth, a 'Nereid in sea-green robes and silver ornaments, with a pale sea-green feather fastened in silver falling backward over her green hat and light-brown hair'. The questioner is Daniel Deronda, an aristocratic young man with an ironic smile. And the answer to his question is, most emphatically, 'beautiful': 'Some faces which are peculiar in their beauty are like original works of art: for the first time they are almost always met with question.'

The novel's central character, Daniel Deronda, is an intriguing and most unusual hero, less acting than acted upon, able to feel the lives of others to an almost painful degree. His apparent lack of self-interest and his compassion for the entire living world make him appear to his friends a perfect being, 'like an Olympian who needed nothing'. But he longs desperately for something: an event that will urge him into action and 'compress his wandering energy'. Deronda lives with his wealthy uncle and has every comfort money can buy, but there is a gaping absence at the heart of his life — he has no idea who his parents are. The secrecy that surrounds his parentage sets him adrift in life: he is unfocused in his intent, burning with unanswered purpose; even his apparent decision to study law 'had been without other result than to deepen the roots of indecision'.

Gwendolen Harleth seems equally at sea in the world. Charged with a nervous intensity, Gwendolen dreams of achieving great-ness, which proves challenging for a woman in Victorian England without fortune or genius. Unlike earlier nineteenth-century heroines, Gwendolen recoils from the idea of marriage, thinking it 'rather a dreary state, in which a woman could not do what she liked, had more children than were desirable, was consequently dull, and became irrevocably immersed in humdrum'. Eliot, an astute psychological observer and sharp social critic, was acutely aware of the constraints of marriage.

If Victorian readers' expectations of a love story between Deronda and Gwendolen were challenged by the arrival of a beau-tiful young Jewish girl, Mirah Lapidoth, they were staggered by the turn the novel takes following Mirah's appearance. For Eliot uses the intersecting lives of these three young people to draw a portrait of Jewish life in England and articulate a dream of a Jewish return to Palestine — and, in doing so, produced one of the most controversial novels of her day. In an era in which the spirit of nationalism was firing across Europe, fuelled by the French Revolution and the recent success of the national liberation movement in Italy (founded in 1847 by Count Camillo di Cavour (1810–61) and culminating in 1871 following the defeat of the last French and Austrian strongholds on Italian soil), Eliot was determined to engage her English readers with the plight of the Jews and their homelessness. As one character says: 'The idea that I am possessed with is that of restoring a political existence to my people, making them a nation again, giving them a national centre, such as the English have, though they too are scattered over the face of the globe.'

Although the public continued to buy the latest instalments of *Daniel Deronda*, the response of non-Jewish readers to its Jewish content was ambivalent. Even her partner, the ever-supportive George Henry Lewes, privately expressed wonder at Eliot's determination to engage so fully with Jewish concerns in a novel. Eliot's interest in the Jews was fired by her friendship with Emanuel Deutsch, a Jewish scholar at the British Museum whom she met in 1866. The character of Ezra Mordecai in *Daniel Deronda* is said to be based on her friend. Like Deutsch, Mordecai is an impoverished scholar and mystic, eaten up by his vision of a Jewish homeland, which at the time was an impossible dream plagued by insurmountable difficulties. As Mordecai says: 'Difficulties? I know there are difficulties. But let the spirit of sublime achievement move in the great among our people, and the work will begin.'

Eliot was an astute observer of her contemporary scene, conversant with the work of Charles Darwin, the philosophy of Spinoza, the music of Richard Wagner — and the Jewish question was a pressing issue of the day. The number of Jews in England increased fivefold during the years 1850 to 1900, and Jews were becoming prominent in English life. In 1857, Sir David Salomons was the first Jew to be elected lord mayor of London. In 1868, Benjamin Disraeli — born a Jew and baptised an Anglican — was elected prime minister of Great Britain, becoming the first Jewish-born prime minister in Europe. And the idea of a Jewish return to Palestine had a long history in England, supported by many prominent Christians and dating back to the publication in 1611 of the first English translation of the Bible, the King James Version, which introduced English readers for the first time to the Jews' origins in Palestine. By the end of the nineteenth century, on a tide of nationalism, the Jews had been emancipated in most European nations except Russia, following the precedent set by Revolutionary France that granted citizenship to Jews in 1791. From the 1840s the English began actively to encourage Jewish settlements in Palestine, despite opposition from orthodox Jews. The Jewish quest for a return to their homeland gained further momentum after Eliot's death, with the establishment of European Zionism in 1897 by Theodore Herzl.

Daniel Deronda was greeted enthusiastically by Jews in England and across Europe. Chaim Guedalla, a leader of London's Jewish community, wrote to Eliot twice in 1876 outlining suggestions for a Jewish colony in Palestine with the possible assistance of Turkish finance (a vision opposed by many orthodox Jews). Rabbi David

Kaufman, from the Jewish Theological Seminary in Budapest, sent Eliot his commentary on *Daniel Deronda*, published in English in 1878 as *George Eliot and Judaism*. As Kaufman wrote: 'None but a poetess . . . would have ventured to animate her work with a sentiment so strange . . . as the longing of the Jews for the re-establishment of their kingdom . . . She shows a taste and a facility of reference really amazing.' For decades *Daniel Deronda*, a novel by a non-Jewish Englishwoman, inspired Jews with a vision that was later realised with the founding of Israel in 1948.

The realisation of dreams of such magnitude requires passion – and, in *Daniel Deronda*, Eliot engages the full force of her considerable intellect and imagination with the many manifestations of passion. For Eliot, those who live beyond their immediate, personal concerns, the 'souls which burn themselves out in solitary enthusiasm', are the great ones, for it is they who accomplish remarkable things, in art, politics, religion, literature, science. As Deronda begins to divine his own impassioned purpose, he reflects:

But were not men of ardent zeal and far-reaching hope everywhere exceptional? – the men who had the visions which, as Mordecai said, were the creators and feeders of the world – moulding and feeding the more passive life which without them would dwindle and shrivel into the narrow tenacity of insects, unshaken by thoughts beyond the reach of their antennae.

Eliot, born Mary Ann Evans in 1819 in Warwickshire, was herself passionate and intellectually gifted. That she felt this as a burden as well as a joy might be seen in the outburst of Princess Halm-Eberstein in *Daniel Deronda*: 'You are not a woman. You may try – but you can never imagine what it is to have a man's force of genius in you, and yet to suffer the slavery of being a girl.' Until her mother's death in 1836, Eliot was sent to various boarding schools, where she became a studious and devoutly religious child. But her religious devotion was challenged when, aged twenty-two, she moved with her father to Coventry, where she met the free-thinkers Charles and Caroline Bray, and Charles Hennell, whose book *An Inquiry Concerning the Origin of Christianity* (1836) encouraged Eliot to abandon orthodox Christianity and declare to her father that she would no longer accompany him to church. The ensuing stand-off between father and daughter could be resolved only by compromise: the daughter could think as she pleased as long as she continued to appear at church. Eliot's linguistic gifts – she read fluently in Italian, French, Spanish, Italian and German – were recognised by Hennell, who arranged for her to translate from German D.F. Strauss's influential book *The Life of Jesus Critically Examined*. The translation was published anonymously in 1846 by John Chapman, and, when Eliot moved to London to become a freelance writer following her father's death in 1849, Chapman made her the managing editor of his journal *The Westminster Review*.

In London, Eliot fell passionately in love with a series of men until in 1851 she met the journalist George Henry Lewes. Lewes was married but with his knowledge his wife was involved with another man, so in July 1854 Eliot and Lewes were free to travel together as lovers to Germany, where they remained until March 1855 while Eliot began her translation of Spinoza's *Ethics* and

Lewes worked on his *Life of Goethe*. On their return to London they continued to live as husband and wife, which caused such a scandal that Eliot's family subsequently rejected her. But despite suffering depression as a result of such a loss, the determined Eliot defied convention and public opinion to live with Lewes until his death in 1878. Encouraged by Lewes, Eliot began to write fiction. Her first book, a collection of three short stories, appeared in 1858 as *Scenes of Clerical Life*, under the pseudonym 'George Eliot'. 'George' was chosen after Lewes's first name, 'Eliot', because she thought it sounded substantial. The publisher John Blackwood did not guess the remarkably gifted author George Eliot was in fact a woman, believing her to be 'a man who had seen a great deal of society'. Eliot's first full-length novel, *Adam Bede*, was successfully published in 1859 and reprinted eight times in its first year. Eliot wrote six more novels, including *Middlemarch*, and scores of essays and articles, becoming one of the nineteenth-century's most acclaimed writers in English.

After Lewes's death, Eliot caused another sensation by marrying, aged sixty, their friend and banker John Walter Cross, an American twenty years younger than herself. She died seven months after their wedding and was buried beside Lewes at Highgate Cemetery.

Since its publication in 1876, *Daniel Deronda* has continued to divide opinion, with many readers lamenting what they consider its divided nature – half love story, half treatise on the homelessness of the Jews. And although it has not received the widespread adulation of the less troubling *Middlemarch*, for many other readers it remains one of the most exciting and challenging imaginative conceptions of the nineteenth-century English novel, and the BBC television version of *Daniel Deronda*, adapted by Andrew Davies and screened in 2002, was immensely popular with viewers and critics alike. Eliot herself knew *Daniel Deronda* would be met with resistance, 'even repulsion', but precisely for this reason she felt compelled to try to understand Jewish life in Victorian England in an attempt to disturb 'the usual attitude of Christians towards Jews' – 'Moreover,' she argued, 'not only towards the Jews, but towards all oriental peoples with whom we English come in contact, a spirit of arrogance and contemptuous dictatorialness is observable which has become a national disgrace to us.'

BRENDA MADDOX

- *Ulysses* by James Joyce
- *Scoop* by Evelyn Waugh
- *Portrait of the Artist as a Young Man* by James Joyce
- *Jane Eyre* by Charlotte Brontë
- *Little Women* by Louisa May Alcott
- *Bleak House* by Charles Dickens
- *A Passage to India* by E.M. Forster
- *The Great Gatsby* by F. Scott Fitzgerald
- *Anna Karenina* by Leo Tolstoy

Brenda Maddox, an award-winning biographer based in London, is the author of many books, including the internationally acclaimed biography of James Joyce's wife, *Nora:*

A Biography of Nora Joyce (1988), *The Married Man: A Life of D.H. Lawrence* (1994), *George's Ghosts: A New Life of W.B. Yeats* (1999) and *Rosalind Franklin: The Dark Lady of DNA* (2002).

Maddox grew up in Boston and studied English literature at Harvard, where she specialised in James Joyce, before moving to London in the 1960s.

13 . *Bleak House*

by

CHARLES DICKENS

(1 8 1 2 – 1 8 7 0)

⚮

CHARLES DICKENS, ONE OF ENGLAND's most prolific, energetic, exuberant and inventive writers, left behind fourteen novels and countless articles and essays when he died suddenly in 1870 aged fifty-eight. Such was Dickens's stature by the time of his death that he was buried in Poets' Corner at Westminster Abbey. And he poured as much energy into the world around him as he did into his writing, turning the full force of his teeming imagination to all aspects of his contemporary scene – politics, law, society, the class system, schools, railways, human relations, London. There's barely a corner of Victorian life Dickens left unexamined. His first novel, *Pickwick Papers*, caused an unexpected sensation. Aged only twenty-five, Dickens was almost overnight trans-formed into a literary celebrity and would later become the most renowned writer in all of Europe and America. Like a nineteenth-century rock star, Dickens gave sell-out readings from his books and even toured America, where he was mobbed in the streets, in hotels and trains. Influential New England Transcendental thinker Ralph Waldo Emerson (1803–1882), who went to one of Dickens's celebrated readings in Boston, was so entertained he laughed as if he 'must crumble to pieces', he said, later adding that he believed Dickens had 'too much talent for his genius; it is a fearful locomotive to which he is bound . . . He daunts me!'

Bleak House, published in 1853, is the story of an interminable legal case – Jarndyce and Jarndyce – being heard in the Courts of Chancery, which involves three wills and a contested property. The malignant reach of Jarndyce and Jarndyce is colossal, casting its gloom across the whole of British society from the country seat of Lady Honoria Dedlock to the alleyways of London, home to the street urchin Jo. The story of *Bleak House* focuses on the lives of three children – Esther Summerson, Ada Clare and Richard Carstone – and their beneficent guardian, John Jarndyce, all of whose lives are indefinitely stalled by the intractable workings of the court.

The novel's twin narrative – one told by Esther Summerson, the other by an anonymous third person – enables Dickens to reach into every strata of English society, as well as to provide the more intimate point of view of a young girl. Esther, a young orphan taken into the care of John Jarndyce on the death of her 'godmother', begins her story apologetically: 'I have a great deal of difficulty in beginning to write my portion of these pages, for I know I am not clever.' The other narrative, portentous in tone, its humour fierce and biting, famously opens with a vision of London choked by mud and fog:

> London. Michaelmas term lately over, and the Lord
> Chancellor sitting in Lincoln's Inn Hall. Implacable
> November weather. As much mud in the streets, as if the
> waters had but newly retired from the face of the earth, and
> it would not be wonderful to meet a Megalosaurus, forty
> feet long or so, waddling like an elephantine lizard up
> Holborn Hill.

In his 1939 essay 'Charles Dickens', George Orwell, an admirer of Dickens and among those responsible for the renewed interest in him in the 1940s and '50s, wrote that Dickens 'attacked English institutions with a ferocity that has never since been approached'. In *Bleak House*, Dickens attacks the fatuous idleness of the aristocracy: 'Sir Leicester is generally in a complacent state, and rarely bored. When he has nothing else to do, he can always contemplate his own greatness. It is a considerable advantage to a man, to have so inexhaustible a subject.' He also attacks the incompetence of Parliament with its carbon-copy MPs: 'Then, giving the Home Department and Leadership of the House of Commons to Joodle, the Exchequer to Koodle, the Colonies to Loodle, and the Foreign Office to Moodle, what are you to do with Noodle?' His fiercest attacks, however, are reserved for the workings of the law, the system that underpins the whole of British society.

In *Bleak House* Dickens creates a dazzling and nightmarish portrait of the English law, with its wills, estates, inheritances, its power to manipulate and to be manipulated, and its potential to destroy lives. The lawyer Mr Kenge, 'who appeared to enjoy beyond everything the sound of his own voice', is stunned to discover that Esther has never heard of Jarndyce and Jarndyce:

> one of the greatest Chancery suits known? Not of Jarndyce and Jarndyce — the — a — in itself a monument of Chancery practice. In which (I would say) every difficulty, every contingency, every masterly fiction, every form of procedure known in that court is represented over and over again? It is a case that could not exist, out of this free and great country.

But John Jarndyce sees the case quite differently:

> The Lawyers have twisted it into such a state of bedevilment that the original merits of the case have long disappeared from the face of the earth. It's about a Will, and the trusts under a Will — or it was, once. It's about nothing but Costs now . . . All the rest, by some extraordinary means, has melted away.

At the corrupt heart of this legal bedevilment — and of *Bleak House* — is Jo the crossing sweeper, a homeless boy who lives in the pestilent slum 'Tom-All-Alone's', which happens to be 'in Chancery, of course'. Tom-All-Alone's, the contested property of Jarndyce and Jarndyce, is now a ruined wasteland, 'a black, dilapidated street, devoid of all decent people', in which the derelict houses, inhabited by vagrants, have descended into squalor. Jo, whose pale form haunts this corrupted realm, has been told by the apparently omnipresent detective Mr Bucket (one of the first detectives in English fiction) to 'keep out of the way'. Fearing that wherever he goes he is being watched, will be seen and 'found out', Jo lives in extraordinary terror of Bucket and 'in his ignorance, he believes this person to be everywhere, and cognizant of everything' — like a nineteenth-century predecessor to George Orwell's Big Brother. At every level, *Bleak House* speaks as powerfully to our times as it did to Dickens's own.

Dickens was born in relative comfort in 1812 in Portsmouth, on England's south coast, but his father, a clerk in the naval pay office, was financially inept and continually troubled by debt. In 1824, when Dickens was twelve, his father was sent to debtors' prison. Dickens, the eldest son of eight children, was sent to work in a blacking factory to support the family. The experience of factory work marked Dickens for life — it exposed him to the deprivations of the working classes and the appalling conditions under which they worked. The reaction of this sensitive, intelligent and highly receptive boy to the suffering of the workers profoundly influenced his worldview, and his novels are fuelled by his outrage at privations and frustrations daily experienced by the poor. At fifteen, Dickens left school and became a solicitor's clerk. He then worked as a court and parliamentary reporter, where he learnt that 'The one great principle of English law, is to make business for itself.' His novels are filled with arresting, richly imagined sentences, written with a journalist's keen eye for the facts and a poet's ear for metaphor and symbolism.

Dickens's personal life, while filled with activity and friends and family, was dark and complex. His separation in 1858 from his wife Catherine, whom he married in Chelsea in 1836, caused a public scandal. It was covered in the press and became the gossip of London, alienating several of Dickens's friends, including Thackeray. Not until many years after his death was it revealed by his daughter Katey, in a taped conversation released after her death, that Dickens had had a secret relationship with a young actress, Ellen Ternan, whom he'd cast in his production of Wilkie Collins's play *The Frozen Deep* in 1857.

Dickens's novels owed much of their popularity to their brilliant characterisation, cliff-hanger plots which unfolded over several monthly instalments and their easy adaptability to the stage. During Dickens's lifetime, up to twenty different stage versions of his latest novel would be playing in theatres around London. His novels have continued to be widely loved by readers and adapted, to cinema and television, for new audiences. In 1985 a film of *Bleak House* was released, starring Denholm Elliott as John Jarndyce and Diana Rigg as Lady Honoria Dedlock.

Elizabeth Knox

- *Pride and Prejudice* and *Persuasion* by Jane Austen
- *David Copperfield*, *Bleak House* and *Little Dorrit* by Charles Dickens
- *Jane Eyre* by Charlotte Brontë
- *Wuthering Heights* by Emily Brontë

- ꙮ *The Master of Ballantrae* and *The Strange Case of Dr Jekyll and Mr Hyde* by R.L. Stevenson
- ꙮ *The Good Soldier* by Ford Madox Ford
- ꙮ *The Great Gatsby* by F. Scott Fitzgerald
- ꙮ *The Radetzky March* by Joseph Roth

New Zealand writer Elizabeth Knox is the author of seven novels, including the bestselling angelic tale *The Vintner's Luck* (1998), *Black Oxen* (2001) and *Daylight* (2003), a murder mystery with saints and vampires.

14. The Marble Faun
by
NATHANIEL HAWTHORNE
(1804–1864)

%

THE MARBLE FAUN IS THE LAST of Nathaniel Hawthorne's five novels, a haunting and tragic story about art and artists, set in Rome. Published in 1860, *The Marble Faun* is Hawthorne's only novel set outside his native America. It opens with three expatriate artists in a Roman museum, examining the sculpture of a faun and noting its likeness to their Italian friend, Donatello. Like Donatello, the faun is 'an amiable and sensual creature, easy, mirthful, apt for jollity, yet not incapable of being touched by pathos'. From this meditation on a faun, that ancient fusion of man and beast, Hawthorne weaves a devastating story of innocence lost that becomes a complex examination of art and nature, and of Europe and its relationship to America. Seduced by the crumbling beauty of the Old World, European civilisation, the novel is at the same time haunted by a wistful longing for that age when 'man's affinity with Nature was more strict, and his fellowship with every living thing more intimate and dear'.

Nathaniel Hawthorne, a friend and contemporary of Herman Melville, came to prominence as a novelist at the age of forty-six with the publication of *The Scarlet Letter* in 1850 — a date that marked the beginning of five dazzling years in American literature. The early 1850s saw the publication of America's first international bestseller, *Uncle Tom's Cabin* (1852) by Harriet Beecher Stowe, as well as Thoreau's *Walden* (1854), Longfellow's *The Song of Hiawatha* (1855) and the first edition of Walt Whitman's *Leaves of Grass* (1855).

Hawthorne's success was confirmed with the publication in quick succession of two more novels, *The House of the Seven Gables* in 1851 and *The Blithedale Romance* in 1852. That same year, Hawthorne also published the campaign biography of his old school friend Franklin Pierce, who was running for presidency. When Pierce became president of the United States in 1853, Hawthorne was rewarded with the prestigious appointment of United States consul in Liverpool, Britain. At the time, Liverpool was England's major Atlantic seaport and America's prime foreign posting. In Liverpool, Hawthorne set out to write a novel about Britain — but instead he found himself so caught up in his public duties that he was unable to write, and suffered a profound crisis of imagination. His friend Herman Melville, himself close to a breakdown and having decided to write no more, visited Hawthorne in Liverpool. Together the two writers walked by the turbulent ocean and discussed their troubled literary fates.

Hawthorne had struggled all his life with this tension between his needs as an artist and his need to be part of the broader civic world. He had accepted a series of prominent government postings and yet these inevitably conflicted with his requirement of 'perfect seclusion' to write. A private and deeply introspective man, his intense imaginative life sat uneasily with his public life. Born on 4 July 1804 into an established New England family, Hawthorne's ancestors had been prominent members of the early Puritan settlement. His great-great-grandfather John Hathorne (Hawthorne added the 'w') was one of the most severe, most zealous judges of the notorious 1692 Salem witch trials, and Hawthorne's novels' preoccupation with guilt and redemption can be seen as part of the burden of this ancestor's dark legacy.

After college, Hawthorne spent twelve years writing and reading, publishing stories and the novel *Fanshawe*, before being appointed to the Boston Custom House. In 1841 he left his job to move to Brook Farm, a socialist cooperative, where he hoped to find a haven for writing. After seven months he left, his hopes unrealised. The following year he married his beloved fiancée, Sophia, and his new responsibilities as husband and father eventually forced him to accept a position at the Salem Custom House (during which time he wrote *The Scarlet Letter*).

When Pierce lost the presidency in 1857, Hawthorne lost his consulship in Liverpool. The following year he travelled to Florence with Sophia and their three children. In Florence, Hawthorne began to work enthusiastically on a new romance, which he continued to sketch out the following winter in Rome. So struck was Hawthorne by the grandeur of Rome that everything else, including America and his New England Puritanism, seemed to him ephemeral: 'Side by side with the massiveness of the Roman Past, all matters, that we handle or dream of, now-a-days, look evanescent and visionary alike.'

The novel Hawthorne sketched out in Italy became *The Marble Faun*, which centres on the community of American artists he found in Rome. It opens in a sculpture gallery where the novel's four central characters are looking at the ancient marbles. Three of the group — Hilda, Kenyon and Miriam — are artists and they have been simultaneously struck by the resemblance of an antique sculpture to their Italian friend Donatello: 'Our friend Donatello is the very Faun of Praxiteles,' remarks Miriam, prefiguring the tragedy that will unfold in the novel — for the Faun, and by extension Donatello, has 'a capacity for strong and warm attachment, and might act devotedly through its impulse, and even die for it at need'. Hilda and Kenyon are innocent Americans, but Miriam is dark and sophisticated, with an air of haunting ambiguity that arises from the fact her origins are unknown. She has been 'plucked out of a mystery, and had its roots still clinging to her'. When Miriam's exotic beauty attracts two Italian men, Donatello and a 'spectre' who appears from the depths of the catacombs, the seeds are sown of the tragic loss of innocence that lies at the heart of the novel.

In the Rome of *The Marble Faun*, the past is more potent than the present. The city appears to strain under the weight of its massive history — its malaria-riddled streets are shadowed by the grandeur of ancient ruins; its rich classical heritage is alive in marble; the Catholic opulence of its Renaissance art is overwhelming. All this in apparent striking contrast to Hawthorne's own New England Puritanism and the artlessness of the young American republic.

In his preface, Hawthorne calls *The Marble Faun* a 'Romance' and explains that he chose Italy as its setting because it could act as 'a sort of poetic or fairy precinct', because 'Romance and poetry, like ivy, lichens, and wall-flowers, need Ruin to make them grow.' Hawthorne wanted to be at liberty in his novel to invoke decadence and dark powers that might not have been acceptable to his readers if planted in American soil. 'No author, without a trial, can conceive the difficulty of writing a Romance about a country where there is no shadow, no antiquity, no mystery, no picturesque and gloomy wrong, nor anything but a common-place prosperity in broad daylight, as is happily the case with my dear native land.' And yet, ironically, while Hawthorne was in Europe grappling with art, nature and history, the 'broad daylight' of his 'dear native land' – the apparent innocence of America – was shortly to be lost forever. One year after *The Marble Faun* was published in 1860, the American Civil War erupted.

The Rome Hawthorne visited was almost untouched by the modern world – 'the lights and shadows were still mediaeval', wrote Harvard scholar, writer and compulsive global traveller Henry Adams of 1860s Rome. It was a Papal city garrisoned with French troops. Napoleon III was in the north of Italy, Count Camillo di Cavour was planning an independent Italy and Giuseppe Garibaldi was fighting with his thousand volunteers in the south. But Hawthorne was so enchanted – 'It is very singular, the sad embrace with which Rome takes possession of the soul' – that he included in *The Marble Faun* numerous details of Rome, its architecture and art. So comprehensive was his portrait of Rome that following the Civil War, when America experienced the beginning of a new age of growth and Americans began to travel to Europe, one of the books they took with them as a guide to Rome was *The Marble Faun*.

One tourist who was struck deeply not only by Rome but by Hawthorne's novel was the young Henry James, who first travelled to Rome in 1869. James discovered through Hawthorne 'that an American could be an artist, one of the finest, without "going outside" about it, as I liked to say'. *The Marble Faun*, with its exploration of the complex, troubled relationship between Europe and America, continued to influence American writers into the twentieth century, and prefigures the work of novelists like Fitzgerald and Hemingway.

Shortly after his return to America in 1860, Hawthorne fell into a deep depression and his hair suddenly turned white. He began to write '64' compulsively on scraps of paper before dying in his sleep while on a walking tour of New Hampshire with Franklin Pierce.

DAVID MAUPIN

- *Swann's Way* by Marcel Proust
- *Vanity Fair* by William Makepeace Thackeray
- *Clarissa* by Samuel Richardson
- *Sister Carrie* by Theodore Dreiser
- *The Custom of the Country* by Edith Wharton
- *Moll Flanders* by Daniel Defoe
- *Evelina* by Frances Burney

- *Giovanni's Room* by James Baldwin
- *A Good Man is Hard to Find* by Flannery O'Connor

David Maupin runs the avant-garde Lehmann Maupin Gallery in Chelsea, New York, which mounted English artist Tracey Emin's first solo show in the USA – *Every Part of Me's Bleeding* – in 1999. Emin achieved notoriety in 1999 with 'My Bed', her piece entered in the high profile Turner Prize exhibition, which consisted of her unmade bed, used condoms and blood-stained underwear.

15. Moby-Dick
by
HERMAN MELVILLE
(1819–1891)
❦

HERMAN MELVILLE'S SIXTH NOVEL, *Moby-Dick* (1851), is one of the most extraordinary novels ever composed. The story it tells is of classic simplicity: Captain Ahab sails on the *Pequod* in search of the white whale Moby-Dick, intent on avenging himself on the beast who has destroyed his leg and now swims before Ahab 'as the monomaniac incarnation of all those malicious agencies which some deep men feel'. Like Ahab's own fixed purpose, *Moby-Dick* is relentless in its focus on Ahab and his quest for the whale; it is also an encyclopedic agglomeration of notes on whales and whaling, boats and the ocean, geography, science, history, literature, religion, philosophy. As one contemporary reviewer commented, 'Who would have looked for philosophy in whales, or for poetry in blubber?' Melville's story contains both.

Moby-Dick opens with the famous declaration 'Call me Ishmael', which introduces its unusual narrator. Ishmael goes on to tell us that 'Whenever I find myself growing grim about the mouth; whenever it is a damp, drizzly November in my soul; whenever I find myself involuntarily pausing before coffin warehouses and bringing up the rear of every funeral I meet . . . then, I account it high time to get to sea as soon as I can.' The oceans of the nineteenth century were home to the Nantucket whaleships that roamed the sea in search of whales, like the *Pequod* on which Ishmael sails. Nineteenth-century life depended on whales – whale oil lit the streets and houses, it lubricated the machinery of industry, and whalebone was stitched into clothes, shaping nineteenth-century fashions. Melville's novel captures the buccaneering spirit of the whale-men who sailed the seas, abandoning dry land, warm homes and family for creaking damp ships and fellow sailors. As Ishmael remarks: 'There is nothing like the perils of whaling to breed this free and easy sort of genial, desperado philosophy.' Ishmael's amused, wry perspective on the world is the basis of much of the humour of *Moby-Dick*, and is essential to the novel's power, as is his loving friendship with the tattooed harpooner Queequeg. Their intimate, off-beat exchanges about whaling, religion and Queequeg's Pacific island life provide a vital human counterpoint to the wild excesses of Ahab.

Captain Ahab is a creation of King Lear–esque proportions, and his extravagant madness prompts Melville to Shakespearean heights of language and rhythm: 'They think me mad – Starbuck does; but I'm demoniac, I am madness maddened!' Ahab's madness has been caused by Moby-Dick, following the destruction of his leg by the malicious whale: 'Ahab and anguish lay stretched together in one hammock rounding in midwinter that dreary, howling Patagonian Cape; then it was, that his torn body and gashed soul bled into one another; and so interfusing, made him mad.' Even the boat Ahab captains is infected by his madness as it sails the troubled seas: 'The ivory-tusked Pequod sharply bowed to the blast, and gored the dark waves in her madness.'

Melville, the third child of Allan and Maria Melvill (the 'e' was added around 1832), was born in 1821 in New York City into an illustrious family whose Scottish and Dutch forebears were among the early settlers of New York. But, following the death of Melville's father, the family's fortunes waned. Melville, who had already started writing, briefly joined his eldest brother in their father's felt and fur business until it went bankrupt. He then decided to find work on the Eyrie Canal, being built at the time, but this plan failed and in 1839 Melville went to sea. In 1841 he sailed aboard the whaler *Acushnet* on a journey that was to shape his first two novels as well as provide rich material for *Moby-Dick*. While at sea, the *Acushnet* drew alongside a passing boat and the two crews mingled, whereupon Melville met a sailor called William Chase. William's father, Owen Chase, had been the first mate on the whaleship *Essex*, which in 1820 had been sunk by a sperm whale with apparent malicious intent. William regaled the 21-year-old Melville with his father's adventures and gave him his father's book, *The Wreck of the Whaleship Essex*, which had been published twenty years earlier. This true story, with its vengeful whale, was the seed of *Moby-Dick*.

When Melville returned to Boston in 1844, his family encouraged him to write his tales of seafaring adventure. His first two novels, *Typee: A Peep at Polynesian Life* (1846) and *Omoo: A Narrative of Adventures in the South Seas* (1847), were so successful that Melville quickly became one of America's most celebrated writers. In 1847 he married Elizabeth Shaw, the daughter of the distinguished Chief Justice of Massachusetts, and they had four children. In the spring of 1850, Melville read Nathaniel Hawthorne's *The Scarlet Letter* and was mesmerised by the portentous darkness of Hawthorne's haunted imagination. The two writers, who were neighbours in Pittsfield, met on a picnic in the summer of that same year and their rapport was immediate. Hawthorne was forty-six, Melville thirty-one. Melville, for whom the connection was intense, began to write impassioned letters to Hawthorne, declaring in one that 'Knowing you persuades me more than the Bible of our immortality.'

Inspired by Hawthorne and his reading of Shakespeare, especially *King Lear*, Melville transformed the whaling story he was working on – *The Whale*, based on Owen's tale – into its final form and renamed it *Moby-Dick*. Written in eighteen frenzied months, *Moby-Dick* was published when Melville was just thirty-two. Melville immediately sent Hawthorne a copy, who praised it in a letter, to which Melville replied with the full force of his Biblical imagination: 'A sense of unspeakable security is in me this moment on account of your having understood the book. I have written a wicked book, and feel spotless as a lamb.' (Hawthorne found Melville's intensity overwhelming and by 1852 the two writers had begun to drift apart. They met for the last time in

Liverpool, England, in 1856, when Hawthorne was the US consul there and Melville visited him during his tour of Europe and the Levant.)

Moby-Dick was published in London in three volumes in 1851 and a month later in America. Although there were some positive reviews, it brought Melville neither fame nor fortune, and following the failure of his next novel, *Pierre*, in 1852, Melville's career as a novelist was effectively over. He was thirty-three. He published only two more novels in his lifetime, and turned instead to writing poetry. In 1866 he published his first volume of poems, on the Civil War. The same year he found a position as a customs inspector on the New York docks, which he held for nearly ten years. Melville's last novel, *Billy Budd*, was completed five months before his death of a heart attack in 1891.

Billy Budd was not published until 1924, following the publication in 1921 of Raymond Weaver's book on Melville, *Herman Melville: Mariner and Mystic*, which reinterpreted Melville for a new era. It seems the literary experimentation of writers such as James Joyce and T.S. Eliot was conducive to the reappraisal of Melville's peculiar talent – for as Carl F. Hovde notes, *Moby-Dick* 'stood up to every scrutiny that modernism could bring'. *Moby-Dick* has since exerted a monumental influence over American literature, from Hemingway's *The Old Man and the Sea* (1952) to the detail of E. Annie Proulx's *The Shipping News* (1993) to Cormac McCarthy's desert voyage in *Blood Meridian* (1985). It has also inspired the work of American visual artists in the twentieth and twenty-first centuries, such as the painter Jackson Pollock and multimedia artist Laurie Anderson.

Melville was writing at a time of festering conflict over abolition and slavery, which in 1861 exploded into civil war. When asked why black Americans don't 'show up' in American novels of the 1840s and '50s, African-American writer Toni Morrison replied: 'Well, they do. They do show up. They're everywhere.' In Morrison's view, the chances of getting 'a truly complex human black person in an American book in the nineteenth century were minimal', but Melville came close to dealing with black Americans: 'Each one of the white men in *Moby-Dick* has a black brother. They're paired together.'

In 1956, John Huston's screen version of *Moby-Dick* was released, starring Gregory Peck as Ahab. Huston directed and co-wrote the screenplay with writer Ray Bradbury. Orson Welles played Father Mapple, whose famous sermon in the novel concludes with the beautiful, resonant line: 'I leave eternity to thee; for what is man that he should live out the lifetime of his God?'

ANNAMARIE JAGOSE

My list of classics shows how books that were once part of a recognised literary canon are open to readings that subvert mainstream cultural values — here, specifically sexual values, those things the canon has more usually been understood to protect and transmit.

- *Emma* by Jane Austen
- *Moby-Dick* by Herman Melville

- ☙ *Little Dorrit* by Charles Dickens
- ☙ *The Bostonians* by Henry James
- ☙ *The Picture of Dorian Gray* by Oscar Wilde
- ☙ *A Passage to India* by E.M. Forster
- ☙ *Mrs Dalloway* by Virginia Woolf
- ☙ *Miss MacIntosh, My Darling* by Marguerite Young
- ☙ *The Twyborn Affair* by Patrick White
- ☙ *Miss Peabody's Inheritance* by Elizabeth Jolley

Annamarie Jagose is an academic and an award-winning novelist. Her books include *In Translation* (1994), *Lulu: A Romance* (1998) and *Slow Water* (2003).

16 . *Madame Bovary*

by

GUSTAVE FLAUBERT

(1 8 2 1 – 1 8 8 0)

⚬

'THE WHOLE OF HER immediate environment – dull countryside,
imbecile petty bourgeois, life in its ordinariness – seemed a freak,
a particular piece of bad luck that had seized on her; while beyond,
as far as eye could see, ranged the vast lands of passion and felicity.'
So life seems to Gustave Flaubert's Madame Bovary, and, like his
most famous creation, Flaubert too longed for the exotic and unattainable, and found life in nineteenth-century provincial France
utterly banal. Early on, the precocious, strikingly beautiful young
Flaubert decided that literature was the means by which he'd
endure the boredom of life: 'The one way of tolerating existence is
to lose oneself in literature as in a perpetual orgy.'

In 1851, following an eighteen-month tour of the Orient he'd
long dreamed of, Flaubert returned to his mother's house on the
Seine near Rouen and began work on a novel about the provincial

life he so despised. For five years he laboured, drumming out the rhythms of his prose with his fingers on his writing desk, producing an agonised five hundred words a week until the manuscript of *Madame Bovary* was completed. So slowly did he work that he wrote to his lover Louise Colet that he was 'like a man playing the piano with lead balls attached to his knuckles'. In 1856, Flaubert's friend Maxime Du Camp published the first of six instalments of *Madame Bovary* in his periodical *Révue de Paris*. The novel sold well but the audacity of Emma Bovary's behaviour so shocked readers that Flaubert was brought to trial, under the repressive censorship of the regime of Louis Bonaparte (Napoleon III), on grounds of offending public morality, religion and decency. Flaubert escaped conviction, but six months later the poet Charles Baudelaire was found guilty of the same charges for *Les Fleurs du Mal*.

What so shocked contemporary readers of *Madame Bovary* was Emma's rebellion against her marriage and her role as the wife of provincial doctor Charles Bovary. Emma, who loves words and literature, is married to a man whose conversation is 'as flat as a street pavement, on which everybody's ideas trudged past, in their workaday dress, provoking no emotion, no laughter, no dreams'. So the restless Emma makes her own dreams. She longs 'to travel — or to go back to the convent. She wanted to die, and she wanted to live in Paris.' She buys a guide to Paris to imagine herself in its boulevards, subscribes to women's papers to immerse herself in the latest fashions and gossip, and loses herself in the romantic novels of Sir Walter Scott, Balzac and George Sand.

Unable — and unwilling — to reconcile herself to her lot, Emma allows herself to be seduced. She remembers 'the heroines of the books she had read and that lyrical legion of adulteresses began to sing in her memory with sisterly voices that enchanted her'. Like Don Quixote, Emma has lost herself in romantic literature and attempts to live her life by its conventions. And, like Don Quixote's friends, Emma's husband and mother-in-law believe the cure for her malaise is to prevent her from reading novels. (Flaubert was reading *Don Quixote* while writing *Madame Bovary*.)

The story of an adulterous wife was suggested to Flaubert by his friend the poet Louis Bouilhet, who had read Flaubert's *The Temptation of Saint Anthony* in 1849 and panned it, urging him instead to write a down-to-earth novel like Balzac's *Parents Pauvres*. Bouilhet suggested a novel based on the tragic true story of Eugène Delamare, a country doctor in Normandy who died of grief after being betrayed and ruined by his wife, Delphine. This story was one source of *Madame Bovary*. Flaubert may also have been influenced by *Mémoires de Madame Ludovica*, the autobiographical adventures of his friend Louise Pradier, the wife of the Swiss sculptor James Pradier at whose studio Flaubert first met his lover Louise Colet in 1846.

Flaubert set *Madame Bovary* in the 1830s, a decade governed by Louis-Philippe (whose overthrow in 1848 Flaubert rejoiced in) and the rise of the bourgeoisie in France. The July Monarchy of Louis-Philippe was installed after the revolution of 1830 and lasted until the revolution of 1848. Louis-Philippe was deliberately called 'Louis-Philippe, King of the French', rather than 'Philip VII, King of France', to denote that he was a man of the people. During the 1830s, French literature flourished and, for the first time, novels, including those of Stendhal and Balzac, began to compete with the work of the Romantic poets for a mass readership.

Madame Bovary is remarkable for the power of its language, its rhythms and the precision and compactness of its metaphors (even in translation). Flaubert was the first writer to treat the novel as a work of art, and to aspire to lift it to the level and significance of poetry. As he wrote to Louise Colet, he wanted his style to be 'as rhythmical as verse and as precise as the language of science'. His novel also contains one of the most beautiful expressions of our inability to contain in language our deepest, most intimate feelings. When Emma's jaded lover mentally dismisses her protestations of love (which she expresses in cliché, despite the depth of her feeling) with the thought 'High flown language concealing tepid affection must be discounted', the narrator, or Flaubert, in a rare intrusion, counters: 'as though the full heart may not sometimes overflow in the emptiest of metaphors, since no one can ever give the exact measure of his needs, his thoughts or his sorrows, and human speech is like a cracked kettle on which we strum out tunes to make a bear dance, when we would move the stars to pity'.

Flaubert was born in Rouen, west of Paris, in 1821. His father was the chief surgeon at the Hôtel-Dieu Hospital in Rouen, and his mother was a doctor's daughter. He was destined, like all good bourgeois men of his day, to become a lawyer, but the onset of a nervous illness (probably epilepsy) at the age of twenty-two forced him to abandon his legal studies in Paris. After his father's death in 1846, followed by his beloved sister Caroline's death the following March, Flaubert retired to an estate in Croisset, on the Seine just south of Rouen, with his mother and niece. There he found the perfect conditions for writing: 'I can imagine nothing in the world preferable to a nice, well-heated room with the books one loves and the leisure one wants.'

Here he spent most of the rest of his life cloistered in his room overlooking the Seine. He did travel to Paris in February 1848 to witness the 'beautiful revolution' – the overthrow of the regime of Louis-Philippe – and, with his friend Maxime Du Camp, was one of the first to tour the liberated Tuileries. And in November 1849 Flaubert journeyed with Du Camp through Egypt, Palestine, Syria, Turkey, Italy and Greece. His travels fired his imagination (according to Du Camp, Flaubert thought of the name 'Emma Bovary' while they were walking above the Nile) and allowed him to indulge his passion for prostitutes. Flaubert never married, but had an intense affair with the poet Louise Colet from 1846 until their breakup in 1855, conducted mostly by correspondence with the occasional 'big fuck', as Flaubert put it, in a railway hotel midway between Croisset and Paris, where Colet lived.

In 1866, Flaubert was awarded the prestigious French medal the Legion of Honour for his novel *Salammbo*. The flamboyant writer celebrated the near completion of that manuscript with a reading and an exotic Oriental dinner for his friends. According to his handwritten menu, the dinner included 'human flesh, brain of bourgeois and tigress clitorises sautéed in rhinoceros butter'. Flaubert managed to combine his monkish existence outside Paris with a busy social life in the capital, where he was feted in literary circles and had many friends. He had a deep and abiding friendship with the writer George Sand and was like a father to Guy de Maupassant, who saw himself as Flaubert's disciple. Flaubert died suddenly of an apoplectic stroke, with an unfinished page on his table.

Flaubert was revered by Vladimir Nabokov (1899–1977) for his 'clinically accurate style' and objectivity. Nabokov included *Madame Bovary* in his short list of eight to ten great European novels and believed that 'Without Flaubert there would have been no Marcel Proust in France, no James Joyce in Ireland, Chekhov in Russia would not have been quite Chekhov.' Nabokov's *King, Queen, Knave* (published in English in 1968) was inspired by *Madame Bovary* (and *Anna Karenina*). Flaubert also influenced Oscar Wilde, T.S. Eliot and Julian Barnes's *Flaubert's Parrot* (1984). Jean-Paul Sartre, on the other hand, hated Flaubert. Sartre spent just over ten years, from 1960 to 1971, writing a great four-volume biography in damnation of Flaubert, called *L'Idiot de la Famille*, which he never finished.

The writer Mario Vargas Llosa wrote a book in praise of *Madame Bovary* – *The Perpetual Orgy* (1975) – in which he diagnoses its enduring power and modernity: 'In *Madame Bovary* we see the first signs of alienation that a century later will take hold of men and women in industrial societies . . . Emma's drama is the gap between illusion and reality.' And the instrument of Emma's undoing, the magic wand she uses to realise her dreams, however temporarily and ultimately unsatisfactorily, is also eerily modern: financial credit. The shopkeeper Monsieur Lheureux insinuates himself into Emma's life, demonstrating to her that far from wanting nothing, as she'd believed, her need for trifles and fripperies is limitless – as, apparently, is the credit he will extend to her.

The continuing resonance of *Madame Bovary* is reflected in its many screen adaptations, including Vincente Minnelli's 1949 cinema adaptation starring Jennifer Jones as Emma, Louis Jourdan as Rodolphe Boulanger, and James Mason, who plays Flaubert defending himself against charges of obscenity. Claude Chabrol's faithful adaptation starring Isabelle Huppert was released in 1991, and in 2000 *Madame Bovary* was adapted by the BBC for television, starring Australian actress Frances O'Connor.

MICHELLE DE KRETSER

- *Persuasion* by Jane Austen
- *Alice in Wonderland* by Lewis Carroll
- *Heart of Darkness* by Joseph Conrad
- *Great Expectations* by Charles Dickens
- *Madame Bovary* by Gustave Flaubert
- *Odyssey* by Homer
- *Against Nature* by J-K Huysmans
- *Turn of the Screw* by Henry James
- *In Search of Lost Time* by Marcel Proust
- *The Waves* by Virginia Woolf

Born in Columbo to a Sri Lankan family which emigrated to Australia when she was fourteen, Michelle de Kretser took an MA at the Sorbonne and worked for several years as an editor. The author of two acclaimed novels, *The Rose Grower* (1999) and *The Hamilton Case* (2003), de Kretser now lives in Melbourne.

17. The Idiot
by
FYODOR DOSTOYEVSKY
(1 8 2 1 – 1 8 8 1)

FYODOR DOSTOYEVSKY'S THE IDIOT is the story of Prince Leo
Nikolayevich Myshkin, a young Russian so honest and ingenuous
that on first sight he is taken for an idiot. His open demeanour
draws people to him and friends feel compelled to confide in him,
yet they are never quite sure if the prince's peculiar, penetrating
perceptions are the fruit of profound wisdom or madness. As one
friend says to him: 'Why, Prince, your simplicity and innocence
are such as were never heard of in the golden age, and then, all of
a sudden, you pierce a fellow through and through, like an arrow,
with such profound psychological insight!' While Dostoyevsky
was struggling with the manuscript of the novel, trying to focus his
vision of the idiot Prince whom he wanted to be a convincing,
perfectly good man, he wrote to himself on 8 April 1868: 'NB The
prince – Christ'.

Shortly after marrying for the second time, in 1867, Dostoyevsky travelled with his wife to Europe. In Basel he saw a painting of Jesus by Hans Holbein which he found so confronting that he stood frozen before it for twenty minutes. His wife recalled that 'the figure of Christ taken from the cross, whose body already showed signs of decomposition, haunted him like a horrible night-mare. In his notes to *The Idiot* and in the novel itself he returns again and again to this theme.' Wracked by debt and debilitating epileptic fits that recurred almost every ten days, and grief-stricken following the death of his baby girl in 1868, Dostoyevsky wrote: 'After all this they demand from me a work of pure art and poetry, without strain, without tearing passions, and point to Turgenev and Goncharov. Let them remember under what condi-tions I do my work.'

Under these excruciating conditions, Dostoyevsky wrote *The Idiot*, working and working at his new novel, tearing up pages and starting again. At the time he was preoccupied by the Gospels, the work of Ernest Renan (whose bestselling *Life of Jesus*, which depicted Jesus as a mortal man, and not the son of God, had been published in France in 1863) and Shakespeare's *Othello*, with its themes of jealousy and passion.

I thought from 4 December to 18 December inclusive. On the average I made six different plans (no less) daily. My head was turned into a windmill. How I did not go mad, I don't understand. At last on 18 December I sat down to write a new novel and on 5 January I had already sent off five chapters of the first part to Moscow.

Unlike his compatriots Tolstoy and Turgenev, Dostoyevsky had no independent income and was forced to earn his living from writing to deadline, so he was forever writing in haste, desperate to earn his next payment.

The Idiot opens with the meeting of two extraordinary young men, Prince Leo Myshkin and Parfyon Rogozhin, on a cold November morning in a carriage of the Warsaw train as it approaches (St) Petersburg at full speed. These two bizarre men are immediately drawn to each other. Their strange passions, and their love for the same woman, ignite Dostoyevsky's intense, explosive novel about love, desire and jealousy, suffering and madness. The novel races along as swiftly as the trains Dostoyevsky's loquacious character Lebedev so abhors, its action consisting predominantly of conversations — heated discussions, intimate confessions, fierce pronouncements — that erupt in set pieces in houses, salons and drawing rooms across Petersburg and the country town of Pavlovsk.

Soon after his arrival in Petersburg from a clinic in Switzerland, the prince visits a distant relative, a Princess Myshkin married to the prominent General Yepanchin. The Yepanchins have three beautiful, accomplished daughters, but the beauty of their youngest daughter, Aglaya, is matched by only one other woman in Petersburg — Nastasya Filippovna. Through the prince, the lives of these two beautiful women become inextricably linked: Aglaya forms a perverse, ambivalent attachment to the prince, but his heart has already been stricken by Nastasya Filippovna. When the prince first sees Nastasya in a portrait, her dazzling beauty pierces him to the depths of his soul. He finds her beauty 'quite unbearable — the beauty of that pale face, those almost hollow cheeks and burning eyes — a strange beauty!' and falls into a peculiar, bold species of love with her.

The prince has been treated in Switzerland by a doctor renowned for his work with idiocy and insanity. Like Dostoyevsky, the prince is an epileptic, and the novel includes a vivid description of the onset of an epileptic fit. The prince's detailed story of a man who faces execution, only to be given a last-minute reprieve, is also based on Dostoyevsky's own life. Born in Moscow in 1821, Dostoyevsky was the second son of a surgeon and a cultured woman from a merchant family. His father expected him to become a military engineer, and he was sent to the Academy of Military Engineering in St Petersburg. But after his father's death in 1839 — he was rumoured to have been murdered by the serfs on his small estate — Dostoyevsky left the army in 1844 to become a writer. His first published work was a translation of one of his favourite authors, Balzac's *Eugénie Grandet*. He then wrote a novella, *Poor Folk*, which so impressed two of his friends that they rushed over to Dostoyevsky's house at 4 am to tell him it was a masterpiece. By his mid twenties, Dostoyevsky had become a prominent literary figure in St Petersburg.

In April 1849, Dostoyevsky and other members of the Petrashevsky Circle, a group of socialist intellectuals dedicated to illegal terrorist agitation with whom he mixed, were arrested and imprisoned. Dostoyevsky's first epileptic fit followed soon after. Eight months later, on 22 December, Dostoyevsky and the other prisoners were led into a square and sentenced to death by firing squad. Only at the very last moment were they told that Tsar Nicholas I had spared their lives. It turned out the mock execution was part of their punishment. The experience of imminent death sent one prisoner mad on the spot and marked Dostoyevsky for the rest of his life. Instead of execution, Dostoyevsky was sent to Siberia for four years of hard labour. Here he spent many hours reading the Bible, which convinced him of the power of the beliefs of ordinary Russians and confirmed his faith in the Russian Orthodox Church. So passionately did Dostoyevsky value his faith in Christ that he later wrote that he would 'prefer to remain with Christ than with the truth'.

While in Siberia, Dostoyevsky married, in 1857, and two years later he was permitted to return to St Petersburg, where his wife died in 1864. His beloved brother died soon after and Dostoyevsky became addicted to gambling, and was plagued by debt and epileptic seizures. After accepting an advance on a new novel, he had still not begun writing it less than a month before the deadline. So he hired a stenographer and, remarkably, dictated *The Gambler* in the remaining few weeks. It was published in 1866. The stenographer was 22-year-old Anna Snitkina, and she and Dostoyevsky were married the following year. Soon after their marriage, they left Russia.

When he returned to Russia in 1873, Dostoyevsky had become famous throughout the world for his novels *Crime and Punishment* (1866), *The Idiot* and *The Possessed* (1871–1872). His last novel, *The Brothers Karamazov*, was completed not long before his death in 1881, by which time he had come to be seen in Russia as a prophet. Like the funeral of his contemporary Tolstoy, whom he never met, Dostoyevsky's funeral was a national event, attended by thirty thousand mourners.

Dostoyevsky wrote during a time of great ferment and upheaval in Russia, a time of modernisation and Westernisation of which Dostoyevsky was deeply suspicious. In *The Idiot*, the onrush of change is symbolised by the ominous presence of the railway – 'this network in which men are entangled' – which is spreading across Europe and Russia. Lebedev sees the railway as the sign of humanity's ruin, and is mocked for his belief:

'Not the railways – no, sir!' retorted Lebedev, losing his temper and at the same time enjoying himself immensely. 'The railways will not pollute the waters of life by themselves alone; but the whole thing, sir, is damned, the whole spirit of the last few centuries, taken as a whole, sir, in its scientific and practical application, is perhaps really damned, sir!'

His damnation of railways has an eerie resonance in our times, for they played so macabre a part in the history of twentieth-century Europe, taking Jews and other prisoners to Auschwitz (and the blazing railways ignited to mark the sixtieth anniversary of Auschwitz seemed to radiate like the apocalyptic star Lebedev invokes in *The Idiot*).

The Idiot is remarkable for Dostoyevsky's profound and un-nerving understanding of the human soul. Nietzsche called Dostoyevsky 'the only psychologist from whom I have anything to learn'. The novel is also remarkable for the brilliant passion yet strange disenchantment of Dostoyevsky's writing, which possesses a harsh, comic, razor-sharp objectivity, an irony, that can be felt in

Kafka, Bulgakov and Nabokov. Two of the twentieth century's greatest filmmakers were haunted by *The Idiot* – Akira Kurosawa and Andrei Tarkovsky. Kurosawa's 1951 film *Hakuchi* is based on *The Idiot*. Set in Hokkaido, in the snow and blizzards of northern Japan, the story takes place following the Second World War and the central Prince Myshkin character is a war veteran. Unfortunately, Andrei Tarkovsky's dream of interpreting *The Idiot* for the cinema was never realised, following the Soviet film authorities' rejection of his proposal. This prompted him to accept an invitation to work in Italy, and he died four years later, in 1986, in Paris. A Russian miniseries made for television in 2002 and screened in 2003 was the first film version of the complete novel.

GEORGIA BLAIN

- *War and Peace* by Leo Tolstoy. Wonderful characters, engrossing story and fascinating thoughts on the absurdity of codifying war. As relevant today as it was when it was written.
- *Crime and Punishment* by Fyodor Dostoyevsky. A dark and horrifying examination of the human psyche.
- *Wuthering Heights* by Emily Brontë. Unforgettable. A Gothic love story that descends into a portrayal of complete cruelty.
- *The Heart is a Lonely Hunter* by Carson McCullers. A novel that is beautifully tender and compassionate.

- *Middlemarch* by George Eliot. A close and intelligent look at what happens when we pair up with the wrong person.
- *The Leopard* by Giuseppe Tomasi di Lampedusa. A wise novel that examines the inevitability of change.

Georgia Blain is the author of *Closed for Winter* (1998), *Candelo* (1999), *The Blind Eye* (2001) and *Names for Nothingness* (2004).

18. *War and Peace*

by

LEO TOLSTOY

(1828–1910)

⚜

'AND ONLY NOW, WHEN I AM LIVING for others – or at least trying to
– only now do I realize all the happiness life holds,' says Pierre
Bezuhov, one of the central characters of Count Leo Tolstoy's novel
War and Peace. Pierre is the character most like Tolstoy himself, and
his realisation reflects the view of life Tolstoy had reached following his marriage, aged thirty-four, to Sofya (Sonya) Andreyevina
Bers, the teenage daughter of the Tsar's physician. After years of
carousing, excessive drinking, gambling and sex, as well as restless
questing for purpose, in 1862 Tolstoy settled into a decade of
domestic bliss. During this decade, he dedicated five frenzied years
to one massive work, which would become *War and Peace*, the realisation of a vast vision. Tolstoy felt himself to be at the height of
his powers – as he said at the time: 'Now I am an author with all
the powers of my soul.'

War and Peace began as several chapters of a novel about an exiled hero of the Decembrist Uprising of 1825, a key revolutionary moment in Russia's history. But, as the work progressed, Tolstoy soon realised that the Decembrist Uprising was so inextricably bound to Napoleon's advance into Russia twenty-three years earlier that he could not write about the uprising without going back to Napoleon's 1812 invasion and the battle of Borodino. As he writes at the opening of Part Three in *War and Peace*: 'The battle of Borodino with the occupation of Moscow that followed and the flight of the French, without any more engagements, is one of the most instructive phenomena in history.' Tolstoy was fascinated by the sudden failure of the French incursion into Russia, by the apparent psychological collapse of the French Army, rather than its military defeat. His fascination with Napoleon's battles led him to the idea of a psychological novel about Alexander I and Napoleon, and the lives of the Russian people during the upheaval of war.

My mind was filled with the possibility of doing a great thing – of writing a psychological novel of Alexander and Napoleon, and of all the baseness, all the empty phrases, the foolishness and the inconsistencies of their *entourage* and of the pair themselves.

The work that resulted is a sweeping portrait of Russia from 1805 to 1820.

Tolstoy's extraordinary achievement in *War and Peace* was to write a novel on a grand scale, featuring over 550 characters, embracing Napoleon's march across Eastern Europe and running to well over a thousand pages in English, from a perspective so intimate it is not only compelling but devastating to read. At the heart of *War and Peace* are the lives of three characters – Pierre Bezuhov, Prince Andrei Bolkonsky and Natasha Rostov – and two families, the Rostovs and the aristocratic Bolkonskys. Together they bring this vast novel to life, animating the broad sweep of history with their love affairs and heartbreaks, their losses, anxieties, quests for meaning and their fortunes on the chaotic fields of war. Tolstoy writes with such affection and understanding of his characters that we become lost in their lives, immersed with them in the wave of history as it uproots them from their homes and loved-ones.

War and Peace opens on a July evening in 1805 at an aristocratic soirée in Petersburg, with a discussion about the inevitability of war and the scourge of Napoleon, held to be 'the Antichrist'. But Pierre Bezuhov commits the sacrilege of praising him: 'Napoleon is great because he towered over the Revolution, suppressed its abuses, preserving all that was good in it.' Pierre, a stout young man who has been educated abroad in Europe, is making his first appearance in society. He takes up with the handsome Prince Andrei Bolkonsky, who finds society tedious and is patently bored: 'Drawing rooms, tittle-tattle, balls, idle conceits and futility – such is the enchanted circle that encloses me. I am setting off now to take part in the war, the greatest war there ever was.' The novel proceeds to unfold the tale of this war, as well as several great love stories, the greatest of which are the loves of its heroine, Natasha Rostov, whom we first meet as a young girl with her doll: 'The little girl with her black eyes and wide mouth was not pretty but she was full of life.'

As well as Tolstoy's stories of Natasha, Andrei and Pierre, and his vivid set pieces of history encompassing battle scenes, diplomatic negotiations and councils with Napoleon and Alexander, Tolstoy digresses to propound his theory of history, a view that is typically idiosyncratic and at odds with the prevailing view of his times. He even applies to history a new branch of mathematics — calculus — developed in the seventeenth century by Isaac Newton in England and Gottfried Leibnitz in Germany. 'Only by assuming an infinitesimally small unit for observation — a differential of history (that is, the common tendencies of men) — and arriving at the art of integration (finding the sum of the infinitesimals) can we hope to discover the laws of history,' writes Tolstoy. In his understanding of the *spirit* of history and the multitudes of people and apparently insignificant events that contribute to its making, Tolstoy went against the intellectual fashions of his day, which were characterised by Thomas Carlyle's hero-based view expounded in *On Heroes, Hero-Worship, and the Heroic in History* (1841). Tolstoy's view is, in fact, closer to our current understanding of the behaviour of complex systems as explained by Chaos Theory.

Over his eighty-two years, Tolstoy lived to see Russia change from a serf-based agricultural economy, through the emancipation of the serfs in 1861 by Tsar Alexander II, to an industrialising nation engaged on the world scene in the early twentieth century. To his dismay, Russia seemed to be abandoning its old ways in favour of the revolutionary spirit of western Europe fired by the great exploits of Napoleon early in the nineteenth century. In *War and Peace*, the soul of old Russia is embodied in the Russian general Kutuzov, whose sense of his own marginal role in the outcome of events is vastly different from the egoistic temperament and heroic dreams of Napoleon as Tolstoy portrays him. Kutuzov understands that battles are decided not by individuals, not by generals, but by 'that intangible force called the spirit of the army, and he kept an eye on that force and guided it as far as lay within his power'. Tolstoy's interpretation of Kutuzov's role ran against the common view of the day, which considered the old general to have been washed up and ineffectual.

Tolstoy was born into an aristocratic family in 1828 on the family estate, Yasnaya Polyana, south of Moscow. His mother died when he was one and his father several years later, so Tolstoy and his four siblings were sent to stay with an aunt in western Russia. There he went to university in 1844 and spent several dissolute years studying Oriental languages before transferring to law because it was less demanding. During these years, Tolstoy read widely and voraciously, particularly enjoying the work of Dickens (he especially loved *David Copperfield* (1849)), Laurence Sterne's *Sentimental Voyage* (1768) and the French philosopher Rousseau's *Confessions* (1782), this last of which had an enormous influence on him. So much did Tolstoy love the work of Rousseau that instead of a cross around his neck he wore a medallion imprinted with the face of Rousseau. When he was nineteen, Tolstoy returned to Yasnaya Polyana. Here he began to keep a diary, filled with strict rules designed to restrain his vigorous appetite for sex and gambling — and harsh outbursts of self-reproach for his failure to stick to his rules.

In 1851, Tolstoy travelled to the Caucasus, where his brother was an army officer. He too joined the army, fighting in the Crimean War of 1853 to 1856, and soon began to write short stories about the war, horrified by the reality of battle and its abysmal failure to live up to his heroic dreams. After the war, Tolstoy resigned from the army in disgust to devote himself to a higher calling – education – and opened a school for the children of his serfs. His first published work, Childhood, appeared in a periodical in 1852. Plagued by crippling doubts about his talent, Tolstoy was overjoyed when he heard Childhood had been accepted for publication in the magazine The Contemporary, founded by the great poet Pushkin. Then in 1865, Tolstoy began work on War and Peace, which he completed in 1869. As Tolstoy wrote, his wife Sonya copied out his pages. She noted in her diary that her husband worked with great emotion, 'the tears starting in his eyes and his heart swelling. I believe his novel is going to be wonderful.'

During their long marriage, Tolstoy and Sonya had thirteen children, although the happy years of their early married life did not last long. Following the completion of Anna Karenina (1874–1876), Tolstoy fell into profound despair. Plagued by thoughts of death and the meaninglessness of life, he read the great works of Christianity, Buddhism and Islam, hoping to find comfort in their pages. He finally found solace in the teachings of Jesus. But, typical of the man, he was not content with the Gospels as they had been written and decided to write his own. Impatient with their miracles and the mystic trinity of Father, Son and Holy Ghost, Tolstoy rewrote the Gospels to forge his own singular version, fusing the four accounts of Jesus' life into one that portrayed Jesus not as the son of God but as a wise man who understood how to live. For this and other heretical behaviour, Tolstoy was excommunicated by the Russian Orthodox Church in 1901.

By the end of his long life, Tolstoy had renounced literature and become a spiritual leader with hundreds of followers around the world, some of whom saw him as a prophet with godlike powers. In 1894, the young Indian revolutionary Mohandas (later Mahatma) Gandhi read Tolstoy's *The Kingdom of God is Within You* and was profoundly influenced by its ideas, especially Tolstoy's pacifist doctrine of non-resistance to evil (in *War and Peace* Tolstoy calls war 'the vilest thing in life'). Gandhi referred to Tolstoy as 'the sage of Yasnaya Polyana' and in his honour founded the Tolstoy Farm near Johannesburg where he spent the final phase of his passive resistance campaign in South Africa, from 1908 to 1914. Dozens of Tolstoy's many followers moved to Yasnaya Polyana to be closer to their idol, which interfered with his family life and put a great strain on his marriage. Eventually, in 1910, aged eighty-two, Tolstoy fled the chaos of his beloved Yasnaya Polyana in the middle of the night with his doctor and one daughter. He died soon after at a deserted railway station on his way to a monastery. Four thousand people lined the streets for Tolstoy's funeral and in Moscow students rallied. The Duma (parliament) was adjourned for the day and all of Russia mourned.

Although Virginia Woolf thought little of James Joyce, the one thing over which the two writers were in perfect agreement was Tolstoy's genius. Joyce worshipped Tolstoy. Woolf called him 'the greatest of all novelists — for what else can we call the author of *War and Peace*?'

BARRY PEARCE

- *A Tale of Two Cities* by Charles Dickens
- *The Brothers Karamazov* by Fyodor Dostoyevsky
- *Tess of the D'Urbervilles* by Thomas Hardy
- *The Great Gatsby* by F. Scott Fitzgerald
- *Madame Bovary* by Gustave Flaubert
- *Ulysses* by James Joyce
- *The Magic Mountain* by Thomas Mann
- *In Search of Lost Time* by Marcel Proust
- *The Red and the Black* by Stendhal
- *Anna Karenina* by Leo Tolstoy

I would have liked to have squeezed Albert Camus' autobiographical novel *The First Man* into the list of ten. An unfinished manuscript found in the car wreck which killed the writer in 1960, it ripped into my heart about the father I never knew and hangs indelibly there more than any of the others. But it's not really a classic, and is perhaps too personal.

Barry Pearce is the head curator of Australian art at the Art Gallery of New South Wales. He is also the author of *Jeffrey Smart* (2005).

19. *Jude the Obscure*
by
THOMAS HARDY
(1840–1928)

THOMAS HARDY ONCE OBSERVED that while in a poem he could
question the nature of God – 'the Supreme Mover or Movers, the
Prime Force or Forces' – without provoking the outrage of readers,
when he did the same thing in a novel it made them 'sneer, or foam,
and set all the literary contortionists jumping upon me, a harmless
agnostic, as if I were a clamorous atheist, which in their crass illit-
eracy they seem to think is the same thing'. The response of the
literary contortionists to *Jude the Obscure* was so vicious that
although Hardy lived another thirty-three years after its publication, it was the last novel he ever wrote. The Bishop of Wakefield
went so far as to burn his copy of the book – 'probably in his
despair at not being able to burn me', Hardy remarked. *Jude the
Obscure* was so violently attacked on its publication in 1895 that it
'completely cur [ed]' Hardy of further interest in novel writing, as

he put it in his 1912 postscript to the novel, and he thereafter devoted his energies to his original passion, poetry. What so angered his critics was that through his story of Jude Fawley, the village boy who dreams of university and a career in the Church, Hardy exposed the soul-crushing rigidity of the laws that bound Victorian society: laws of class, wealth, marriage and religion.

Hardy was born in Dorset in 1840, the eldest of four children of Thomas Hardy Snr, a stonemason, master builder and violinist, and his wife, Jemima; and he grew up in a small cottage bordered by wild heathland. His mother encouraged his precocious intellect and passion for learning, his father taught him the violin, and he received a good grounding in Latin, French and mathematics at school in the nearby town of Dorchester. Although he longed to go to university, he followed his father's trade and was apprenticed to a local architect. At twenty-one, Hardy went to work in London as a draftsman with a leading ecclesiastical architect, where he remained until illness drove him back to Dorset in 1867. Three years later, his architectural work took him to an isolated church in Cornwall and there he met the lively Emma Lavinia Gifford. Against both families' wishes − Hardy's ambitious mother advised her children never to marry and Emma's family thought Hardy beneath her − they were married in 1874, eventually settling in Dorchester in 1883 where Hardy designed 'Max Gate', the rambling house in which he lived until his death, aged eighty-seven. After selling his novel based on his romance with Emma (*A Pair of Blue Eyes*) to *Tinsley's Magazine* in 1872, Hardy gave up architecture to devote himself completely to writing. The brilliant editor Leslie Stephen (father of Virginia Woolf) was struck by

Hardy's talent and asked him to write a novel for his prestigious *Cornhill Magazine*. Hardy responded by writing *Far From the Madding Crowd*. He worked with such manic urgency that he wrote on anything, even dead leaves, woodchips and stone fragments when he could find no paper. *Far From the Madding Crowd* was published in 1874 and brought Hardy fame and fortune.

By the time he came to write *Jude the Obscure*, from scribbled notes in 1887 to its completion in 1894, Hardy was one of the most feted writers in England and had long before left behind his humble origins as the son of a stonemason. As a young aspiring writer with one rejected manuscript and desperate to be published, Hardy had followed the advice of novelist George Meredith on how to tailor his work to suit the reading public. Almost thirty years later, as an established writer weathering the storms of outrage that had greeted *Tess of the D'Urbervilles* in 1891, Hardy could write what he wanted. *Jude the Obscure* seethes with Hardy's long-nursed outrage at the hypocrisy of Victorian England.

Like Hardy, Jude Fawley is a country boy determined to move beyond the stifling confines of village life to the university town on the horizon, 'city of light and love'. But although Victorian society was overlaid by visions of progress and industry, many like Jude who attempted to progress beyond the circumstances of their birth were thwarted on their path, damned from the start by their poverty. Hardy himself lived out the Victorian ideal of self-improvement, rising from poor country boy to celebrated, well-off writer through diligence, hard work and perseverance, virtues expounded by Samuel Smiles in his bestselling book *Self-Help* published in 1859. Self-help groups flourished in Victorian

England, like Jude's 'Artisans' Mutual Improvement Society' that assists young men to 'enlarge their minds'. But, through Jude, Hardy launched a furious attack on the self-help philosophy, exposing its terrible flaws. *Jude the Obscure* is a devastating portrait of love, marriage and poverty, of aspirations crushed by lack of material resources, in which the poor of industrial England are like the Indian peasants in Rohinton Mistry's *A Fine Balance* (1995) – trapped in an endless cycle of circumstances beyond their control, there is an overwhelming sense of doom hanging over their every effort to better themselves. As Jude despairs, 'I'm an outsider to the end of my days!' His tragedy is born of a conflict between his aspirations, the pressures of poverty, his illicit sexual passions and the bonds of marriage.

In response to his critics, who attacked his book for its treatment of marriage and the religion that sanctifies it, Hardy wrote that contemporary marriage laws – 'the forced adaptation of human instincts to rusty and irksome moulds that do not fit them' (which he knew from personal experience, as his own marriage was deeply troubled) – seemed to him 'a good foundation for the fable of a tragedy'. Jude and his cousin and soul-mate Sue Bridehead, a 'New Woman', come from a family cursed to marry unhappily and so they attempt to live outside its suffocating laws. Sue, who sees a bride's flowers as 'sadly like the garland which decked the heifers of sacrifice in old times', goes further, by attempting to live outside the comfort of the Church, and finding solace in pagan symbols and literature. Instead of reading the Bible before bed, she reads the contemporary poet Swinburne, quoting from his 'Hymn to Proserpine', the lament of a fourth-century pagan Roman on the advent of Christianity as state religion and the outlawing of his own beloved gods: 'Thou hast conquered, O pale Galilean: / The world has grown grey from thy breath!' When Jude suggests they sit in the cathedral to find peace and shelter, Sue responds that she'd rather sit in the railway station, now the centre of town life: 'The Cathedral was a very good place four or five centuries ago; but it is played out now.' Although the world Jude and Sue have been born into is rapidly changing, it is not ready for their new thinking — 'the time was not ripe for us! Our ideas were fifty years too soon to be any good to us.'

Jude the Obscure also reveals the inexorable tide of material progress that is senselessly destroying the world of Hardy's childhood, the English countryside and hamlets with their ancient sacred grounds. New churches rise up in modern Gothic design, 'unfamiliar to English eyes', while the ruined site of an 'ancient temple to the Christian divinities was not even recorded on the green and level grass plot that had immemorially been the church-yard'. The composer of a hymn so beautiful that Jude is haunted by it for days decides to give up music entirely, telling Jude: 'You must go into trade if you want to make money nowadays. The wine business is what I am thinking of.'

And yet the hierarchies of university and Church that serve the upper classes remain as inaccessible to Jude as 'planets across an object glass'. This is typical of Hardy's metaphors, which draw extensively on his vast reading of contemporary writers, including the scientists Charles Darwin, T.E. Huxley (grandfather of Aldous Huxley) and Herbert Spencer (who coined the term 'survival of the fittest'). The language Hardy uses to apprehend nature reflects their theories of evolution and the apparent absence of God or pattern in its work. Jude considers 'the wilfulness of Nature', its 'inexorable laws', and sees 'with more and more frequency, the scorn of Nature for man's finer emotions and her lack of interest in his aspirations'. Of Hardy's generation of poets, Ford Madox Ford called Hardy 'the most passionate and the most learned of them all'. The same might be said of Hardy the novelist.

At Hardy's instruction, his two volumes of autobiography were published under the name of his second wife, Florence Hardy, his longtime secretary whom he married after Emma's death. On his own death, Hardy was cremated and his ashes now lie next to those of Charles Dickens in Westminster Abbey. But, fittingly, Hardy's heart lies buried in the soil of his country parish.

D.H. Lawrence wrote a long essay on Hardy, 'Study of Thomas Hardy', which was published posthumously in *Phoenix: The Post-humous Papers of D.H. Lawrence* (1936). In a letter written in 1916, while he was working on the study, Lawrence dismissed the great European novelists in favour of one American and one Englishman: 'They are all – Turgenev, Tolstoi, Dostoyevsky, Maupassant, Flaubert – so very *obvious* and coarse, beside the lovely, mature and sensitive art of Fenimore Cooper or Hardy.'

Jude, a film of *Jude the Obscure*, starring Kate Winslet as Sue Bridehead and Christopher Eccleston as Jude, was made in 1996.

2 0 . The Wings of the Dove

by

HENRY JAMES

(1 8 4 3 – 1 9 1 6)

❧

'THERE ARE SUBJECTS AND SUBJECTS, and this one seemed particularly to bristle,' wrote Henry James in his Preface to *The Wings of the Dove*. The bristling subject is classic James – the dove of the title is an innocent American girl, Milly Theale, who falls under the spell of a sophisticated English couple, the beautiful Kate Croy and journalist Merton Densher. The peculiar, fragile love triangle that results becomes, in James's telling, a complex probing of motivation and desire, of the value of life and beauty, and, above all, of the power of money. For Milly has something that draws people inexorably to her – a stupendous fortune. As Kate says of her, 'If you can imagine an angel with a thumping bank-account you'll have the simplest expression of the kind of thing.' Milly's millions are the wings of the title – they give her a freedom the other characters in the novel can only dream of, allowing her to take flight from mundane concerns and self-interested machinations: 'that element of wealth in her which was a power, which was a great power, and which was dove-like only so far as one remembered that doves have wings and wondrous flights, have them as well as tender tints and soft sounds'.

The Wings of the Dove, set around 1900 in London and Venice and, fleetingly, New York, opens with Kate Croy visiting her father in his miserable lodgings. Immediately we are plunged into the poverty of Kate's family, from which she alone has been rescued. After her mother's death, her mother's wealthy sister, Aunt Maud, took Kate to live with her. Installed in Aunt Maud's mansion at Lancaster Gate, on the northern edge of Kensington Gardens, Kate has been elevated beyond her family's financial woes and Aunt Maud plans to marry her to the aristocratic Lord Mark. The highly intelligent, strong-willed Kate, however, has other plans. At a bohemian party in a gallery hired by a hostess who 'fished with big nets', a tall, young, impoverished journalist, Merton Densher, catches Kate's eye. Six months later they meet again by chance on the London Underground and Densher walks with Kate to Lancaster Gate – 'and then she . . . walked with him away from it . . .' Of course, Aunt Maud disapproves of the liaison.

Then Milly arrives in London. Kate and Densher enter her orbit with the intention of using her for their own ends, of tapping her enormous wealth. They plan to construct a trap for 'great innocence to come', manipulating the truth of their circumstances – 'Didn't we long ago agree that what she believes is the principal thing for us?' – to lure Milly into marriage. But, unexpectedly, Milly acts on Kate and Densher as much as they plan to act on her, and her life becomes an essential element in their bond:

> Milly, from the other side, happened at that moment to
> notice them, and she sent across towards them in response
> all the candour of her smile, the lustre of her pearls, the
> value of her life, the essence of her wealth. It brought them,
> with faces made fairly grave by the reality she put into their
> plan, together again.

James lived through 'the Gilded Age' of America, a term coined by Mark Twain and Charles Dudley Warner for the period of massive change that saw America's transformation from a predominantly rural, agrarian economy into a booming industrial capitalist one (manufacturing quadrupled in America between 1865 and 1900). The last three decades of the nineteenth century were characterised by relentless capitalism, corruption and vulgar displays of wealth. On a visit to America at the time, the French prime minister Georges Clemenceau remarked, 'America is the only nation in history which, miraculously, has gone directly from barbarism to degeneration without the usual interval of civilization.' The great wealth such as Milly Theale's that had been amassed from this phenomenal period of growth was soon being wantonly lavished on diamonds and pearls. This rampant materialism deeply troubled James, and provoked the leading American economist Thorstein Veblen to coin the term 'conspicuous consumption' to describe spending geared to enhancing status, spending that 'makes a statement', in his 1899 book *The Theory of the Leisure Class*.

The idea of a novel based around a doomed young girl with everything — vast wealth, breeding, intelligence, beauty, freedom — except for a future, had been plaguing James for years, perhaps ever since his cousin Minny Temple died at age twenty-four from tuberculosis. James wrote: 'I can scarce remember the time when the situation on which this long-drawn fiction mainly rests was not vividly present to me.' Minny had begged her beloved cousin Henry (James) to take her to Rome when he first went as an adult independently of his family. He refused her request and she died before having seen the city of her dreams. James wanted to write about a young person 'conscious of a great capacity for life, but early stricken and doomed' who sets out to achieve, 'however briefly and brokenly', the sense of having lived. Another significant loss in James's life that may have coloured *The Wings of the Dove* was the death — apparent suicide — of his friend and confidant, the writer Constance Fenimore Woolson, who fell to her death from the window of a Venetian palazzo in 1894.

James was born in 1843 in New York, the second son of Henry James and Mary Robertson Walsh. James's grandfather William had come to America from his tenant farm in Ireland in the eighteenth century and settled in Albany, New York, where he soon amassed a spectacular fortune in trade, banking and investment. His son, the unconventional Henry James Snr, a social theorist and lecturer, spent his inheritance on touring Europe, giving his five children an eclectic education in Paris, London and Geneva. The family returned to New York before the Civil War broke out and settled in Newport. Henry's two younger brothers fought in the war but a back injury prevented Henry from joining them. This was but one instance of his lifelong feeling of exclusion from the events of his times.

While Henry Snr permitted his eldest son, William (later famous as a philosopher and psychologist), to study science at Harvard, he disapproved of college life for his second son, Henry, a reserved, bookish boy. But at nineteen James went to Harvard Law School, and ended up spending most of his time reading, especially Balzac and Hawthorne (whose young American innocent abroad, Hilda, in *The Marble Faun*, is like Milly Theale associated with doves). Two years later, James's first story and first book review were published and during his twenties, he became known for his short stories, reviews and articles. In 1869, he went to Europe for the first time as an adult, travelling to Italy, France and England, and realised he could work better and live more cheaply in Europe. In 1875, his first published novel appeared – *Roderick Hudson* – as well as his first book of travel writing and a collection of tales. James continued to produce work at an astonishing rate, publishing some one hundred volumes over the next forty years.

In 1875, James spent a year in Paris, where he met Turgenev, Flaubert, Zola and Guy de Maupassant before moving to London. In 1878, his novella *Daisy Miller* was published by Leslie Stephen in his influential *Cornhill Magazine* and became James's only best-seller. It was so popular that editor William Dean Howells remarked that he'd heard New York society had been divided into 'Daisy Millerites' and 'anti-Daisy Millerites'. In London, James was a man about town, and famously dined out 140 times during 1878 and 1879. James's approach to fiction was transformed by his devastating, failed attempt to write successfully for the stage, a doomed play, *Guy Domville*. Following this shattering experience, he focused in his novels on a small number of characters constellated in highly charged situations and told his stories from a shifting, multiple viewpoint.

The first of three novels to be published following this period of transformation was *The Wings of the Dove*, in 1902 (although it was written after *The Ambassadors*, which was published the following year, and in 1904 the third novel, *The Golden Bowl*, appeared). These last three novels James dictated, to save his hand, while living comfortably and happily away from the demands of London life in Rye, Sussex. James, always a fastidious writer, later spent three years revising his main novels (of which he wrote a total of twenty), which were published in twenty-four volumes as 'the New York Edition'. In 1934, the prefaces James wrote for eighteen of his novels, including *The Wings of the Dove*, were published together as *The Art of the Novel*, which became an essential text for the New Critics, such as I.A. Richards and F.R. Leavis. James believed the novel, because of the freedom it offered a writer, was the ultimate art form.

Reading *The Wings of the Dove* is like entering a hall of mirrors, filled with baroque images and shimmering surfaces, dazzling, elusive, seductive. And yet James's opulent prose is razor sharp, capable of teasing out distinctions of hair-breadth subtlety. James found his greatest lessons as a writer in Balzac and Hawthorne. He also admired Dickens, Turgenev and George Eliot. James's novels are densely written and said to be challenging, but as James himself wrote, believing the enjoyment of art to be our highest luxury: 'the luxury is not greatest, by my consequent measure, when the work asks for as little attention as possible . . .'

James's last visit to America, in 1904–05, confirmed his disenchantment with his native land. On his return to England he wrote *The American Scene*, recording his impression of the country's excessive urbanisation, pollution and wanton waste of resources. James became a British subject in 1915, the year before his death, to demonstrate his support for Britain's involvement in the First World War and his disapproval of America's refusal to join the war in Europe.

One hundred years after the publication of *The Wings of the Dove*, there has been an unprecedented resurgence of interest in its author (perhaps because his fin-de-siècle complexity, opulence and ambiguity resonate with our times), including four new books which engage with James in one way or another: Colm Tóibín's acclaimed biographical novel *The Master* (2004), David Lodge's *Author, Author* (2004), Emma Tennant's *Felony* (2002) and Alan Hollinghurst's Booker Prize–winning *The Line of Beauty* (2004). David Lodge called the sudden interest in James 'a contagion'. In 1997, a brilliant film of *The Wings of the Dove* was released, starring Helena Bonham-Carter, Linus Roache, Alison Elliott and Charlotte Rampling.

Gore Vidal has given James the highest praise, calling him 'the master of the novel in English' from 1881, the year *The Portrait of a Lady* was published, in a way that was unequalled before and has remained unequalled since.

KATHY MOSSOP

- *Pride and Prejudice* by Jane Austen
- *Middlemarch* by George Eliot
- *War and Peace* by Leo Tolstoy
- *Great Expectations* by Charles Dickens
- *To the Lighthouse* by Virginia Woolf
- *The Wings of the Dove* by Henry James
- *To Kill a Mockingbird* by Harper Lee

Kathy Mossop is the former editor of *Good Reading*, a popular Australian magazine for book lovers. She has worked in publishing for over twenty years.

21 . *The Awakening*
by
KATE CHOPIN
(1 8 5 1 – 1 9 0 4)
ꝏ

'I suppose this is what you would call unwomanly; but I have got into a habit of expressing myself.' This illicit confession is made by Edna Pontellier to Robert Lebrun, a young man who is not her husband. *The Awakening*, set in 1890s Louisiana, is the haunting tale of a young married woman, Edna Pontellier, and her growing struggle to express herself beyond her roles of wife, mother, daughter, sister. While holidaying with her servants and two young sons at the seaside resort of Grand Isle on the Gulf of Mexico, under the sway of the languorous sea and her easy Creole companions (her husband visits from New Orleans only on weekends), Edna Pontellier becomes aware of deep, desperate urgings in her soul and sexual being. Long after midnight, as she sits on the porch, she finds herself crying for reasons she could not have told, except that 'An indescribable oppression, which seemed to generate in some unfamiliar part of her unconscious, filled her whole being with a vague anguish.' In her sure, relentless unfolding of Edna Pontellier's crisis, Kate Chopin exposes the soul of a woman struggling within the confines of other people's needs — those of her husband, children, society, religion — to find some ground on which to exist in her own right.

Kate Chopin was born in 1851 in St Louis, Missouri, the daughter of a wealthy Irish merchant, Captain Thomas O'Flaherty, and Eliza Faris, whose family was part of the French Creole aristocracy of the South. When Chopin was only four years old, her father was killed tragically in a railway accident, and, like her own widowed mother and grandmother before her, Chopin's mother never remarried. So Chopin was raised in a household of strong, independent, intelligent women, and was especially close to her great-grandmother, who taught her piano, encouraged her to read French literature and told her old Creole stories.

Unusually, in an era when few girls went to school, Chopin received a rigorous, intellectual education at the Sacred Heart Convent. Although her education was interrupted by the outbreak of civil war in 1861, Chopin eventually graduated in 1868 a star student. Two years later, aged nineteen, she married Oscar Chopin, the son of a wealthy Creole Louisiana cotton grower. When their honeymoon in Europe was cut short by the outbreak of the Franco-Prussian War, they returned to America to settle in New Orleans, where Oscar was a cotton merchant. But the Civil War had almost destroyed the cotton industry and ruined many of the old Creole families, and financial pressures eventually forced the couple to return to Oscar's family home in

Natchitoches Parish, one of the oldest French plantation communities in America. Three years later, Oscar died of swamp fever, leaving Chopin with huge debts and six children.

Eventually Chopin took her children back to her home town of St Louis, and, soon after their arrival in 1884, encouraged by her close friend and family doctor, she devoted herself to writing. Fiercely intelligent, Chopin lived an independent, bohemian life, smoking Turkish cigarettes, drinking alcohol and walking alone through the city streets – unheard of for women at the time. She read Darwin, Zola, Ibsen and Maupassant (her literary model), and had named her only daughter Leila after George Sand's rebellious heroine. Chopin soon earned a reputation for her beautifully written, perceptive stories, which were published in magazines such as *Vogue*, *Harper's* and *Atlantic Monthly*. Her stories seemed to fit neatly into the genre of 'local color' that was popular in America between the Civil War and the end of the nineteenth century, and Southern local color stories like Chopin's were particularly sought after, their portraits of French Creole and Southern life being exotic in an increasingly industrialised, urbanised, homogenised post–Civil War America.

But, with the publication of *The Awakening* in 1899, Chopin was to overstep the bounds of acceptability. As one of the earliest novels to portray the troubled consciousness of a woman who finds that her full sexual, creative and intelligent being has no place in the world of nineteenth-century Christian morality, *The Awakening* was greeted by most critics with astonishment and regret that so fine a short-story writer should have entered 'the overworked field of sex fiction' (*The Times-Herald*, Chicago,

June 1899). As one reviewer lamented: 'It is with high expectations that we open the volume, remembering the author's agreeable
short stories, and with real disappointment that we close it. The
recording reviewer drops a tear over one more clever author gone
wrong' (*The Nation*, 3 August 1899). Another reviewer considered
that Chopin's novel about a married woman's sexual adventures
could 'hardly be described in language fit for publication' (*The
Providence Sunday Journal*, 4 June 1899).

Even the writer Willa Cather, then in her mid twenties,
declared in her review of *The Awakening*: 'I shall not attempt to say
why Miss Chopin has devoted so exquisite and sensitive, well-
governed a style to so trite and sordid a theme' (*The Leader*, July
1899). Cather called *The Awakening* a Creole 'Bovary' and since
then it has often been seen in this light. But Chopin's novel was
written by a woman, forty-three years after Flaubert's *Madame
Bovary*, and Edna Pontellier's rebellion possesses a substance and
defiant self-awareness that go far beyond Emma Bovary's romantic
yearnings. Edna Pontellier will not be owned. 'I don't want
anything but my own way. That is wanting a good deal, of course,
when you have to trample upon the lives, the hearts, the prejudices
of others,' she declares. 'I would give my life for my children; but I
wouldn't give myself.' This subtle but profound distinction lies at
the heart of Chopin's devastating novel. Mme Pontellier is not a
'mother-woman', those women who 'efface themselves as individuals and grow wings as ministering angels'. Chopin locates
'mother-women' firmly in our fantasies — she can find no words to
describe these supreme beings, 'save the old ones that have served
so often to picture the bygone heroine of romance and the fair lady

of our dreams'. This ideal woman is as real as a knight in shining armour, she is an outdated model, and Mme Pontellier is determined to live her way out of the clichés.

Chopin writes with an extraordinarily rich yet simple and direct manner, inspired initially by the French writer Guy de Maupassant. In her selection of the detail of life, Chopin's ear and eye are as unerring when they portray moments of the domestic round as they are in conveying the caprices of Mme Pontellier's moods, such as when M. Pontellier checks on his sleeping sons after a day at the beach: 'He turned and shifted the youngest about in bed. One of them began to kick and talk about a basket full of crabs.' By the end of the nineteenth century, city living had become the prevailing mode of life and this is reflected in the novel in M. Pontellier's mother's concern for her grandsons. She doesn't want them to be 'children of the pavement', wishing instead for them 'to know the country, with its streams, its fields, its woods, its freedom, so delicious to the young'.

The negative reviews and subsequent poor sales of *The Awakening* effectively ended Chopin's writing career. Her third book of short stories was rejected soon after publication of *The Awakening* and Chopin died five years later, in August 1904. Her only other published novel, *At Fault*, was self-published in 1890. *The Awakening* soon went out of print and Chopin's work drifted into obscurity until the 1930s, when the first biography of her life was written by, ironically, a Christian minister, Father Daniel Rankin, and published in 1932. A French translation of *The Awakening* was published in 1953, arranged by the French writer Cyrille Arnavon, who considered Chopin a major writer. When

Norwegian scholar Per Seyersted discovered Chopin's stories, he was so struck by their beauty that he combed the libraries of St Louis, seeking out her work, copying her stories down by hand and eventually publishing her complete works in two volumes in 1969, along with his biography of her, *Kate Chopin: A Critical Biography*.

The 1991 film *Grand Isle*, produced by and starring Kelly McGillis, directed by Mary Lambert, is based on *The Awakening*.

J.K. ROWLING

Among J.K. Rowling's favourite classics are the novels of Jane Austen.

- *Sense and Sensibility*
- *Pride and Prejudice*
- *Mansfield Park*
- *Emma*
- *Northanger Abbey*
- *Persuasion*

J.K. Rowling is the author of the bestselling Harry Potter books.

by

J O S E P H   C O N R A D

(1 8 5 7 – 1 9 2 4)

As a child, Joseph Conrad pointed his finger to the heart of a map of Africa and declared: 'When I grow up I shall go there.' Two decades later, in 1890, Conrad sailed as mate on a river steamer up the Belgian Congo, into the heart of Africa. Having joined the French merchant navy aged sixteen and spent sixteen years at sea, this was Conrad's first freshwater navigation – and it was to be his last. Conrad was so deeply disturbed by what he experienced in the Congo, by the greed and cruelty exercised by the regime of Belgium's King Leopold II, and perhaps by the stirring of his own blood, that he was left a broken man, physically, mentally and to the depths of his soul, and never went to sea again.

Having spent four months in the Congo, Conrad returned to Europe, where he spent his first weeks in hospital recovering from a debilitating illness that was to plague him for the rest of his life in fevers and gout. It was not only his physical health that failed in Africa; in the Congo, Conrad suffered psychological and existential shock so profound that he was permanently altered. 'Before the Congo I was a mere animal,' he said. His friend Edward Garnett believed Conrad's Congo experiences were 'the turning-point in his mental life' and transformed him from a sailor to a writer, for on his return to England, Conrad gave away his life as a sailor and began his 'second' life, as a writer. It is possible to see in Conrad's existential crisis a clash between the culture of Victorian England, with its sexual suppression, and that of the Congo, renowned for the erotic power and beauty of its music, particularly its drumming. Conrad's character Charlie Marlow finds the music and dancing of the people along the Congo requires his deepest strength to behold: a man 'must meet that truth with his own true stuff – with his own inborn strength'.

In 1899, the first of three instalments of a story based on Conrad's voyage up the Congo – then named *The Heart of Darkness* – was published in *Blackwood's Edinburgh Magazine*, one of Britain's most prestigious literary journals. The story appeared in full three years later as *Heart of Darkness*, the second story in Conrad's collection *Youth: A Narrative; and Two Other Stories*. Conrad described the novel as 'the spoil I brought out from the centre of Africa, where, really, I had no sort of business'. In the century since its first publication, *Heart of Darkness* has become emblematic of moral ambiguity and European cultural decadence. So familiar is Conrad's haunting novella believed to be that in 2005 a television critic can use it as a touchstone of 'corruption and moral uncertainty' when reviewing a drama series (*Lost*, reviewed by Michael

Idato in *The Sydney Morning Herald*, 31 January 2005). *Heart of Darkness* has lived out its author's own hopes that his tale would resonate long after its telling: 'That sombre theme had to be given a sinister resonance, a tonality of its own, a continued vibration that, I hoped, would hang in the air and dwell on the ear after the last note had been struck.'

The story of *Heart of Darkness* is simple – it recounts the journey of a sailor, Charlie Marlow, up the Congo in the 1890s, during its brutal rule by King Leopold II of Belgium. It is in the telling that the story's complexities and ambiguities arise. An unnamed narrator sits aboard the *Nellie* in the Thames Estuary with four other men, waiting for the tide to turn. As they wait, the only one of their number to be named, the haunted, sunken-cheeked Marlow, embarks on a troubled tale of his Congo voyage. The narrator recounts to us Marlow's story as Marlow tells it on the darkening Essex marshes, recalling his experience of Africa and the infamous Mr Kurtz.

Marlow's journey into the Congo begins as Conrad's own did. Both hiked on foot along the lower reaches of the river to the registration port on the upper Congo to meet their assigned steamers. Both found on their arrival that their boats had sunk days earlier. In *Heart of Darkness*, Conrad suggests the sinking is deliberate, part of a covert plot to isolate the fictional Kurtz further upriver. Here, truth and fiction diverge – Conrad was impatient to be afloat and took a position on another boat, the captain of which taught him the art of freshwater navigation. But Marlow stays at the station while his assigned boat is being mended, waiting months for a handful of rivets to arrive from downstream for the work to be completed, during which time he plumbs the depths of the cruelty of colonial life in Africa, finding it increasingly bizarre, increasingly surreal.

The manager of the station appears to have his own agenda, entirely focused on undermining the star of the Belgian colonial venture, the 'universal genius' Mr Kurtz, the chief of the Inner Station. Although Marlow will later find on meeting him that Kurtz has become 'hollow at the core', he was once considered a prodigy, the most promising man of the colonial administration, 'an emissary of pity, and science, and progress' rumoured to be destined for great things. The station manager, in stark contrast, inspires neither love nor respect, but uneasiness. But as Marlow soon realises: 'You have no idea how effective such a . . . a . . . faculty can be.' In the debilitating Congo climate rife with sleeping sickness, robust health is the key to success and the manager's only distinction. 'His position had come to him − why? Perhaps because he was never ill.' The devil of imperialism that Marlow witnesses laying waste to the land and its people is Dostoyevsky's decadent, modern devil − 'a flabby, weak-eyed devil of rapacious and pitiless folly'.

From its earliest days, Conrad's life was one of travel and exile, until he eventually found a home in southeast England: 'I have been all my life − all my two lives − the spoiled adopted child of Great Britain and even of the Empire; for it was Australia that gave me my first command.' Conrad was born Jozef Teodor Konrad Korzeniowski in 1857 in Poland, at the time part of the Russian Empire, now the Ukraine. When Conrad was four his father, Apollo, a poet and Polish patriot, was exiled for his involvement with an anti-Russian movement, which later organised the 1863 uprising against Russian rule. Conrad and his mother joined Apollo in northern Russia and, following his mother's death four years later, the boy lived a solitary life in exile with his father. Conrad spent his days reading Sir Walter Scott, James Fenimore Cooper, Dickens and Thackeray in Polish and French while his father translated Shakespeare and Victor Hugo to earn a living. On his father's death in 1869, Conrad was cared for by a maternal uncle, who sent him to school in Cracow and Switzerland. In 1874, Conrad left Switzerland for Marseilles, dreaming of becoming a sailor. Following a failed suicide attempt in February 1878, Conrad joined a British freighter, served in the British merchant navy for many years and became a British subject in 1886.

On his return to England from Africa, Conrad sent the story he'd been working on for five years, *Almayer's Folly* (written in English, his third language), to a London publisher and in April 1895 it appeared under the name 'Joseph Conrad'. The following year he married Jessie George and they eventually settled in Kent. Not until the publication of *Lord Jim* (1900), *Nostromo* (1904) and *Under Western Eyes* (1911) did Conrad find financial security with his growing success as a writer. In April 1924, Conrad refused a knighthood from the British Prime Minister, Ramsay MacDonald, and he died in August of the same year.

The shock and uncertainty that struck Conrad in Africa shapes the way *Heart of Darkness* is told. There is no secure foundation to his story. In a much quoted line, the narrator observes that Marlow is no typical seaman:

> to him the meaning of an episode was not inside like a
> kernel but outside, enveloping the tale which brought it
> out only as a glow brings out a haze, in the likeness of one
> of these misty halos that sometimes are made visible by the
> spectral illumination of moonshine.

This quality in Marlow pervades *Heart of Darkness*: his circumlocution — coupled with the narrator's retelling — gives the novel a haunted and haunting allusiveness. The novel's vagueness is called to account as morally irresponsible by the Nigerian writer Chinua Achebe in his influential essay 'An Image of Africa: Racism in Conrad's *Heart of Darkness*', first published in 1977. Achebe argues that Conrad's much noted insistence on 'inexpressible and incomprehensible mystery' must not be dismissed lightly, 'as many Conrad critics have tended to do, as a mere stylistic flaw; for it raises serious questions of artistic good faith'. According to Achebe, Conrad's mystery in fact works to induce 'hypnotic stupor' in his readers, numbing them to the racism inherent in his story. Achebe calls Conrad a 'thoroughgoing racist' for his portrayal of Africa and its people: 'Conrad saw and condemned the evil of imperial exploitation but was strangely unaware of the racism on which it sharpened its iron tooth.'

More recently, the German writer W.G. Sebald, who also moved from Europe to settle in England, shares in his writing Conrad's shifting, multi-layered approach to truth and the impossibility of its direct telling. Like Conrad, Sebald was deeply engaged with an attempt to articulate profound, unsettling truths about the European psyche. His novel *The Rings of Saturn* (published in

English in 1998), is, among many things, a reflection on Conrad's voyage to the Congo and his troubled life lived apart from his birth country.

Conrad's strange, beautiful novel, *Heart of Darkness*, has influenced many writers, including T.S. Eliot, Hemingway, F. Scott Fitzgerald, Sartre and Sebald. Francis Ford Coppola's film *Apocalypse Now* about the Vietnam War famously draws on *Heart of Darkness*.

A BRIEF HISTORY OF THE CONGO

The land through which Conrad navigated was once the kingdom of Kongo, ruled from the fifteenth to the early eighteenth century by a king from Mbanza (now Damba, Angola) and divided into six provinces, each with its own governor. In 1482, Portuguese sailors arrived on the Kongo coast and diplomatic relations developed between the two kingdoms. Under the influence of the Portuguese, the King of Kongo, Nzinga Nkuwu, converted to Christianity and Roman Catholicism became the official religion. But in the early sixteenth century the Portuguese began to take slaves from the Kongo and ignored King Nzinga Mbemba's appeals to King John III of Portugal to stop the slave trade. For the next three hundred years, European powers enslaved hundreds of thousands of people from the region and in 1665 Portugal invaded the Kongo, slaughtering the king and nobles.

The Welsh journalist and adventurer Henry M. Stanley (of 'Dr Livingstone, I presume' fame) crossed the Congo (as it became) in 1876, gathering detailed information and becoming a reputed expert on the region. Two years later, King Leopold II of Belgium hired Stanley to establish Belgian trading posts along the Congo River. In 1885, Leopold took over the region, having by skilful negotiation with other European powers positioned himself as sole ruler of the Congo Free State (the 'Free' denoted free trade for all nations, but Leopold managed to create his own monopoly), which then became Leopold's own private kingdom. By the mid 1890s, the Congo — its people, rubber, ivory — had become the source of Leopold's massive wealth, which he used to beautify his capital, Brussels ('a city that always makes me think of a whited sepulchre', as Marlow calls it in *Heart of Darkness*, because beyond its outer beauty lie the wasted bones of Africa). Leopold's rule swiftly became notorious for its exploitation of the local people.

Its brutality was first revealed by the investigative journalist E.D. Morel, whose reports led to questions being raised in the British House of Commons. In 1904, the British consul Roger Casement's influential report on 'the Administration of the Congo Free State' (1903) was published to the world, revealing the atrocities perpetrated by Leopold's agents. Among the horrors it noted were: the prevention of local trade, the destruction of village life, the spread of sleeping sickness exacerbated by poverty and poor health, the torture and mutilation of men, women and children who refused to work. Casement's report eventually led to the Congo's being passed to the Belgian government, which formally took over 'the Belgian Congo' in August 1908. (The fate of Casement himself, however, was tragic. Roger Casement was hanged for treason by the British government in 1916 following his negotiations in Berlin on behalf of the Irish struggle for independence.)

23 . Pan: From Lieutenant
Thomas Glahn's Papers
by
KNUT HAMSUN
(1 8 5 9 – 1 9 5 2)

'I love three things,' I say then. 'I love a dream of love I
once had, I love you, and I love this patch of earth.'
'And which do you love best?'
'The dream.'

LIEUTENANT THOMAS GLAHN, the eccentric, solitude-loving
narrator of *Pan*, prefers the dream to flesh and blood, prefers it to
the earth itself. At the end of the nineteenth century, the
Norwegian writer Knut Hamsun's passionate urge to articulate
dreams, the dark shadows of the mind, the deviant and poetic
dimensions of life, charged the European novel with a new energy
– one that would power writers and artists into the next century,
like Edvard Munch, Franz Kafka, Thomas Mann, Ernest
Hemingway and Henry Miller. In 1888, Hamsun caused a sensa-

tion when a fragment of his novel *Hunger* was published in the Danish literary journal *New Earth*. Hamsun's lyrical, impressionistic tale of a young writer starving in Kristiania (now Oslo) electrified the literary world with its stark originality and subtle psychological perceptions. In his introduction to a later edition of *Hunger*, the writer Isaac Bashevis Singer called Hamsun 'the father of the modern school of literature in his every aspect – his subjectiveness, his fragmentariness, his use of flashbacks, his lyricism. The whole modern school of fiction in the twentieth century stems from Hamsun.'

Following the publication of the completed version of *Hunger* in 1890, Knut Hamsun was celebrated across Europe. Three years later he moved to Paris and here he began work on a cool, unnerving love story set in a remote mountain village in northern Norway, published in 1894 as *Pan: From Lieutenant Thomas Glahn's Papers*. In *Pan's* intimate, first-person narrative, Lieutenant Glahn recalls his summer holiday in the mountains two years earlier, accompanied by his dog Aesop. Hunting in the woods with Aesop, Glahn is filled with ecstatic joy, until one day he meets a tall girl with curved eyebrows – 'someone who for a short while filled my thoughts' and disturbs his solitude. The alluring, petulant girl is in turn attracted to Glahn's animal look. Their affair is awkward, intense and perverse, as 'bewitching and ephemeral' as the short Arctic summer, as beautiful and elusive as the lovers themselves.

Pan is remarkable for the clear-cut poetry of Hamsun's prose, which is so spare, so pure and direct, and yet so suggestive of incandescent dreams and evocative of shifting moods. He writes beautifully about the mountains and forests of Norway, the long summer of daylight, the dark winter beyond: 'Indian summer, Indian summer. The paths ran like ribbons in through the yellow-ing woods, every day a new star appeared, the moon showed dimly like a shadow, a shadow of gold dipped in silver . . .' Hamsun's writing is also remarkable for its profound, new psychological acuity. He understands that the human soul is irrational and untamable, that it is this that shapes our apprehension of the world and not the world itself, 'For it is within ourselves that the sources of joy and sorrow lie.'

Knut Hamsun was born Knut Pedersen in a remote mountain hamlet in the Gudbrandsdal Valley in central Norway. His family was of peasant stock and his father was a travelling tailor. When Hamsun was three they moved to an estate called 'Hamsund', near the Lofoten Islands north of the Arctic Circle, with its long winter darkness and months of summer daylight. Although Hamsun had little formal education, he soon became an avid reader and began writing his own stories. In 1877, not yet twenty, he used his hard-earned savings to publish his first book, *The Enigmatic One*, which appeared under the name 'Knut Pedersen Hamsund' (a printer's error later dropped the 'd' to make 'Hamsun', which the author liked and decided to adopt). Inspired by Dostoyevsky, Nietzsche and Strindberg, determined to make a living as a writer, Hamsun quit his apprenticeship and spent the next ten years on the road, embracing a precarious, itinerant life. In 1878, he moved to Kristiania, and in 1882 he made the first of his two journeys to the United States, hoping America would offer him better prospects of becoming a writer than Europe. During his travels, he worked as a teacher, a labourer, a journalist, a tram conductor in Chicago, and a farmhand in North Dakota. He returned permanently to Europe in 1888, and the following year published his satirical account of America, ironically titled *The Spiritual Life of Modern America*.

Hamsun married twice. His first marriage ended in divorce in 1906, then three years later he married the actress Marie Andersen and they had four children. In 1918, they moved to an old manor house on a large estate in southern Norway where Hamsun lived until after the Second World War. The demands Hamsun made of his writing were exacting, as he wrote in 1888: 'Language must resound with all the harmonies of music. The writer must always, at all times, find the tremulous word which captures the thing and is able to draw a sob from my soul by its very rightness.' Hamsun needed utter solitude for his work and, although he had a separate hut for writing, he was a difficult, temperamental man to live with, and was plagued by depression, as his wife, Marie Hamsun, tells in her memoir of their turbulent marriage, *Rainbow*, published in 1953.

In 1920, Hamsun was awarded the Nobel Prize for his novel *The Growth of the Soil* published in 1917. He became one of Norway's most lauded citizens, celebrated for his literary genius and for his portrayal of the natural beauty of his country, a young nation which had only fifteen years earlier, in 1905, achieved full independence from Sweden. But Hamsun's national celebrity was to be short-lived. In the 1930s he wrote a series of pro-Fascist articles and when the German forces occupied Norway during the Second World War, Hamsun gave them his full support. Following the war, he was taken into custody for collaboration with the Nazis. Owing to his old age – he was nearly ninety – the charges were dropped. Instead he was ordered to pay a large fine to the Norwegian government and was sent to a psychiatric clinic in Oslo. But Hamsun remained unrepentant and wrote an account of his political views and his trial, *On Overgrown Paths*, which was published in 1949. Three years later he died, aged ninety-two.

24 . *The Age of Innocence*
by
EDITH WHARTON
(1 8 6 2 – 1 9 3 7)

'OUR IDEAS ABOUT MARRIAGE and divorce are particularly old-fashioned. Our legislation favours divorce – our social customs don't,' says Newland Archer to the Countess Olenska, attempting to explain the subtle but rigid unspoken conventions of the patrician New York society to which they belong. The Countess Olenska, née Ellen Mingott, arrives in New York from Europe as Archer is about to announce his engagement to her cousin May Welland, a beautiful, athletic and irreproachable society girl. Ellen Olenska has fled her philandering husband, a Polish count, and returned to her family in New York to seek a divorce. 'The individual, in such cases, is nearly always sacrificed to what is supposed to be the collective interest: people cling to any convention that keeps the family together,' continues Archer, dismayed to find himself forced to resort to such platitudes.

The passion with which the Countess longs for her freedom from her husband, her inability to be surprised by anything, her bold talk and eccentric style – 'Madame Olenska, heedless of tradition, was attired in a long robe of red velvet bordered about the chin and down the front with glossy black fur' – conjure for Archer a mysterious European world that grows to fill the void in his life, which is rapidly becoming apparent to him with the approach of his society marriage. Brought together by May's family, Ellen and Archer find themselves consumed by desire for one another. In the unfolding of Archer's story and his divided heart, Wharton teases out the tensions between individual needs and social obligations – the shame of divorce, the pain of marriage, the restrictive codes of society, its damning of outsiders and yet its generosity to its own, the irresistible charm of its ways – and draws a complex and subtly delineated portrait of upper-class New York in the 1870s. Only in its quiet closing moments does the novel reveal the full truth of May's lucid understanding of her husband and marriage, and demonstrate the ambiguity of Wharton's rounded perception of life.

Wharton was in her late fifties when she wrote *The Age of Innocence*. She had experienced in her own life the pain of loveless marriage, the shame of divorce, the pleasure of illicit sexual passion and the unyielding power of New York's upper class. She had also experienced at first hand the devastation of the First World War. The war broke out when Wharton was living in Paris and she immediately became energetically involved in assisting those whose lives it had ruined, helping refugees from northeastern France and Belgium, travelling to the front in her motorcar to help. (Wharton loved driving and bought her first automobile in 1904.) In 1916, Wharton edited *The Book of the Homeless*, an anthology with contributions from Thomas Hardy, John Galsworthy and W.B. Yeats, to raise money for the refugees. In recognition of her wartime relief work, Wharton was made a Chevalier of the Legion of Honour by the French government. Following the war, totally consumed by an urge to write about its overwhelming intensity, almost as an aside Wharton began to work on a new novel about the New York of her childhood. If before the war Wharton had seen society exclusively in terms of its power to crush the individual, her experience of the war years opened her eyes to the benefits of civilisation, the ways in which family, history and tradition can provide the context and security essential for life. Her new insight can be felt in *The Age of Innocence*.

Born in New York in 1862, during the Civil War, Wharton was the youngest child (by twelve years) and only daughter of George and Lucretia Jones, members of the New York upper class whose English and Dutch ancestors had acquired their vast wealth in business, law and banking. (They were the Joneses with whom the term 'keeping up with the Joneses' originated.) In Wharton's milieu, a woman's only conceivable ambition was to make a successful society marriage and become an exemplary wife and mother. Wharton's family was not at all interested in literature and was surprised by Edith's passion for reading and writing. Educated at home and on the family's travels through Europe (which began in 1866 and lasted six years), Wharton wrote poetry and finished her first novella, *Fast and Loose*, when she was fifteen.

A few years after the death of her beloved father, Wharton, at the ripe old age of twenty-three (at which she was considered almost on the shelf), married Boston banker Edward Wharton in 1885. Her first notable book was published in 1897; written with a friend, architect Ogden Codman, her book *The Decoration of Houses* advocated simple, classical design and immediately influenced designers throughout America. Wharton also designed her own house, 'The Mount', in Lenox, Massachusetts. Completed in 1902, the house was described by Wharton's friend Henry James as 'a delicate French chateau mirrored in a Massachusetts pond'. Wharton was passionate about her house and garden, and wrote in her diary that architecture and flowers (as well as books, dogs and a good joke) were among her ruling passions. In 1905, the popular and critical success of *The House of Mirth* established Wharton as a prominent American writer, but she felt enormous tensions between her position as a society matron and her vocation as a writer. This may have contributed to the breakdown of her health, which took the Whartons to France and Italy, where her health was restored, and in 1907 Wharton moved with her husband to Paris, a city she felt was in her blood.

Following her move to Europe, Wharton flourished as a writer but her marriage foundered. In France, she wrote in bed, dropping page after page onto the floor for a secretary to type. Her daily output was massive and she produced a book a year for forty years. But in 1913 Wharton and her husband Edward were divorced, prompted by his mental instability, financial irresponsibility and numerous affairs with other women.

In 1908, at the age of forty-six, Wharton fell in love with American expatriate Morton Fullerton, a journalist on the London

Times who'd had many affairs with men and women, and they had a passionate sexual affair as well as a meeting of minds. Henry James had introduced her to Fullerton, with whom Henry was also in love and on whom he modelled Merton Densher in *The Wings of the Dove*. Wharton was a lifelong supporter of Henry James, which included campaigning for him to win the Nobel Prize and secretly diverting some of her own more abundant royalties to him via her publisher.

Contracted for publication by *The Pictorial Review*, a popular magazine for women, *The Age of Innocence* appeared in four large instalments from July to October 1920. The book, published the same year, was an immediate success. In 1921, *The Age of Innocence* won the Pulitzer Prize. In what was to be her only journey home following the war, Wharton returned to America to receive the award. Two years later, in 1923, she became the first woman to receive a Doctorate of Letters from Yale University. For a girl born into a society in which women writers were unheard of, that Wharton had become a writer at all was a remarkable feat of courage and determination. That she had risen to such heights of critical acclaim was testament to her abundant talent and fierce intellect.

Martin Scorsese's sumptuous 1993 cinema adaptation of *The Age of Innocence* starred Daniel Day-Lewis as Newland Archer, Winona Ryder as May Welland and Michelle Pfeiffer as Countess Olenska. Apparently Scorsese was passionately committed to directing Wharton's great novel and brings to his film all the subtle characterisation, complex social mores, signs and codes, all the claustrophobia and beauty of Wharton's original.

HELEN BARNES

In no particular order:

- *Keep the Aspidistra Flying* by George Orwell
- *The Information* by Martin Amis

(These first two are essential reading for writers. It's important to keep checking whether you really are a writer, or just a flake.)

- *The Leopard* by Giuseppe Tomasi di Lampedusa
- *The Age of Innocence* by Edith Wharton
- *Vineland* by Thomas Pynchon
- *1984* by George Orwell
- *Wuthering Heights* by Emily Brontë
- *Money* by Martin Amis
- *Brighton Rock* by Graham Greene
- *Cities of the Red Night* by William S. Burroughs

Australian writer Helen Barnes is the author of *The Crypt Orchid* (1994), *The Weather Girl* (1996) and *Killing Aurora* (2000).

25. *Maurice Guest*

by

HENRY HANDEL RICHARDSON

(1870–1946)

MAURICE GUEST, HENRY HANDEL RICHARDSON'S first novel, is the story of a young music student, Maurice Guest, who travels from his 'cheerless', middle-class home in provincial England to Leipzig to study the piano, and is soon caught up in a dissolute love triangle. The novel opens with Maurice filled with the ecstasy of music, wandering into the woods beyond the town following a public concert rehearsal:

He was under the sway of a twofold intoxication: great music and a day rich in promise. From the flood of melody that had broken over him, the frenzied storm of applause, he had come out, not into a lamplit darkness that would have crushed his elation back upon him and hemmed him in, but into the spacious lightness of a fair

blue day, where all that he felt could expand, as a flower
does in the sun.

Maurice arrives in Leipzig filled with hopes for a brilliant
career as a concert pianist: 'He felt so ready for work, so fresh and
unworn; the fervour of a deep enthusiasm was rampant in him . . .'
But Leipzig was one of the most sophisticated centres of music
and culture in 1890s Europe, and, since Maurice is a decent
provincial boy, the mix proves fatal for him. As the novel
unfolds, Maurice drifts further and further from the spacious
lightness of the fair blue days into the recesses of a lamplit
darkness, for his enthusiasm and 'anxiousness to oblige' cloak a
'deathly indifference'.

The agent of Maurice's undoing is a fiery, provocative, gifted
Australian music student, Louise Dufrayer. Richardson based Louise
on a celebrated actress of the day with whom the author was
obsessed, Eleonora Duse, whose tempestuous ten-year affair with
Italian writer Gabriele D'Annunzio was the talk of Europe. Louise
Dufrayer, that 'scentless tropical flower, with stiff, waxen petals', is
to shape Maurice's life. And tragically so, for Louise is in love with
another man, the insolent opportunist and genius violinist Shilsky,
whose great symphonic poem he names 'Zarathustra'. One portentous day, Louise's beauty enchants Maurice as powerfully and irreversibly as any Wagnerian love philtre: 'The beauty, whose spell
thus bound him, was of that subtle kind which leaves many a one
cold, but, as if just for this reason, is almost always fateful for those
who feel its charm.' *Maurice Guest*, with its remarkable portraits of
student life and passionate debate about love and art and music,

unerringly charts Maurice's corruption as he succumbs to the allure of Louise and abandons music for the dictates of sexual desire.

Henry Handel Richardson, born Ethel Florence Lindesay Richardson in Melbourne in 1870, was herself a gifted musician. Her father, Walter Richardson, was an Irish medical graduate from Edinburgh and her English mother, Mary, had followed her brothers to the Victorian goldfields, where she met her future husband. Richardson's musical distinction brought some much-craved recognition to her otherwise unhappy boarding-school years at Presbyterian Ladies' College in Melbourne (the subject of her second novel, *The Getting of Wisdom* (1910)), but her life was forever marked by the slow, traumatic deterioration of her father's health from the tertiary syphilis and associated dementia that led to his death in 1879.

In 1888, Richardson sailed with her mother and sister to England. The following year she began a three-year course to train as a concert pianist at the famed Conservatorium of Music in Leipzig, founded by Mendelssohn Bartholdy. Leipzig, in the new nation of Germany (founded in 1871, just eighteen years before Richardson's arrival), was one of the great cultural centres of Europe, renowned for its age-old choir, St Thomas's Boys Choir, where J.S. Bach had once been choirmaster, and as the birthplace of Richard Wagner. Here, Richardson immersed herself completely in music. In 1890 she met J.G. Robertson, a shy, brilliant, Wagner-loving, 23-year-old science graduate from Glasgow who was writing his PhD in philology at Leipzig University. Robertson invited Richardson to a series of Wagner operas, which she later said was the real beginning of her musical education. They quickly discovered their shared love of music and books, and in 1891 they were engaged.

The following year Richardson graduated and abandoned her plans to become a concert pianist, deciding to become a writer instead. Perhaps she discovered in Germany that her talent, so prodigious in isolated Australia, was not great enough for the world stage. And she began to suffer agonies when exposed on the concert stage, like Krafft in *Maurice Guest* who speaks 'with a morbid horror — yet as if the idea of it fascinated him — of the publicity of the concert-platform'. In December 1895, Richardson and Robertson were married, and the following year Richardson began work on *Maurice Guest*, based on her student life in Leipzig. In 1903, the couple moved to London when Robertson was appointed to a German chair at the University of London. Here, with Robertson's unfailing moral support, Richardson threw herself into her manuscript and finally finished it in 1907.

Maurice Guest was published in 1908 under the pen name 'Henry Handel Richardson'. The novel's European sensibility was influenced by Richardson's reading of Scandinavian literature, particularly Ibsen and Jacobsen (whose *Niels Lynne* she had translated from German, published in 1896), Dostoyevsky and Nietzsche, and the music of Wagner. Nietzsche's influence can be felt in her portrait of the genius artist Shilsky, and in the views of the eccentric, sexually fluid music student Krafft:

No, there's no such thing as absolute truth. If there were, the finest subtleties of existence would be lost . . . Truth? —

it is one of the many miserable conventions the human brain has tortured itself with, and its first principle is an utter lack of imaginative faculties.

Richardson was a passionate, driven, unconventional woman, and perhaps formed a love triangle of her own when the musically gifted Olga Roncoroni (whom she met in Lyme Regis, Dorset, in 1919) moved in with her and Robertson, remaining with Richardson as her secretary and constant companion until her death in 1946. Richardson returned only once to Australia, in 1912, to research her trilogy *The Fortunes of Richard Mahony*, based on her father. The third volume, *Ultima Thule*, published at Robertson's expense because Richardson's publisher rejected it, finally brought her the fame and commercial success she had dreamt of all her life. A review in *The Daily News* (14 January 1929) gave *Ultima Thule* high praise: 'if our age has produced a masterpiece at all, this is a masterpiece.'

MARDI McCONNOCHIE

- *Daniel Deronda* by George Eliot
- *Villette* by Charlotte Brontë
- *Maurice Guest* by Henry Handel Richardson
- *To the Lighthouse* by Virginia Woolf
- *The House of Mirth* by Edith Wharton
- *The Golden Notebook* by Doris Lessing
- *Nights at the Circus* by Angela Carter

🐛 *Alias Grace* by Margaret Atwood

The Australian novelist, playwright and screenwriter Mardi McConnochie is the author of three novels: the acclaimed *Coldwater* (2001), *The Snow Queen* (2003) and *Fivestar* (2005).

26 . *Death in Venice*
by
THOMAS MANN
(1 8 7 5 – 1 9 5 5)

DEATH IN VENICE IS A HIGHLY STYLISED, richly suggestive story of the last days of Gustav Aschenbach, a feted writer suddenly uncharacteristically overwhelmed, at age fifty-three, by the urge to travel. 'It was simply a desire to travel, but it had presented itself as nothing less than a seizure, with intensely passionate and indeed hallucinatory force, turning his craving into vision.' The vision he sees, of tangled tropical undergrowth, fills him with terror and mysterious longing. Haunted by his inner impulse, he travels to an island in the Adriatic where, as if by revelation, his fated destination becomes apparent to him: he must travel to Venice, that incomparable city, that 'fantastic mutation of normal reality'.

Unerringly, Thomas Mann recounts the one last blazing upsurge of passion in Gustav Aschenbach, his artist hero, brilliantly unfurling the subtle blossoming of his desire as he falls madly in love with a young boy. Aschenbach's life has been one of 'cold, inflexible, passionate duty'. Intent on fame, for the sake of his talent, Aschenbach has 'curbed and cooled his feelings' – and his discipline and forbearance have been rewarded with accolades and universal admiration. He has fascinated twenty-year-old readers with his 'breath-taking cynicisms about the nature of art and the artist himself'; his prose is read by children in prescribed school readers. Yet, in Venice, the foundations of his lofty career begin to falter as he finds a world increasingly 'deranged and bizarre'.

On first beholding the young boy in his hotel on the Lido, Aschenbach notices with astonishment that he is 'entirely beauti-ful'. The boy, Tadzio, appears god-like. With curls of dark gold, he is Eros, a 'divine sculptural shape' with the 'creamy lustre of Parian marble'. As Aschenbach's response to Tadzio transmutes from one of 'cool professional approval' to utterly abandoned longing, Mann's Christian metaphors – Aschenbach's passive suffering is St Sebastian's – are usurped by those of classical Greece; his rhythms become hymnic and his prose explodes into a paean to physical beauty. Aschenbach discovers that it is passion that exalts artists, that 'the longing of our soul must remain the longing of a lover – that is our joy and our shame . . .' In essence, *Death in Venice* is a supremely modulated outpouring of suppressed homoerotic passion – both Aschenbach's and Mann's own. For as Mann later wrote of *Death in Venice*: 'Nothing is invented.' Although Mann married in 1905, the most intense relationship of his life was with the painter and violinist Paul Ehrenberg, which lasted from their meeting in 1899 until around 1903.

In May 1911, Thomas Mann travelled from Munich with his wife and brother Heinrich to the Adriatic island of Pola. From Pola they journeyed by boat to Venice to vacation on the glamorous resort island the Lido. Here, like Aschenbach, for a fleeting moment Mann became enchanted by a beautiful young Polish boy holidaying with his mother and three sisters. But Mann was in his prime, almost twenty years younger than the fictional Aschenbach, and was not facing an irrevocable creative and physical decline.

Following his Venetian holiday, Mann returned to an idea he'd had for a story based on Goethe's infatuation at seventy-four with a young seventeen-year-old girl, while holidaying in 1823. Between July 1911 and July 1912 Mann worked on the story, transposing the theme of an aging man's passion for a girl to his passion for a boy. He later described the driving force of *Death in Venice* as: 'Passion that drives to distraction and destroys dignity — that was really the subject matter of my tale.' First published in two instalments in October and November 1912, the book edition of *Death in Venice* appeared in 1913 and the first printing of 8000 sold out in a month.

Death in Venice opens on an unseasonably warm spring afternoon in 'the year in which for months on end so grave a threat seemed to hang over the peace of Europe'. Two years after Mann completed *Death in Venice*, the First World War erupted. In an uncanny way, the novel explores the role of the artist in an age apparently intent on its own destruction. Aschenbach's fate is aligned with the fate of Europe; both are destined to be overwhelmed by chaos. For Aschenbach's work has struck a chord with the public – and what is his work but 'elegant self-control' concealing 'a state of inner disintegration and biological decay', like European civilisation itself. And, as the narrator observes, 'For a significant intellectual product to make a broad and deep immediate appeal, there must be a hidden affinity, indeed a congruence, between the personal destiny of the author and the wider destiny of his generation.' Reflecting this, Mann later described his pre–World War I self as someone who recorded and analysed decadence, a lover of beauty obsessed with the pathological, darkness and death.

Born in Lubeck, Germany, in 1875, Mann, like Aschenbach, had an exotic mother and a successful, upright father. His mother, the beautiful and musically gifted Julia da Silva Bruhns, was born in Brazil to a Portuguese Creole mother and a German planter father. Aged eighteen, she married consul Heinrich Mann, a successful businessman. Under the influence of his mother, who played Chopin on the piano, Mann grew up with a passion for music, above all Wagner, who had a profound influence on Mann's writing. As a boy, he produced his own operas in a puppet theatre. Mann writes of Aschenbach, echoing his own artistic provenance: 'It was from this marriage between hard-working, sober conscientiousness and darker, more fiery impulses that an artist, and indeed this particular kind of artist, had come into being.' Soon after his father's death in 1891, Mann moved to Munich, where he remained until 1933.

Mann found extraordinary and immediate success with his first novel, *The Buddenbrooks*, published in 1901. In 1905 he married Katia Pringsheim, and together they had six children. In 1933 they were in Switzerland when Hitler became chancellor, and their children warned them not to return to Germany. They remained in Switzerland until 1938, when they moved to the United States. Mann became an American citizen in 1944 but returned to Switzerland in 1952, where he died three years later. Mann is considered to have been the greatest German writer of the twentieth century, and in 1929 he won the Nobel Prize for Literature.

The identity of the boy who had fascinated Mann on the Lido was revealed in 1964 as Wladyslaw, Baron Moes, whose real-life friend – the fictional Jasiu – visited the set of Visconti's celluloid adaptation of *Death in Venice* (1971). Visconti's sumptuous film starred Dirk Bogarde as Aschenbach and Björn Andresen as Tadzio.

The great English composer Benjamin Britten devoted his last years to an opera based on *Death in Venice*. Britten's *Death in Venice* had its London premiere in Covent Garden in October 1973, three years before the composer's death.

27. Narcissus and Goldmund

by

HERMANN HESSE

(1887–1962)

※

HERMANN HESSE'S SIXTH NOVEL, *Narcissus and Goldmund*, is the story of two young men in medieval northern Europe who bear 'special marks of fate' — Narcissus, a handsome prodigy admired for his intellect and refinement, and Goldmund, a radiant, golden-haired youth filled with dark secrets, driven by passion and creative yearning. Still in his early twenties, Narcissus's extraordinary intelligence has secured him a position as teacher at the Mariabronn cloister on the edge of the Black Forest. He is also gifted with the ability to see into the souls of those around him, able to sense their character and destiny. When Goldmund arrives at the cloister on horseback accompanied by his stern father, both father and son determined that Goldmund will train for the priesthood, Narcissus soon intuits that the delicate youth's destiny does not lie within the Church. A curious, illicit friendship grows between teacher and student, until they become inseparable.

But their friendship is destined to cause pain, to others and to themselves. As Narcissus says: 'our friendship has no other purpose, no other reason, than to show you how utterly unlike me you are . . .' They are opposites, sun and moon – 'No road will bring us together.' Narcissus feels called to show Goldmund his soul's purpose and in the process breaks both their hearts. Unlike Narcissus, who is born for scholarship and cloister life, Goldmund belongs in the world beyond. He has a secret bond with wood and stone, an affinity for 'the flowers and thickets of sprouting leaves that burst forth from the stone of the columns and unfolded so eloquently and intensely', and his learning lies not in books but in 'the petal of a flower or a tiny worm on the path'.

Narcissus and Goldmund is told with a fable-like simplicity and the influence of Carl Gustav Jung is apparent in many of the novel's themes and motifs. Narcissus acts as Goldmund's confessor and medieval psychoanalyst, pushing him to crisis point: 'you've forgotten your childhood; it cries for you from the depths of your soul. It will make you suffer until you heed it.' Hesse's own life was a series of crises and new beginnings, and one such crisis struck him during the First World War. The pressures of the war, against which Hesse worked energetically, the stresses in his marriage, and his father's death in 1916, led Hesse to physical and emotional collapse. To recover, he went to Lucerne for psychoanalysis with J.B. Lang, a student of Jung. Based on this experience, he wrote *Demian*, the novel that brought him international fame, published in 1919 under the name of its narrator, Emil Sinclair.

In the spring of 1927, having suffered a physical breakdown and spent much of the previous four years at Baden health spa on medical advice, Hesse started work on *Narcissus and Goldmund*. He had become increasingly concerned by the crippling effects of industrial civilisation and technology, and preoccupied by what he considered the duality of life, particularly the pull between the contemplative life of the spirit and the life of the flesh he felt keenly in himself. His previous novel, *Steppenwolf* (1927), explores this pull. In *Narcissus and Goldmund*, Hesse returns to this tension but can now sympathetically express both tendencies in himself — scholarly hermit and worldly artist.

Hesse was born in Calw, on the northern edge of the Black Forest, in 1877, six years after the unification of Germany by Otto von Bismarck. His mother, Marie, was born in India, the daughter of Hermann Gundert, a Protestant missionary and gifted linguist. Hesse's father, Johannes Hesse, was also a missionary in India, but returned to Germany to work in the publishing house of the Basel Missionary Society with Gundert, where he met and married Gundert's daughter. A precociously gifted, multi-talented and rebellious child, Hesse exhausted his parents and was sent to several boarding schools before returning to Calw, at sixteen, in October 1893. He had run away from the Maulbronn seminary aged fifteen, where he was supposed to train for the priesthood, because he suffered a religious crisis. After being entrusted to the care of a Protestant pastor for a cure, he bought a shotgun and disappeared, leaving a suicide note, but reappeared later the same day. On his return home to Calw, Hesse spent his days reading in his grandfather's extensive library, gardening, and helping his father in the publishing house.

Following a brief apprenticeship as a machinist in a tower-clock factory, at the age of eighteen Hesse was apprenticed in a bookshop. He devoted himself to study and wrote poetry, and his first volume of poems, *Romantic Songs*, appeared in 1899. In 1904 his first novel, *Peter Camenzind*, was published and Hesse became famous overnight. His book sold so well he was able to give up his job to write full time. He married Marie Bernoulli in 1904, and they had three children. But domestic life did not suit Hesse, and he soon became restless. In 1911 he went to India, hoping for a religious experience, which he did not find, and his journey inspired his novel *Siddhartha*, published in 1922. During the First World War, Hesse and his family lived in Berne, Switzerland. Fiercely opposed to the war, Hesse worked for the Prisoners of War Welfare Organisation to ensure that German prisoners of war had access to books and journals. In 1918, Marie was hospitalised for mental illness and their marriage collapsed. The following year Hesse moved to Montagnola, Switzerland, where he spent the rest of his life, and became a Swiss citizen in 1923.

After a brief and unhappy second marriage, Hesse married Ninon Dolbin in 1931 and began writing his last major work, *The Glass Bead Game*, which was refused publication by the Nazis. In 1943 he was put on the Nazi blacklist and, following the war, in 1946, Hesse was awarded the Nobel Prize for Literature. All his life Hesse worked passionately for books and literature, believing that reading the literature of the world was essential for an understanding of the past. In this cause, between 1920 and 1936 he reviewed about 1000 books and following the First World War he helped to establish the magazine *Vivos Vico*, which was designed to assist with the rebuilding of post-war Germany by educating its young people. Hesse died in his sleep in 1962.

Hesse was the original teenage rebel. During his life he received thousands of letters and visits from young readers, who responded to the confessional tone of his novels and looked to him for spiritual guidance. In 1967 the musician John Kay formed a rock band in San Francisco and named it Steppenwolf after Hesse's novel. Born Joachim Krauledat, Kay had escaped post-war East Germany in a daring midnight flight with his mother and arrived in Canada aged thirteen, dreaming of rock 'n' roll. Steppenwolf's hit song 'Born to be Wild' – which opens the cult movie *Easy Rider* (1969) – defined the generation that looked to Hesse's novels of teenage angst and rebellion against family and society in their search for their 'true self'.

ANDREW MCGAHAN

J.R.R. Tolkien. I don't think you could argue that it's the greatest literature ever, but no other writing has given me as much pleasure over the years as the works of Tolkien. *Lord of the Rings*, sure, but that's only a fraction of what he created, and when I study all the other volumes and essays and fragments concerning Middle Earth that have appeared since his death – an entire world history so vast and yet so deeply incomplete and problematic – that's when I wish he was the one writer who could come back to life and finish what he started.

Andrew McGahan is the author of four novels, including the *Australian*/Vogel Award–winning *Praise* (1992) and *The White Earth* (2004), which won the 2005 Miles Franklin Award.

28 . *Howards End*
by
E . M . FORSTER
(1 8 7 9 – 1 9 7 0)

✑

THE ESSENCE OF E.M. FORSTER's fourth novel, *Howards End*, can be summed up in the two words of its much quoted epigraph: 'Only connect . . .' E.M. Forster began work on *Howards End* in 1908, after he had been reading the American poet Walt Whitman, who had 'started speaking to me'. With the force of revelation, Whitman spoke to Forster of the possibility of a connection between the unseen and the seen, between the soul and the body, passion and prose, art and money. Forster was thrilled: 'That the spiritual world might be robust – !' he wrote. The possibilities of a robust spiritual world are teased out in *Howards End* through the improbable coming together of two quite different families, one robust and one spiritual. The London lives of the Schlegels, sisters Margaret and Helen, are filled with art, literature and soirées with their bohemian friends; their wealth is inherited. The lives of the

Wilcoxes are filled with business; they are committee men, their conversation restricted to sport and politics, their wealth earned, via the Imperial and West African Rubber Company.

The novel opens abruptly with a series of letters from Helen, the more impulsive of the Schlegel sisters, to her sister, Margaret, declaring her love for the Wilcoxes, Paul Wilcox in particular. But romantic love is not destined to unite the two families. Instead, an affinity between two women, Margaret Schlegel and Mrs Wilcox, brings the families together in an unlikely fusion that ends in marriage. Margaret and Mrs Wilcox are hybrids – one not pure Schlegel spirit, the other not pure Wilcox matter.

Mrs Wilcox, like her husband, two sons and daughter, under-stands the value of bricks and mortar, but, unlike them, she is attuned to the spiritual power of her house and the material world. Born at 'Howards End', she is profoundly connected to her home, forever wandering across the lawn with handfuls of hay, trailing her longs skirts across the damp grass: 'she seemed not to belong to the young people and their motor, but to the house, and to the tree that overshadowed it'. Howards End and Mrs Wilcox are the great moral core of Forster's novel; they provide the sacred connec-tion between the earth and the imagination that Forster so valued and that was being lost in a new world so intent on motion.

London was but a foretaste of this nomadic civilization which is altering human nature so profoundly, and throws upon personal relationships a stress greater than they have ever had before. Under cosmopolitanism, if it comes, we shall receive no help from the earth. Trees and meadows and mountains will only be a spectacle, and the binding force that they once exercised on character must be entrusted to Love alone. May Love be equal to the task!

Margaret combines a pragmatic acceptance of the importance of money with her knowledge of the central place in life of art and friendship, the sisters' credo. In what is a heresy to Helen, and 'horrid' even to Margaret herself, Margaret begins to wonder if 'the very soul of the world is economic, and that the lowest abyss is not the absence of love, but the absence of coin'. Her realisations come from her meeting with two forces, the Wilcoxes and Leonard Bast, an impoverished insurance clerk. She begins to realise that the energy and grit of the Wilcoxes keep the world going: without them 'life might never have moved out of proto-plasm'. The Schlegel sisters meet Leonard Bast by chance at a Beethoven concert and invite him to tea. Leonard is desperately striving to educate himself, but his hackneyed attempts at culture are, like Leonard himself, doomed to failure. Leonard's life, a life Margaret would never ordinarily meet, forces her to consider the wealth she and her family take for granted: 'You and I and the Wilcoxes stand upon money as upon islands. It is so firm beneath our feet that we forget its very existence.'

The rapid changes and rampant materialism of the Edwardian world in which Forster was writing, sickened him: 'It really is a new civilization', he wrote in 1908. 'I have been born at the end of the age of peace and can't expect to feel anything but despair.' The times were characterised by a 'craze for motion', money and work, and the increasing activities of trade unionists and suffragettes. And a war with Germany was brewing. King Edward VII succeeded his mother, Queen Victoria, in 1901 and ruled until his death in 1910, a period that roughly spans the years in which Forster wrote his first four novels. *Howards End* was published in 1910, at the height of a constitutional crisis over the creation of a large number of new Liberal peers requested by the Liberal Prime Minister Asquith. This would have given the reforming Liberal Party the parliamentary power to wage war on poverty, much needed in an era in which five million people received over half the national income, while the other thirty-eight million struggled on what remained. In this time of social reform, the first subsidised secondary education was introduced in 1902; old-age pension in 1908; and the first truly middle-class parliament, in which most MPs worked for a living, was elected in 1906.

Forster was born in London in 1879. His father, an architect, died when Forster was only one. At four, Forster moved with his mother to 'Rooksnest', a house in the country north of London, where they lived for ten years until their lease ran out. Rooksnest was the model for Howards End, and Forster described it as 'my childhood and my safety'. After difficult schooldays, Forster went to King's College, Cambridge, to study classics, and met kindred spirits Leonard Woolf, Lytton Strachey and Maynard Keynes. On leaving Cambridge, Forster decided to be a writer, and spent a year in Italy and Greece with his mother.

Back in England, Forster published his first novel, *Where Angels Fear to Tread*, in 1905, then *The Longest Journey* (1907) and *A Room with a View* (1908). But not until the publication of *Howards End* in

1910 to critical acclaim did Forster become one of the most feted novelists in England. In 1912 he travelled to India, where he found his spiritual home, and returned in 1921. On the eve of the First World War, Forster wrote *Maurice*, a novel on homosexual love. During the war, Forster worked for the Red Cross in Alexandria for three years. Here he met the love of his life on a tram, Muhammad al-Adl, with whom, in his late thirties, he had his first sexual affair. While in the Egyptian port, he also befriended the Greek poet Cavafy, and later persuaded T.S. Eliot to publish his poems. After the war, inspired by Proust, Forster wrote his last novel, *A Passage to India*, published in 1924. The year after his mother's death in 1945, King's College gave Forster a fellowship and he moved to Cambridge. He died in Coventry in 1970 and *Maurice* was published the following year.

Howards End is a beautifully written, considered novel about Edwardian England, a world in transition. It is remarkable for the assuredness of its writing, its delicate sensitivities, subtle observations of class and manners, and the intimacy of its prose, with its acute awareness of Englishness and its gently teasing and ironic tone. It is also remarkable for the courage with which the aesthete Forster faced the realities of the material conditions of his time, and the importance of money:

> The imagination ought to play upon money and realize it vividly for it's the — the second most important thing in the world. It is so slurred over and hushed up, there is so little clear thinking — oh, political economy, of course, but so few of us think clearly about our own private incomes,

and admit that independent thoughts are in nine cases out of ten the result of independent means.

In 1992, the Merchant Ivory cinema adaptation of *Howards End* was released. It is a poignant interpretation of Forster's novel, brilliantly cast with Vanessa Redgrave as Mrs Wilcox, Emma Thompson in her Academy Award–winning role as Margaret, Helena Bonham Carter as Helen, and Anthony Hopkins as Mr Wilcox.

PAUL KELLY

Remembrance of Things Past by Marcel Proust is ten books more or less depending on how you divide it — a great long meditation on memory, desire and time. Reading it took up a great chunk of the twenty-second year of my life. Every once in a while I go back to the first few pages and the sound of the swinging gate and dream of shutting out the world and re-reading it all the way to the end, but, like Marcel, I know I'll never, ever have the time again.

Paul Kelly is a great Australian singer-songwriter whose songs include classics 'Before Too Long', 'Winter Coat', 'From St Kilda to Kings Cross' and 'From Little Things Big Things Grow'.

29 . T h e   W a v e s
by
V I R G I N I A   W O O L F
(1 8 8 2 – 1 9 4 1)

✂

BY THE TIME VIRGINIA WOOLF came to write *The Waves*, her seventh
novel, she was at the height of her creative powers, riding on the
success of a period of intense work that had given birth to *Mrs
Dalloway* (1925), *To the Lighthouse* (1927), *Orlando* (1928) and *A Room
of One's Own* (1929). In 1927, two years before starting *The Waves*,
Woolf had written to her sister, the painter Vanessa Bell: 'I think
we are now at the same point: both mistresses of our medium as
never before.' The artistic confidence that accompanied her new-
found fame and fortune can be seen in the creative daring and
inventiveness she brought to the novel that would be published in
1931 as *The Waves*.

Originally titled *The Moths*, *The Waves* was inspired by a letter
from Vanessa, written in 1927 from the South of France about
moths, in particular a giant moth that had banged heavily against

the window of their farmhouse. 'My maternal instinct,' Vanessa wrote, 'which you deplore so much, wouldnt let me leave it'; so, on behalf of her bug-loving children, Vanessa and her companions, after many attempts, finally managed to kill and set the monstrous moth. Virginia wrote back that Vanessa's moth story had so intrigued her that she could think of nothing else for hours afterwards and planned to write a story about it.

Woolf transformed Vanessa's moth tale beyond recognition, constructing from it an extraordinary and poignant novel in six voices with prose interludes – a prose poem of great beauty. *The Waves* is Woolf's most ingenious attempt to solve the creative problems she had set herself: of conveying in words the flow of experience and identity and the passing of time; of writing the spiritual stuff of existence rather than its material trappings. The novel is composed of the voices – 'dramatic soliloquies', as Woolf called them – of six characters from their earliest childhood observations of the dawning day through to the complex utterances of their middle age. The seventh, silent character, Percival, 'remote from us all in a pagan universe', is the one around whom revolve the lives of the six other characters: Bernard, Susan, Louis, Rhonda, Neville and Jinny.

The seven sections, spoken in the six characters' gradually maturing voices, are intercut with fragments in italics that mark out the phases of the sun as it moves across the sky in the course of a day, the first recording the dawn: '*The sun had not yet risen. The sea was indistinguishable from the sky, except that the sea was slightly creased as if a cloth had wrinkles in it.*' Woolf's novel is remarkable not only for the extent to which we come to know its six distinct yet interfused voices and characters, but for how intimately we become connected to the flow of their lives and feel their loves, longings and losses.

While writing the novel, Woolf referred to *The Waves* as auto-biography – and yet she worked hard to take it beyond the personal to express the collective flow of life, to write prose as compact, intensely wrought and rhythmic as poetry. 'I am writing the Waves to a rhythm not to a plot,' she commented. The result is a novel composed of sentences of great beauty, the accumulated effect of which is mesmerising: '"I will take my anguish and lay it upon the roots under the beech trees."'; '"But when we sit together, close," said Bernard, "we melt into each other with phrases. We are edged with mist."' Like C.G. Jung, Woolf thought the joining of the internal male and female was essential for artistic creativity: 'It is when this fusion takes place that the mind is fully fertilized and uses all its faculties. Perhaps a mind that is purely masculine cannot create, any more than a mind that is purely feminine.' With its three male and three female voices, *The Waves* articulates Woolf's hypothesis. It is an opera based on her inner creative workings, a symphony of her own various inner male and female voices, and those of her family and friends – her sister Vanessa shaped Susan; T.S. Eliot informed Louis; her beloved brother Thoby, who died tragically young, inspired Percival – as they merge and separate, ebb and flow, are part of Woolf and yet are not her.

The Waves was published by Virginia and Leonard Woolf at the Hogarth Press in 1931 to critical acclaim and commercial success. Leonard considered *The Waves* the best of Woolf's books, her masterpiece. Woolf herself was surprised by the response of reviewers and the public: 'How odd this is — so far most of the low-brow reviewers (whose sense I respect) find the Waves perfectly simple: and it is selling beyond all my other books! Now why?'

Woolf was born in London in 1882, the daughter of renowned writer and editor Leslie Stephen, and his second wife, Julia Stephen. Julia had three children from her first marriage, Leslie had one, and together they had four more children, so their Kensington house was busy, crowded and intimate. Woolf was educated at home by her father, who was struck by his youngest daughter's dazzling intellect and verbal brilliance. 'The greatest disaster that could happen' occurred when Woolf was thirteen: in 1895 her mother died and, soon after, Woolf had her first break-down. Following their father's death in 1904 (which provoked Woolf's second breakdown), the Stephen siblings, now young men and women, moved together from their dark childhood home across London to unfashionable Bloomsbury, where they found unprecedented freedom in a spacious, light-filled, sparsely furnished terrace. Here writers and artists gathered, including Roger Fry and Lytton Strachey, and the notorious Bloomsbury Group evolved. And here Woolf began to write in earnest, devoting herself to journalism from 1904 to 1909 before beginning her first novel.

An exhibition organised by Roger Fry in 1910 — *Manet and the Post-Impressionists* — brought the bold-stroked paintings of Van Gogh, Gauguin and Cézanne to London en masse for the first time. The exhibition shook the foundations of the London art world and Woolf later wrote: 'On or about December 1910, human character changed.' In her view, the change required a radical new approach to novel writing. Three years after her arrival in Bloomsbury, at the age of twenty-six Woolf had written: 'I shall re-form the novel and capture multitudes of things at present fugitive, enclose the whole and shape infinite strange shapes.' With the critical support and encouragement of Vanessa's husband, Clive Bell, Woolf's first novel, *Melymbrosia*, was published in 1915 as *The Voyage Out*. In 1912, Woolf married Leonard Woolf and two years later they established the Hogarth Press, which became successful beyond their greatest expectations, publishing T.S. Eliot, E.M. Forster, Katherine Mansfield, economist Maynard Keynes and the first English translations of Freud. Dividing her time between the press and her own writing, London and her house in Sussex, Woolf continued to work hard to realise her ambition to reform the novel, producing a novel every three or four years until after *The Waves*.

After completing her last novel, *Between the Acts*, in 1941, fearing the loss of her creative powers like Bernard in *The Waves* ('When I cannot see words curling like rings of smoke round me I am in darkness — I am nothing'), Woolf drowned herself. Leonard, devastated, decided to bury Virginia's ashes under one of the two elms that grew side by side by the pond in their garden at Rodmell, which Virginia had named Leonard and Virginia. The memorial on the tree is engraved with the quotation: 'Death is the enemy. Against you I will fling myself unvanquished and unyielding. O Death!' — spoken by Bernard, his last lines in *The Waves*.

Michael Cunningham's 1998 novel that was inspired by Woolf's *Mrs Dalloway* — *The Hours: A Novel* — became a bestselling sensation and won the Pulitzer Prize. A film, *The Hours*, based on his book was released in 2002, starring Nicole Kidman, Julianne Moore and Meryl Streep. *The Hours* was nominated for nine Academy Awards and won Nicole Kidman the Academy Award for Best Actress in 2003.

JANE MESSER

- *Autumn of the Patriarch* by Gabriel García Márquez. A book drenched with the author's imaginings, his elaborate and rhythmic language – that made me understand how a dictator fills the minds of a people with his presence, day and night.
- *Underworld* by Don DeLillo
- *Kristin Lavransdatter* by Sigrid Undset
- *The Yellow Wallpaper* by Charlotte Perkins Gilman
- *Little Horses of Tarquinia* by Marguerite Duras
- *Delta of Venus* by Anaïs Nin. Erotic writing that's subtle and sexily unnerving even now, forty years after it was written (good sex doesn't date).
- *The Words to Say It* by Marie Cardinal
- *Sanctuary* by William Faulkner
- *Visitants* by Randolph Stowe
- *Pale Fire* by Vladimir Nabokov

Jane Messer teaches creative writing at Macquarie University. She is the author of *Night by Night* (1994) and editor of *Bedlam* (1996) and *Certifiable Truths* (1998).

30 . *Kristin Lavransdatter*

by

SIGRID UNDSET

(1 8 8 2 – 1 9 4 9)

≪

SIGRID UNDSET'S MEDIEVAL TRILOGY, *Kristin Lavransdatter*, is the story of the fiery Kristin Lavransdatter from her girlhood to old age. Kristin is the eldest daughter of Ragnfrid and Lavrans (hence Lavrans-*datter*), a God-fearing farmer whose knowledge of animals and plants and skill at hunting have made him a wealthy land-holder. Like her father, Kristin is beautiful and strong; her soul is deep and attuned to the natural world. She is also headstrong, intrepid and passionate – fired by her love for the black-haired knight Erlend Nikulausson of Husaby, Kristin defies her father, her community and her God to bind herself to Erlend, boldly assuming all the dangers and adventure of his turbulent life. As her admirer Simon Andresson says: 'You trod all underfoot and braved all that you might come together.'

Set in fourteenth-century Norway, the novel opens with

Kristin as a young girl of seven, 'a lily-rose', setting out with her adored father into the mountains to tend the cattle. By a mountain stream, a mysterious woman — 'pale with waving, flaxen hair', dressed in leaf-green — offers Kristin a wreath of golden flowers. Kristin's horse neighs in alarm, alerting her to the danger, and her father rushes to save her from the enchanted wreath. The mountains above Kristin's home are haunted by fairy people, alive with ancient tales and pagan gods, existing alongside the Roman Catholic Church and priest of the village. Against a background of violent upheaval — in 1319, a minor, three-year-old Magnus VII, succeeded to the thrones of both Norway and Sweden, causing dissent in Norway — are the lives of Kristin and her family, their loves and betrayals, the dangers of childbirth and war, the devastation of the Black Plague and the consolation of a Christian god new to a land still steeped in Norse traditions.

Christianity became firmly established in Norway from the mid eleventh century, following the death and martyrdom of Christian King Olaf Haraldsson (St Olaf) at the Battle of Stiklestad in 1030. His subsequent sainthood encouraged the widespread adoption of the new religion.

The coming to Christianity was something Undset knew from her own life. On 1 November 1924, two years after the publication of the third volume of the Lavransdatter trilogy, Undset was received into the Catholic Church, having been brought up an atheist. In *Kristin Lavransdatter*, Undset explores the movement towards the Roman Catholic Church not only of Norway, caught between Christianity and its ancient Norse beliefs, but also of Kristin: from the agonies she suffers through her love for Erlend and their children, she increasingly finds comfort in the Church. This is reflected in the titles of the three volumes of the trilogy – *The Bridal Wreath*, *The Wife* and *The Cross* – which trace out the arc of Kristin and Erlend's love, from their early abandon to erotic passion to Kristin's growing understanding of her deeper relation to Erlend and the essential place of God in her life.

Sigrid Undset was born in 1882 in Denmark to a Danish mother and a Norwegian father. When she was two, her father, a distinguished Norwegian archaeologist, took up a post at the Museum of Antiquities in Kristiania (now Oslo), where Undset grew up with her two younger sisters in an intellectual, atheist household. Her father's love of old Norse sagas inspired his daughter's extensive knowledge of Old Norse and Old Icelandic and her passion for history. Undset and her sisters were sent to the first co-educational school in Oslo, but its progressive views filled Undset with unease. Only many years later, following the First World War, was she able to clarify her discomfort, concluding that 'liberalism, feminism, nationalism, socialism, pacifism, would not work, because they refused to consider human nature as it really is . . .' By the 1920s she had become convinced, from her study of history, 'that the only thoroughly sane people, of our civilization at least, seemed to be those queer men and women the Catholic Church calls Saints' – and it was then that Undset converted to Catholicism, most unusual in Protestant Norway.

Following the early death of her beloved father in 1893, Undset left school aged fifteen. She longed to become a painter, but was forced to earn a living and entered a commercial academy. At the age of seventeen she went to work as a secretary for the German Electrical Company in Oslo, where she remained for ten years. In her scant spare time she wrote an historical novel, which was rejected by a leading publisher with the words: 'Don't try your hand at any more historical novels. It's not your line.' Although she responded to his advice by writing a novel set in contemporary Norway (*Frau Marta Oulie*, which was published in 1907), Undset was later to win the Nobel Prize for Literature in 1928 for the very thing she was told she had no talent for — her historical novels. *Frau Marta Oulie*, which opens with the bold declaration 'I have been unfaithful to my husband', caused an immediate sensation in Norway. Following the publication in 1909 of her second novel, set in the eleventh century, Undset left her job and travelled to Germany and Italy on a writer's scholarship.

In Rome, Undset met the Norwegian painter Anders Svarstad, and based her novel *Jenny* (1911) on their passionate affair. They married in Belgium in 1912 and returned to Norway, where they had three children. With little help from her unsupportive husband, Undset was left to care for their children and three stepchildren and eventually she left him and moved with her children to Lillehammer, north of Oslo. Her marriage was annulled in 1924 when she converted to Catholicism. Following the German occupation of Norway in 1940, Undset, a fierce opponent of Nazism, joined the Resistance and her books were banned. She soon left Norway to spend the war years in the United States, where she became a prominent identity, lecturing on behalf of her country. She returned to Norway in 1945 and died of a stroke four years later.

The publication of *Kristin Lavransdatter* in Norway from 1920 to 1922, fifteen years after Norway's independence from Sweden in 1905 (following five centuries of domination first by Denmark then by Sweden), gave twentieth-century Norwegians a rousing tale of their past, with an indomitable heroine and a courageous knight who fought against a king shared with Sweden. The trilogy was an immediate success. *Kristin Lavransdatter* was published in English from 1923. In 1997 the first volume of a new, updated English translation by Tiina Nunnally appeared. The remaining two volumes of Nunnally's translation, said to be true to the spirit of Undset's original, were published in 1999 and 2000.

Undset's trilogy is remarkable for its fiery portrait of the passionate, independent Kristin and her undying love for the dashing Erlend, and for its rich evocation of fourteenth-century Norway. Considered to be among the greatest historical novels of the twentieth century, *Kristin Lavransdatter* was adapted for the cinema in 1995 by Liv Ullmann, Ingmar Bergman's muse and the star of many of his films, including *Persona*, *Cries and Whispers* and *Scenes from a Marriage*. Ullmann's film of *Kristin Lavransdatter*, featuring Elisabeth Matheson as Kristin and Björn Skagestad as Erlend, was seen by over half the population of Norway in the year of its release.

DON DELILLO

This is one man's memory of reading the first three chapters of *Ulysses* in a small room, those pages in particular, and

feeling, in the sun-cut prose, that here was a world, perhaps dreamily attainable — the English language in all its
malleable beauty, capable of being shaped, hammered,
molded, reformulated.

American writer Don DeLillo is the author of two plays and
thirteen novels, including *Underworld* (1997) and *White
Noise* (1984).

31 . *Ulysses*
by
JAMES JOYCE
(1 8 8 2 – 1 9 4 1)
⁕

WHEN JAMES JOYCE WAS A SCHOOLBOY, he wrote an essay on his favourite hero – Ulysses. Joyce probably first met the hero of Homer's *Odyssey* through Charles Lamb's children's version, *The Adventures of Ulysses,* and so gave Odysseus the Latin version of his name, Ulysses, in the massive work he began to consider while in his early thirties: *Ulysses,* his novel that would mine the riches of Homer's original by re-conceiving the 3000-year-old story of Odysseus's long Mediterranean travels, transporting them to Dublin over one day in the life of that twentieth-century Odysseus, Leopold Bloom.

What so intrigued Joyce about Ulysses? 'Why was I always returning to this theme . . .? I find the subject of Ulysses the most human in world literature . . . Observe the beauty of the motifs: the only man in Hellas who is against the war, and the father.' The theme of fatherhood is the overarching refrain of *Ulysses*. It is Joyce's great preoccupation as an artist and the great preoccupation of Leopold Bloom and Stephen Dedalus. There is a certain ambiguity associated with fatherhood that biological mothers cannot feel, which recurs in the paranoia that pervades Bloom's thoughts and the novel's ramblings. How does a father know he is truly a father to a child? 'What links them in nature? An instant of blind rut.' Has this paranoia alone fired men's long history of artistic and intellectual creative output? When in *Ulysses* John Eglinton scoffs to Stephen Dedalus, what useful discovery could Socrates have learned from his wife? Stephen replies with dazzling wit and insight: 'Dialectic, Stephen answered: and from his mother how to bring thoughts into the world.'

It is said that when the great American writer F. Scott Fitzgerald met James Joyce at one of Gertrude Stein's dinner parties in Paris, Fitzgerald, drunk and overawed, knelt at his feet, kissed his hand and asked him how it felt to be a genius. The undoubted genius of James Joyce had been apparent years earlier at school in Dublin. In 1897, at fifteen, Joyce had topped the whole of Ireland in English composition. By the time he graduated from University College in 1902, aged twenty, he had rejected Catholicism, found 'the eternal affirmation of the spirit of man in literature', taught himself Dano-Norwegian to read his revered Henrik Ibsen in the original, and decided to exile himself in Paris. In 1903, Joyce was called home from Paris to the bedside of his dying mother. The following year, on a Dublin street he met a young Galway girl and several days later the two walked together through the city towards the mouth of the River Liffey.

There the girl unbuttoned his trousers, put her hand in his pants, and Joyce fell in love. The girl, with whom Joyce spent the rest of his life, was Nora Barnacle; the date was probably 16 June 1904 – and Joyce immortalised both the woman and the date in his extraordinary second novel, *Ulysses*. 'June that was too I wooed. The year returns. History repeats itself ... Life, love, voyage round your own little world.'

Three months after they met, Joyce and Nora sailed to Europe, eventually settling in Trieste in 1905. The following year Joyce wrote to his brother about a short story he was planning for *Dubliners*, his book of stories, called 'Ulysses'. The story did not appear, but in 1914 Joyce began work on *Ulysses*, a novel, in which he intended to forge from the city of his birth – 'Dear, Dirty Dublin' – a modern telling of Homer's *Odyssey*. Joyce absorbed himself completely in the novel for the next seven years, working and living with Nora and their two children in cramped hotel rooms in Trieste, Zurich (during the First World War), and eventually in Paris. (Only after the appearance of *Ulysses* did Joyce marry Nora, in the Kensington Registry Office, London, in 1921.)

While domestic chaos reigned around him, Joyce would sit utterly transported by the demands of his complex new novel. *Ulysses* is written in eighteen chapters, each in a different style, each picking up a different thread of the *Odyssey*. It was a Herculean task, as Joyce wrote in 1921:

My head is full of pebbles and rubbish and broken matches and bits of glass picked up, 'most everywhere. The task I set myself technically in writing a book from eighteen different

points of view and in as many styles, all apparently
unknown or undiscovered by my fellow tradesmen, that
and the nature of the legend chosen would be enough to
upset anyone's mental balance.

In Homer's epic poem, the diplomat and warrior Odysseus
voyages home to Ithaca, to his wife Penelope and son Telemachus,
following the razing of Troy. In Joyce's *Ulysses*, the Jewish advertising man Leopold Bloom cooks breakfast kidneys for his wife Molly
before voyaging out through the streets of Dublin, where he visits
a newspaper office, goes to a funeral, goes to the pub, a maternity
hospital and a brothel, before returning home with the 'son'
Stephen Dedalus, who has found him on his way, and eventually
heads upstairs to Molly Bloom and their marital bed. The *Odyssey*
is an epic tale of a war hero's ten-year voyage home; *Ulysses* is an
account of the daily motions of an ordinary family man on 16 June
1904. Joyce once observed: 'Surely living with a woman is one of
the most difficult things a man has to do'; this is the heroic task that
Joyce sets Leopold Bloom — marriage. Bloom must navigate the
deep, siren-filled waters of marriage.

Joyce's vision embraces the whole of Western culture from
Homer, and includes one of the most intriguing ruminations
ever conceived on Shakespeare, *Hamlet* and paternity: 'When
Rutlandbaconsouthamptonshakespeare or another poet of the
same name in the comedy of errors wrote *Hamlet* he was not the
father of his own son merely but, being no more a son, he was and
felt himself the father of all his race.' (Shakespeare was 'no more a
son' because his father had recently died.) Composed of multiple

narratives and voices, rich in experiment, intellectual speculation and lucid insights ('Wait. Five months. Molecules all change. I am other now . . .'), Joyce's novel is also a hymn to the body and its functions – eating, urination, defecation, masturbation, copulation. Even the novel's basic structure takes account of the body, with each chapter devoted to a different organ.

Joyce's first novel, *A Portrait of the Artist as a Young Man* (1916), had established him as the new literary star of the moment, and his second novel was eagerly awaited. Sections of *Ulysses* appeared in an avant-garde American magazine from 1918 (and the following year in a London journal), but in 1921 the magazine was found guilty of obscenity and *Ulysses* was banned. When the novel was eventually published in full in Paris on 2 February 1922 (Joyce's fortieth birthday), it achieved overnight fame and within months was declared a masterpiece.

The acclaim of *Ulysses* as a modernist masterpiece has been accompanied by its reputation as a difficult and inaccessible novel. But while Joyce filled *Ulysses* with all his vast learning, his profound understanding of his modern world and all his linguistic trickery, his great novel remains supremely human. The many joys of *Ulysses* include: Joyce's uncanny ear for language; the novel's enormous vitality and modernity; its bawdy humour, wit and humanity; and the poignant portrait of a man and his marriage that lies at the heart of the story. Samuel Beckett wrote of Joyce that 'His writing is not about something. It is the thing itself.' The 'thing itself' alluded to by Beckett is life, and just as life is a tangled, complex set of happenings, thoughts, feelings, memories, anxieties, food, dreams, conversations, ablutions, and so on, so is Joyce's novel

Ulysses. Joyce was so convinced that his book was not only about the common man but for the common man, that he gave away copies to waiters and hotel porters. And Nora Joyce's biographer, Brenda Maddox, might add that *Ulysses* is also for the common woman, arguing that Joyce 'gave his country and his century the voice of female desire'. Molly Bloom's famous soliloquy that concludes *Ulysses* — and looks forward to a century of women's voices — oozes sensuality: 'I wish some man or other would take me sometime when hes there and kiss me in his arms theres nothing like a kiss long and hot down to your soul almost paralyses you.'

T.S. Eliot (1888–1965) thought Joyce's 'mythical method' — his approach to writing novels — was a discovery of such magnitude that it was equivalent to Einstein's discoveries in physics. Ezra Pound (1885–1972) and F. Scott Fitzgerald revered Joyce. Djuna Barnes was fascinated by his linguistic play and said that after *Ulysses* it was fruitless for anyone else to try to write. Ernest Hemingway smuggled copies of *Ulysses* out of Paris into America, where it was banned. It became fashionable for American tourists returning home from Paris to hide a copy of *Ulysses* in their luggage.

Joyce was fascinated by the cinema and in 1909 he opened the first cinema in Dublin, the Volta. Joyce didn't think *Ulysses* could be adapted to film with 'artistic propriety', but he did discuss a film of his novel with pioneering Russian film director Sergei Eisenstein, which was never made. The first film of *Ulysses* was directed by an American, Joseph Strick, in 1967, but it was banned in Ireland until 2001, when its scenes of ablution and Molly's monologue finally met the censor's approval. Strick believed Joyce was a great cinematic writer and his inventions in *Ulysses* contributed to modern cinema. In 2003, a second film, *Bloom*, was completed by Dublin filmmaker Sean Walsh, who took ten years to film the book. To make his film, Walsh read *Ulysses* about fifty times and wrote about 800 drafts of the screenplay. Driven by his passion for the book, Walsh was determined to bring *Ulysses* to a wide audience, to 'show them the story, show them all the humanity and humour of this masterpiece'.

BLOOMSDAY AND THE JOYCE INDUSTRY

Joyce famously wrote of *Ulysses*: 'I've put in so many enigmas and puzzles that it will keep the professors busy for centuries arguing over what I meant, and that's the only way of ensuring immortality.' Joyce not only succeeded in keeping numerous departments of professors busy unravelling the threads of *Ulysses* (thus ensuring him immortality), but his novel has also spawned a whole literature of guides to reading it, including books such as Harry Blamires's *The New Bloomsday Book*, a commentary on the novel, which has itself become a classic.

James Joyce has become an Irish industry, a tourist business in the country from which he exiled himself – and 16 June, the date on which he cast his novel, has been sanctified as 'Bloomsday'. On 16 June, pilgrims travel to Dublin from all over the world to walk its streets as Leopold Bloom walked them in fictional 1904. Bloomsday was first celebrated in Paris on 27 June 1929 by Joyce and his friends, including Samuel Beckett (1906–1989) and Paul Valéry (1871–1945), with a lunch to commemorate the twenty-fifth anniversary of 16 June 1904 and the publication of the French translation of *Ulysses*. In the twenty-first century, Bloomsday is celebrated with street festivals, readings and music; and breakfasts of Leopold Bloom's favourite food — fried kidneys and offal — are eaten in countries across the globe, including Ireland, Italy, Australia, the USA, Canada and China (the extraordinary feat of translating *Ulysses* into Chinese was completed in the 1980s). In 2004, the centenary of the original Bloomsday was celebrated in 'ReJoyce Dublin 2004', a festival that ran from April until August.

3 2 . The Trial

by

FRANZ KAFKA

(1 8 8 3 – 1 9 2 4)

❧

'SOMEBODY MUST HAVE MADE A FALSE ACCUSATION against Josef K., for he was arrested one morning without having done anything wrong.' This much-quoted opening sentence of *The Trial* sets the tone – one of cool, lucid observation of increasingly bizarre events – of Franz Kafka's novel about a senior bank officer, Josef K., who on the morning of his thirtieth birthday, out of the blue and for no apparent reason, is charged with an unnamed criminal offence. *The Trial* recounts K.'s growing sense of helplessness as he seeks to uncover the truth of his case from a labyrinthine legal machine whose reach appears to be limitless, whose agents are revealed behind every door, from the door of K.'s own apartment to the door of an impoverished painter's studio in a derelict tenement. As K. observes quietly to the court: 'There is no doubt that behind all the utterances of this court, and therefore behind my arrest and today's examination, there stands a great organization.'

Franz Kafka was born in 1883 in Prague (then in the Austro-Hungarian Empire) into a middle-class Jewish family. When his two older brothers died in infancy, Kafka became the eldest child, with three younger sisters. He was sent to German schools, where he excelled, and went on to study law at the German University, graduating in July 1906 with a Doctorate in Jurisprudence. Following university, Kafka worked in the law courts before finding a semi-legal position in 1908 in the Workers' Accident Insurance Institute, where he worked until 1922 when tuberculosis forced him to retire. For most of his four decades, Kafka lived in his parents' cramped apartment, working at the insurance office by day and writing by night: 'Since I am nothing but literature and can and want to be nothing else, my job will never take possession of me,' he wrote. His father, a merchant, was utterly unable to comprehend his pale, thin son's complete devotion to so unprofitable and so unworldly an occupation as literature.

In 1902, Kafka met the writer Max Brod, who was to become his closest friend and literary executor, and through whom in 1912 he met Felice Bauer, a businesswoman from Berlin. Kafka's noncommittal relationship with Felice, conducted mostly via letters between Prague and Berlin, resulted in two broken engagements and coincided with an extraordinary period of creative outpouring. Several weeks after their meeting, Kafka wrote 'The Judgement', one of the few stories to be published in his lifetime, which appeared in 1913 with a dedication to Felice. In the months after their meeting he also wrote six chapters of the novel published posthumously as *America* (1927) and the story 'The Metamorphosis', published in 1915.

In 1923, Kafka moved to Berlin to escape his family and focus on his writing. He died in June 1924 near Vienna, shortly before his forty-first birthday, leaving Brod with instructions to destroy his writing after his death. Instead, Brod famously published and promoted Kafka's stories, starting in 1925 with *The Trial*, and Kafka achieved worldwide posthumous fame during the Nazi era, as his three sisters were being deported and killed in concentration camps.

The Trial does not make comfortable reading, as might be expected from a man who believed we ought to read 'only the kind of books that wound and stab us. If the book we're reading doesn't wake us up with a blow on the head, what are we reading it for? . . . A book must be the axe for the frozen sea inside us. That is my belief.' *The Trial* is remarkable for the clarity of Kafka's vision of a world ruled by anonymous bureaucracy, and for his prose that so lucidly articulates both K.'s apparent state of paranoia and the potent, impeccable logic pitted against him to justify the court's commonsense-defying behaviour. Like *Bleak House*, in which the language of the law has become hollow sophistry capable of great destructive power, at its most literal interpretation *The Trial* is a study of the power of words and the impotence of the individual at the mercy of a vast legal system that, through its power to judge right and wrong, ultimately becomes the arbiter of meaning. The portrait painter — whose painting of Justice is reminiscent not of Justice or Victory, but 'looked exactly like the goddess of the Hunt' — explains to K. there is no point hoping to persuade the court to change its opinion, for the court is utterly unresponsive:

'If I paint all the judges in a row on a canvas, and you argue your defence before this canvas, you'll have more success than you would have before the actual court.'

But gradually K. begins to understand that his innocence is beside the point — he is trapped in a system in which his every protestation of innocence only increases his aura of guilt: 'What matters are the many subtleties in which the court gets lost. But in the end it produces great guilt from some point where originally there was nothing at all.' There is also a mad humour in Kafka's vision, in the ludicrous antics of the court and K.'s efforts to cooperate with it: '"You are an interior decorator?" "No," said K., "I am a senior administrator in a large bank." This answer provoked such a hearty laugh from the right faction down below that K. had to laugh too.'

So rich and open a story is *The Trial* that it has been all things to all people: a religious allegory; a story of divine justice, original sin, fate, capitalism, a totalitarian nightmare, an impotent son overwhelmed by an omnipotent father; a tale of the absurdity of existence. None of these interpretations is able to encompass the full brilliance of the story itself. The remarkable thing about *The Trial* is that Kafka has transformed his own experience of impotence and strange thrall to his captors — his parents; his teachers; his fiancée, Felice Bauer; his employers; his society; life itself — and distilled it into a lucid and resonant multi-layered parable that has the force and irreducibility of truth.

So acute was Kafka's vision that almost one hundred years after his death the word 'Kafkaesque' conveys more vividly than any other word a world governed by impassive agents who may or may not be obeying orders from faceless superiors for no apparent reason. And further, its descriptive powers are uncannily applicable to almost every dimension of our contemporary world – able to evoke our feelings of helplessness when dealing with authority, like the frustrations of automated telephone-answering services, or the general absurdity of modern life, such as the multi-levelled 'parking cavern' of the giant new Ikea in Sydney, described as 'Kafkaesque' by the writer Malcolm Knox in his review of the shopping centre for the pointlessness of its many parking attendants waving 'cars all over the place, with little apparent purpose, as the car park is mostly empty' (*The Sydney Morning Herald*, 17 February 2005).

Orson Welles surmounted numerous challenges, including running out of money, to bring his nightmare vision of *The Trial* to the screen, starring Anthony Perkins as Josef K. It was supposed to be filmed in Zagreb, but finally, fortuitously, one moonlit night Welles discovered the perfect location in Paris – the abandoned railway station Gare d'Orsay. Welles considered *The Trial* (1963) the best film he'd made. Although, perhaps unlike Kafka, Welles viewed Joseph K. as 'a little bureaucrat' and therefore guilty: 'I consider him guilty . . . He belongs to a guilty society; he collaborates with it.'

ANNA FUNDER

- ❧ *Pride and Prejudice* by Jane Austen
- ❧ *Madame Bovary* by Gustave Flaubert
- ❧ *The Trial* by Franz Kafka

- *Mrs Dalloway* by Virginia Woolf
- *The Master and Margarita* by Mikhail Bulgakov
- *The Member of the Wedding* by Carson McCullers
- *The Man Who Loved Children* by Christina Stead
- *1984* by George Orwell
- *Independence Day* by Richard Ford
- *A Home at the End of the World* by Michael Cunningham

Australian writer Anna Funder is the author of the best-selling *Stasiland: Stories from Behind the Berlin Wall* (2002), which won the 2004 BBC FOUR Samuel Johnson Prize for Non-Fiction.

33 . Women in Love
by
D . H . Lawrence
(1 8 8 5 – 1 9 3 0)

IN 1913, HAVING RECENTLY ELOPED to Europe with a married woman, D.H. Lawrence began work on a novel that would encompass his vision of nineteenth-century English provincial life. Set in the Midlands, it focused on the changing fortunes of the Brangwen family, farmers in a region being slowly overrun by coal mining, and on the associated problems faced by modern men and women as their traditional ties to the land were increasingly severed. As Lawrence wrote at the time: 'I am so sure that only through a readjustment between men and women, and a making free and healthy of this sex, will she [England] get out of her present atrophy.'

Originally called *The Sisters*, the manuscript became too big for a single work, and Lawrence turned it into two novels. The first, the story of three generations of the Brangwen family, was published as *The Rainbow* in September 1915. Two months later in a notorious trial, it was prosecuted for obscenity for its immoral portrayal of sex, and the publisher was forced to withdraw it from sale. Crushed by the trial and filled with despair by the continuing world war he had expected would end in 1915, Lawrence returned to his Brangwen saga in 1916 and reworked the remaining material into a fierce and powerful sequel he eventually called *Women in Love*.

Determined to make sense of the destruction of the war years, Lawrence struggled through his novel to articulate his vision of marriage and sexual love for the twentieth century. *Women in Love* takes up the story of the two Brangwen sisters, Ursula and Gudrun, now sophisticated, worldly women. It opens with Ursula embroidering and Gudrun drawing as they sit together in the window-bay of their father's house. The first words come from Gudrun, who asks her sister, 'Ursula, don't you *really want* to get married?' Ursula replies that she doesn't know, 'It depends how you mean.' Like most things in Lawrence's world, marriage no longer has a fixed meaning, and Ursula's ambivalence to marriage is one of the driving forces of the novel: 'When it comes to the point, one isn't even tempted — oh, if I were tempted, I'd marry like a shot. I'm only tempted not to.'

Ursula's contrariness compels and frustrates her lover, the school inspector Rupert Birkin (based on Lawrence). She resists Birkin's urge to dominate her and there is a chance these two might find the quivering, delicately balanced union of independent beings — 'two single beings constellated together like two stars' — that Lawrence believed was possible between men and women. But Gudrun's passionate affair with the mining magnate Gerald Crich is an expression of something much darker in the human psyche and of the broader dissolution of the war years. Their relationship is founded on a shared, magnetic coldness — as a pet rabbit struggles in Gudrun's hands, Gerald sees, 'with subtle recognition, her sullen passion of cruelty'. On finishing *Women in Love* in November 1916, Lawrence said the novel frightened him because 'it's so end of the world . . .' As Lawrence's friend John Middleton Murry acknowledged (despite not liking *Women in Love*), Lawrence was one of the few writers who 'struggled with the spiritual catastrophe of the war in the depths of their souls'. Lawrence did not find a publisher for *Women in Love* until 1920, and, when it finally appeared in London in May 1921, it was attacked by the conservative, jingoistic newspaper *John Bull* as 'a loathsome study of sex depravity leading youth to unspeakable disaster'.

David Herbert Richards Lawrence was born in Nottinghamshire in 1885, the fourth child of a barely literate coalminer and his educated, religious wife. Aged twelve, he won a scholarship to Nottingham High School in 1898, but left school at sixteen to work as a clerk in a factory. Forced by pneumonia to give up his job, Lawrence found work as a teacher in 1902 and began writing poetry in 1905. Ford Madox Ford published Lawrence's poetry in *English Review* and recommended Lawrence's first novel, *The White Peacock*, to publisher William Heinemann, who published it in 1911. Soon after, Lawrence fell passionately in love with the German aristocrat Frieda Weekley, who was married to a professor at Nottingham University College. The lovers eloped to Germany before moving to Italy where Lawrence began *The Sisters*. Following Frieda's divorce, they were married in London in 1914 in the Kensington Registry Office (where James Joyce and Nora

Barnacle were married). Their witnesses were Katherine Mansfield and her lover, John Middleton Murry, who moved with the Lawrences to Cornwall. Here, Lawrence worked on *Women in Love*, drawing the charged relationship between Birkin and Gerald Crich from his intense love for Murry. So potent is the homoerotic undercurrent between the two men that in Ken Russell's 1969 film of *Women in Love*, the wrestling scene between a naked Alan Bates as Birkin and naked Oliver Reed as Gerald caused a sensation on its release. (The film also starred Glenda Jackson as Gudrun, for which she received the Academy Award for Best Actress in 1970.)

Lawrence and Frieda were expelled from Cornwall in 1917, accused of spying for Germany on the suspicion they were supplying provisions to the German submarines along the Cornish coast, and forbidden to leave England. Disillusioned with England and believing life to be elsewhere, after the war they moved to Italy and never lived in Lawrence's homeland again. They spent the years until Lawrence's death in 1930 travelling the world in search of a better life, visiting the United States via Sri Lanka and Australia (where in six weeks Lawrence wrote *Kangaroo*, published in 1923). In 1925, they returned to Italy, where Lawrence began *Lady Chatterley's Lover*, which was published privately in 1928 and banned the same year. He died five years later in Vence, France, aged forty-four. *Lady Chatterley's Lover* only became freely available after 1959 (New York) and 1960 (London).

Women in Love is notable for Lawrence's probing analysis of human relationships and the dazzling precision with which he observes the natural world and transforms it into symbols to evoke the almost inexpressible insights of his blood. His words remain vividly alive, as when he describes Ursula watching Birkin throw stones into a moonlit pond:

> Ursula was aware of the bright moon leaping and swaying, all distorted, in her eyes. It seemed to shoot out arms of fire like a cuttlefish, like a luminous polyp, palpitating strongly before her . . . Then again there was a burst of sound, and a burst of brilliant light, the moon had exploded on the water, and was flying asunder in flakes of white and dangerous fire.

'Oh, there is something so lovable about him and his eagerness, his passionate eagerness for life — that is what one loves so,' said Mansfield of Lawrence. The passionate eagerness of Lawrence the man is everywhere apparent in *Women in Love* — both in his character Birkin, as well as in the fierceness of his writing and the urgency with which he insists on his vision, rhythmically pounding it out like a preacher:

> And why? Why should we consider ourselves, men and women, as broken fragments of one whole? It is not true. We are not broken fragments of one whole. Rather we are the singling away into purity and clear being, of things that were mixed.

In 1913, D.H. Lawrence wrote to a friend: 'My great religion is a belief in the blood, the flesh, as being wiser than the intellect . . . All I want is to answer my blood, direct, without fribbling intervention of my mind, or moral, or what-not.' For Lawrence, sex was the key to understanding life and the universe: 'I shall always be a Priest of Love and a glad one.'

❄ EDMUND CAPON ❄

Here are my ten favourite novels. And I know what you'll think — quite understandably — what an odd lot.

- ⚘ *The Leopard* by Giuseppe Tomasi di Lampedusa. Because it's one of those rare books which I can always return to and I still love the film version too — by Visconti, with Burt Lancaster, Alain Delon and Claudia Cardinale. Decaying pageantry at its most eloquent.
- ⚘ Kazuo Ishiguro: read everything of his — just done the new one. But *The Unconsoled* is arguably my favourite book at the moment. Story of a pianist of renown who arrives in an unidentified central European city for a gig — but nothing, neither the performance nor anything else quite comes into fruition. It's quite real and plausible but ultimately baffling, uncertain and elusive.
- ⚘ *The Masterpiece* by Emile Zola. As autobiographical as Zola gets, and fascinating about him and Cézanne.
- ⚘ Thomas Bernhard: really whacky bloke he is — or was. *Wittgenstein's Nephew* is probably number one ... but so too is ...
- ⚘ *Woodcutters* by Thomas Bernhard. Happy family vitriol (also known as *Cutting Timber*).

- ❦ J.G. Ballard: read absolutely everything of his — the best subterfuge in town. *Cocaine Nights* is a classic and has the best title of all.
- ❦ Antonio Tabucchi: not much known, it seems — professor of Portuguese at Siena University but writes wonderful quiet mysteries. Favourite is *Declares Pereira* but *Indian Nocturnes* is equally absorbing and brief too.
- ❦ *The New Machiavelli* by H.G. Wells. You have to have wit and cynicism to foresee as Wells did.
- ❦ *Lord Jim* by Joseph Conrad. Well, it takes place in my kind of territory, and what's more you have to read it at least three times to find out what is really going on.
- ❦ *Eucalyptus* by Murray Bail. My favourite Australian book. Saved from the silver screen, for the moment at least . . .

Born in England, Edmund Capon has been based in Sydney as the director of the Art Gallery of New South Wales for over twenty-five years. A specialist in China, Capon's art interests and scholarship are wide-ranging.

34 . *P r e l u d e*

by

K A T H E R I N E   M A N S F I E L D

(1 8 8 8 – 1 9 2 3)

❧

IN 1917, WHEN VIRGINIA WOOLF asked Katherine Mansfield for a story for the Hogarth Press, Mansfield reworked a piece she had begun during the First World War intended to be a novel about her childhood in New Zealand. Renamed 'Prelude', the story Mansfield sent Woolf is based on her family's move from Wellington to nearby rural Karori. Hand-printed and published as a 68-page booklet by the Hogarth Press in July 1918, *Prelude* was the Woolfs' second publication. Two years later it was published in Mansfield's collection *Bliss and Other Stories* (1920).

Set in New Zealand, *Prelude* is a beautifully evocative, lucid story told in twelve parts with a fluid point of view that shifts effortlessly from two little girls, Kezia and Lottie Burnell, to their languid dreamy mother, Linda; their romantic energetic father, Stanley; grandmother; servant; and longing-filled aunt, Beryl. The carefully observed deliberate strokes of Mansfield's prose were enriched by the 1910 Japanese exhibition in London and Roger Fry's exhibition *Manet and the Post-Impressionists*, particularly the sunflowers of Vincent Van Gogh, which inspired a new sense of freedom in Mansfield. Her story's discontinuous structure, with its twelve intercut sections, was shaped by the movement of cinema, and its multiple perspectives were influenced by Mansfield's observation of Cubist painting, especially Picasso's. Mansfield's urge to create new forms for the short story was intensified by her sense that following the war, which in 1915 had taken the life of her beloved brother Leslie, nothing could ever be the same again: 'I can't imagine how after the war these men can pick up the old threads as tho' it had never been.'

Prelude opens abruptly, with the arrangement of baggage, children and two women, on a buggy: 'There was not an inch of room for Lottie and Kezia in the buggy.' Their mother is willing to forsake her two little girls for her mountainous luggage of 'absolute necessities': the girls can stay behind to follow later, the luggage cannot. Immediately, Mansfield plunges the reader into the drama of her story. In spare, sharp prose, she vividly evokes the two little girls: 'Hand in hand, they stared with round solemn eyes first at the absolute necessities and then at their mother.' Mansfield can evoke whole emotional histories in one sentence, so precise and economical is her writing. As she said of her process: 'I feel as fastidious as though I wrote with acid.' Yet from acid she creates stories of haunting suggestiveness. She wanted to 'speak to the secret self we all have – to acknowledge that'.

In Mansfield's hands, the material world and the otherworldly merge, and her prose is as adept at conjuring solid substance and landscape as it is at evoking the unformed hinterlands of experience, the half-glimpsed shadowy worlds of dreams, longings and visions: 'Linda looked up at the fat swelling plant with its cruel leaves and fleshy stem. High above them, as though becalmed in the air, and yet holding so fast to the earth it grew from, it might have had claws instead of roots.' And, in her economic prose, Mansfield powerfully conveys her characters, with much affection and humour, as well as the subtle interweaving of their relationships. Her portrait of Stanley, the worldly, hasty man of action, is brilliant: '"Oh, damn! Oh, blast!" said Stanley, who had butted into a crisp white shirt only to find that some idiot had fastened the neck-band and he was caught.' Stanley and his family also come vividly to life in Mansfield's story of their beachside holiday, *At the Bay*, a companion piece to *Prelude*.

Mansfield, born Katherine Mansfield Beauchamp in 1888 in Wellington, New Zealand, experimented all her short life with different names, looks, styles of dress – her fluid identity a natural source of her stories' skilful, shifting narrative point of view. Mansfield first left New Zealand in 1903 with her family to study with her two sisters at Queen's College in London. Three years later she returned to New Zealand, where she had a number of passionate affairs with men and women, and took up music, planning to become a cellist. Although she became a writer, not a musician, Mansfield brought a musical ear to her stories, attending to the length and sound of her sentences, reading them aloud 'just as one would *play over* a musical composition', as she wrote after completing her compact short story 'Miss Brill'. In 1908, aged nineteen and with an annual allowance from her banker father, Mansfield left New Zealand again, never to return.

In England, Mansfield married George Bowden in 1909 (he thought she looked like her hero, Oscar Wilde) but left him the day after their wedding to resume her affair with violinist Garnet Trowell (T.S. Eliot warned Ezra Pound she was a dangerous woman). Her first stories were published in 1910 by A.R. Orage, the influential editor of *The New Age*, London's first socialist weekly, and then in 1911 in her first collection of stories, *In a German Pension*. The same year, Mansfield sent a story to John Middleton Murry, editor of the cutting-edge magazine *Rhythm*, which aimed among other things to 'familiarize us with our outcast selves'. Murry rejected her story but published the next one, 'The Woman at the Store'. Soon Murry and Mansfield became lovers, known as 'The Two Tigers' for their passionate belief that art must be brutal in order to renew its humanity, and in 1916 they moved to Cornwall, near D.H. and Frieda Lawrence. Mansfield and Murry had a tempestuous relationship characterised by separations, affairs and jealousy, but they remained ardently attached to each other. Mansfield completed the first draft of *Prelude* when she was at her happiest with Murry, writing opposite him at the same table while he worked on his first book, on Dostoyevsky. After her divorce from Bowden, Mansfield and Murry were married in 1918.

Mansfield's health, always fragile, deteriorated in 1918 when she began to spit blood; she was diagnosed with tuberculosis. From then on, Mansfield travelled constantly on the Continent, unable to spend winters in England, and in 1920 she moved to Menton on the French Riviera. After periods with Murry in Switzerland, Mansfield travelled to Gurdjieff's Institute for the Harmonious Development of Man at Fontainebleau in October 1922 to seek a cure for her tuberculosis. Here she died aged thirty-four in January 1923, on the evening after Murry's arrival from England.

After Mansfield's death, Woolf wrote: 'When I began to write, it seemed to me there was no point in writing. Katherine wont read it.' Mansfield was perhaps the only woman Woolf knew who cared as much about writing as she did, and was the only writer of whom Woolf confessed jealousy, for the beauty and exactness of her prose. The British journalist, novelist and critic Rebecca West (1892–1983), famous for her reports of the Nürnberg war trials, considered *Prelude* to be a work of genius.

MARGARET FINK

- *The Pilgrim's Progress* by John Bunyan. Read when I was eleven or twelve, Bunyan's masterpiece showed me one can be moral without being religious.
- *Brideshead Revisited* by Evelyn Waugh. Although I enjoyed most of Evelyn Waugh's novels, this is the one I've selected.
- *Madame Bovary* by Gustave Flaubert
- *Crime and Punishment* by Fyodor Dostoyevsky
- *The Man Who Loved Children* by Christina Stead
- *The Mill on the Floss* by George Eliot
- *Jude the Obscure* by Thomas Hardy

- ❧ *Earthly Powers* by Anthony Burgess
- ❧ *Bleak House* by Charles Dickens
- ❧ *Wuthering Heights* by Emily Brontë

Australian Margaret Fink is a film producer whose films include the acclaimed *My Brilliant Career* (1979), *For Love Alone* (1986) and *Candy* (2006).

35 . *Wide Sargasso Sea*
by
JEAN RHYS
(1 8 9 0 – 1 9 7 9)

ॐ

IN 1939 JEAN RHYS'S SECOND HUSBAND gave her a copy of Charlotte
Brontë's *Jane Eyre*, an act that would shape Rhys's writing life for the
next three decades. So haunted was Rhys by the shadowy figure of
Rochester's mad Jamaican wife in Brontë's novel that she struggled
for over twenty years to write this first Mrs Rochester's untold story.
This she finally achieved with the publication in 1966 of *Wide
Sargasso Sea* – her fifth, final and most devastating novel – which
tells the story of Mrs Rochester from her childhood in the West
Indies to her incarceration in Rochester's attic in England, a journey
from warm tropical lushness to cold that Rhys knew well from her
own life. In bringing to life the spectre that haunts *Jane Eyre*, Rhys
gives voice to the woman whose lunacy shapes one of Victorian
England's most acclaimed novels, and brings to centre stage the
colonial foundations on which the British Empire was built.

Wide Sargasso Sea, set in 1830s Jamaica and Dominica, tells the tragic story of Antoinette Cosway, as Rhys names Brontë's Bertha Antoinetta Mason, who married Mr Rochester. Narrated in multiple voices, *Wide Sargasso Sea* tells Antoinette's story in three parts. The first part, narrated by the young Antoinette, tells the story of her life before marriage, of her beautiful mother and the family's fading fortunes. The second part, narrated by the unnamed Rochester, tells the story of his married life in 'Granbois', Antoinette's mother's house in the Windward Islands. Rochester finds life there overwhelming: 'Everything is too much, I felt as I rode wearily after her. Too much blue, too much purple, too much green. The flowers too red, the mountains too high, the hills too near.' And his wife disturbs him: 'The girl is thought beautiful, she is beautiful. And yet . . .' The brief third part is told by Antoinette in England: 'In this room I wake early and lie shivering for it is very cold.' Here Rochester has renamed her Bertha, which for Antoinette is some kind of magic, a way for Rochester further to reshape her identity and possess her. As Antoinette says: 'Names matter, like when he wouldn't call me Antoinette, and I saw Antoinette drifting out of the window with her scents, her pretty clothes and her looking-glass.' For Rhys's novel, written with the beauty and precision of poetry, is predominantly a tale of possession, of love and haunting: 'She's mad but *mine, mine*. What will I care for gods or devils or for Fate itself. If she smiles or weeps or both. *For me*.'

Rhys draws on a rich history of early-nineteenth-century Caribbean life for her portraits of Antoinette and her mother, in particular on the phenomenon of Creole heiresses who had gone mad as a result of their inbred colonial society, their sanity further tested by their sudden impoverishment following the emancipation of the slaves on whom their fortunes depended and by their beliefs in local voodoo superstitions. The Emancipation Act of British Parliament of 1833 originally stipulated emancipation over a seven-year transitional phase to allow a period of adjustment, but this was amended and the slaves were granted full emancipation in August 1838 (although in Dominica, Rhys's home, slavery ended in 1834). The local planters felt betrayed by the British government, and their loss of free labour and the halving of sugar prices following the introduction of free trade destroyed their fortunes. Times were hard and many plantation families were ruined, like Antoinette's, and their estates were bought up by wealthy interlopers from Britain such as Mr Rochester, who knew nothing about island life.

Jean Rhys was born Ella Gwendolen Rees Williams in 1890 in Roseau, Dominica, a Caribbean island that had been sold to England by France in 1805. Her father was a Welsh doctor, her mother a white Creole whose grandfather had owned a plantation and been part of Dominica's white colonial elite. Dominica is a small, rugged island, densely vegetated and mountainous, with a violent history. As Rhys's Rochester longingly observes: 'It was a beautiful place – wild, untouched, above all untouched, with an alien, disturbing, secret loveliness. And it kept its secret. I'd find myself thinking, "What I see is nothing – I want what it *hides* – that is not nothing."'

Rhys left Dominica when she was sixteen to go to school in Cambridge, where her grandfather had gone to university. After a brief term at the Royal Academy of Dramatic Art in London, she dropped out to become a chorus girl. In 1912, after a passionate affair, Rhys began to write. In 1919 she married the Dutch writer Jean Lenglet, and they lived a bohemian life, mostly in Vienna and Paris, where artists, writers and musicians congregated following the end of the First World War. They had two children, a son who died at three weeks and a daughter, Maryvonne. When Lenglet was jailed in Paris in 1924 for embezzlement, Rhys moved in with writer Ford Madox Ford and Australian painter Stella Bowen, and Rhys and Ford soon became lovers (in her autobiography, *Drawn from Life* (1941), Bowen refers to the unnamed Jean as 'the real Wild One'). Ford published Rhys's first short story in his magazine, *The Transatlantic Review*, in 1924, and in 1927 a collection of her stories, *The Left Bank*, was published under her pen name 'Jean Rhys'. This was followed by the publication of her first novel, *Quartet*, based on her affair with Ford. Between 1928 and 1939 she published four novels, about beautiful, fading women in Paris and London during the 1920s and '30s. In 1928, she returned to England and moved in with her agent, Leslie Tilden Smith, whom she married in 1934. They moved to Cornwall when war broke out in 1939 — and Rhys then disappeared from the literary world for nearly three decades.

In 1939, after receiving *Jane Eyre* from Tilden Smith, Rhys began excitedly to write the missing story of Mrs Rochester: 'It is that particular mad Creole I want to write about, not any of the other mad Creoles,' she wrote. She originally called the story *Le Revenant* (one returned from the dead), but burnt the typescript after an argument with her husband. She then spent the next twenty years labouring over her story: 'I must write. If I stop writing, my life will have been an abject failure. It is that already to other people, but it could be an abject failure to myself. I will not have earned death.' Impoverished and isolated in Cornwall, Rhys poured a lifetime of separation and division into her only novel set in the West Indies, eventually called *Wide Sargasso Sea*. She named it after the Sargasso Sea, a free-floating sea in the North Atlantic adrift between the West Indies and the Azores, unique among the world's seas because it has no coastline.

Despite her rumoured death, Rhys was finally discovered in Cornwall by the outside world in 1957. Impressed by a broadcast version of her novel *Good Morning, Midnight*, the editor Francis Wyndham finally tracked down Rhys and wrote to her, wondering if she had any new work. She replied that she was working on a new novel 'unlike anything I've attempted before'. Sustained by a group of supportive editors and agents, including Wyndham, Diana Athill, Sonia Orwell (George Orwell's widow) and Olwyn Hughes (Ted Hughes's sister), Rhys eventually managed to shape from her obsession with Bertha Mason a novel, in cool lucid prose, as haunting as it is beautiful. So profoundly did Rhys struggle with Antoinette Cosway's story that, according to Diana Athill:

> It is no exaggeration to say that it nearly killed her: her heart went into failure on the day she was supposed to hand the book over to me, and it was two years before she recovered enough to add the two or three little finishing touches without which she would not let us publish it.

When she discovered that Jean Rhys had spent several days in Holloway Prison, the English playwright Polly Teale knew she wanted to write a play about her life. She was fascinated by the fact that this gifted writer had assaulted a neighbour, whom Rhys believed had been making too much noise, then bitten the policeman who arrived on the scene to deal with the matter. This story of Rhys's violent behaviour is eerily evocative of the fictional Mrs Rochester; fittingly, Teale named her play *After Mrs Rochester*.

MARGARET MERTEN

In no particular order:
- *Catch 22* by Joseph Heller
- *Bleak House* by Charles Dickens
- *Vanity Fair* by William Makepeace Thackeray
- *The Garden Party* by Katherine Mansfield
- *1984* by George Orwell
- *Pride and Prejudice* by Jane Austen
- *Heart of Darkness* by Joseph Conrad
- *The Tin Drum* by Günter Grass
- *The Great Gatsby* by F. Scott Fitzgerald
- *Death in Venice* by Thomas Mann

Australian journalist Margaret Merten is the associate editor of *Harper's Bazaar* and was previously features editor for *Vogue* magazine.

36. *The Master and Margarita*

by

MIKHAIL BULGAKOV

(1891–1940)

ॐ

MIKHAIL BULGAKOV SPENT NINE DIFFICULT YEARS working on *The Master and Margarita*, writing eight different versions and only completing the final manuscript shortly before his death in 1940. The novel is a fierce satire of Stalinist Russia, a love story of cosmic dimensions, and a story of Pontius Pilate and Jesus Christ. Not surprisingly, given its explosive subject matter, *The Master and Margarita* was not published until twenty-seven years after Bulgakov's death. The serialised publication in 1967 of a censored version of the novel caused a literary sensation in Soviet Russia for its daring engagement with a taboo subject, Christianity; its rich, outrageous black comedy; and the outlandish behaviour of its supernatural characters – Satan disguised as the foreign Professor Woland and his retinue of two grotesque demons, a gigantic black cat and a beautiful, naked woman.

The novel opens on a strange spring day at Patriarch Ponds, a park in inner Moscow. Two Communist Party literary hacks — Berlioz, the editor of a highbrow literary magazine, and Bezdomny, a poet — walk together discussing the poet's latest work, an anti-religious poem about Jesus commissioned by Berlioz. Like all good Soviet citizens, they are committed atheists, and Berlioz is concerned that Bezdomny has made Jesus too convincing in his poem, as if he really existed, when the point of the poem is to show he is pure myth. '"There is not one oriental religion," said Berlioz, "in which an immaculate virgin does not bring a god into the world. And the Christians, lacking any originality, invented their Jesus in exactly the same way."' But Patriarch Ponds (named 'Patriarch' after the head of the Russian Orthodox Church, an institution under ruthless attack in the 1930s) sets the scene for the sudden arrival of a character from this outlawed theology — Satan: 'He looked slightly over forty. Crooked sort of mouth. Clean-shaven. Dark hair. Right eye black, left eye for some reason green. Eyebrows black, but one higher than the other. In short — a foreigner.'

When the man — who describes himself as a professor of black magic and tells them he was with Pontius Pilate during his interrogation of Jesus — predicts an improbable event that rapidly comes to pass, Bezdomny is terrified and tries to warn the people of Moscow and his fellow writers that a mad professor and foreign spy is on the loose and will wreak havoc unless he is caught. For his efforts, Bezdomny is bound in tea towels and carted off to a psychiatric clinic. Here he is visited by a dark-haired man with restless eyes from the neighbouring room who calls himself 'a master', and the two men discover they have both been locked up because of Pontius Pilate. The Master then tells his extraordinary tale about falling in love with a beautiful woman who urges him to finish his novel about Pilate, which she believes is the work of a master. He does, but 'When I emerged into the world clutching my novel, my life came to an end.'

With brilliant dexterity, Bulgakov weaves together the three strands of his story: the tale of the Master and his lover, Margarita; the story of Pontius Pilate and his failure to act courageously (a story written by the Master, narrated by Satan, read by Margarita, dreamt by Bezdomny); and the surreal nightmare of the satanic invasion of Moscow. In the last of these strands, greedy, petty officials are transported or imprisoned on a whim, their apartments invaded, their lives destroyed, as the terror wreaked by Stalin's regime is turned on the instruments of state (including one of Moscow's literary clubs at whose hands Bulgakov suffered). Bulgakov writes with dazzling, knife-like precision and wild originality, with a violence that lurks even in his love scenes. When the Master and Margarita meet, 'Love leaped up out at us like a murderer jumping out of a dark alley. It shocked us both – the shock of a stroke of lightning, the shock of a flick-knife.'

Mikhail Bulgakov was born in 1891 in Kiev, Ukraine, in the Russian Empire, into a theological family (his father was a theology professor at the Kiev Theological Academy). He studied medicine at Kiev University and, following his graduation in 1916, joined the White Army as a doctor, but in 1920 gave up medicine to work as a journalist. The following year, aged thirty, Bulgakov moved to Moscow to devote himself to literature. He worked as a freelance journalist, writing comic pieces for newspapers and journals, but found little success with his novels in an increasingly repressive Soviet regime, of which his work was sharply critical. His first novel, *The Heart of a Dog*, was not published in his own country until 1987. His novel about the Civil War, *The White Guard*, was published in serial form in 1924 but the last instalment never appeared because the journal was closed down for failing to toe the Communist Party line. Bulgakov briefly became a successful playwright, but in 1929 his plays were banned. Even his adaptation for the stage of *The White Guard*, which was reputedly among Stalin's favourite plays, was eventually banned. Forced into isolation and poverty, Bulgakov was so frustrated by the impossibility of getting his work published in the Soviet Union that he wrote to Stalin requesting permission to emigrate (his brothers had emigrated to Paris). In response, Stalin personally telephoned him to offer him a post as literary consultant at the Moscow Arts Theatre, which he accepted. At this time he met Elena Shilovskaia, and they were married in 1932 (she was his third wife). He started work on *The Master and Margarita* and it is said that the beautiful, intrepid Margarita was modelled on Elena. Eight years later, Bulgakov died in despair, leaving behind his great unpublished indictment of his times and fervent call for love and compassion, not power, to shape human lives – *The Master and Margarita*. As Yeshua (Jesus) tells Pilate: "'Among other things," continued the prisoner, "I said that all power is a form of violence exercised over people and that the time will come when there will be no rule by Caesar nor any other form of rule.'"

In 2004, the first Russian film version of *The Master and*

Margarita was made, to be screened as a ten-part television series. Directed by Vladimir Bortko, the film had to be made secretly in the Crimea because Bulgakov's story now risks offending an entirely different section of Russian society – the Church. As Father Mikhail Dudko (head of the Secretariat for Church and Society) told the English newspaper *The Guardian*: 'We Christians know four gospels, and in Bulgakov's book we see a kind of fifth: a gospel narrated by Satan, [who is called] Woland in the book. And the interpretation is in Satan's favour. Our reaction to such an interpretation can be nothing but negative.'

NICHOLAS SHAKESPEARE

- *Le Morte d'Arthur* by Sir Thomas Malory
- *The Mayor of Casterbridge* by Thomas Hardy
- The works of Marcel Proust
- *The Master and Margarita* by Mikhail Bulgakov
- *Literature or Life* by Jorge Semprun
- *Labyrinths* by Jorge Luis Borges
- *Danube* by Claudio Magris
- *Love in the Time of Cholera* by Gabriel García Márquez

Nicholas Shakespeare is the award-winning author of four novels: *The Vision of Elena Silves* (1989), *The High Flyer* (1993), *The Dancer Upstairs* (1995) and *Snowleg* (2004). He is also the author of an acclaimed biography of Bruce Chatwin (1999) and *In Tasmania* (2004).

37 . Nightwood
by
DJUNA BARNES
(1892–1982)

❧

IN 1920, THE AMERICAN WRITER and artist Djuna Barnes moved
from New York to Paris, where she met the love of her life, Thelma
Wood. Their passionate eight-year love affair, fired by sex, drugs
and violent emotion, came to an explosive end in 1929. Two years
later, Barnes left Paris for England and moved into Peggy
Guggenheim's country manor, where she wrote out her devastation in a haunting novel of erotic obsession and torment, *Nightwood*,
which Barnes called the soliloquy of 'a soul talking to itself in the
heart of the night' and said was written in blood. The extraordinary baroque richness of her novel, about the unleashed passion of
Nora Flood for the boyish woman Robin Vote, led the poet
T.S. Eliot to compare it to Elizabethan drama: 'What I would leave
the reader prepared to find is the great achievement of a style,
the beauty of phrasing, the brilliance of wit and characterisation,

and a quality of horror and doom very nearly related to that of Elizabethan tragedy.'

Nightwood, told in eight disjointed chapters, opens early in 1880 with the birth in Vienna of Felix Volkbein. Felix's Jewish father, Guido, has attempted to 'span the impossible gap' between himself and his Christian wife, between his Jewish blood and that of his adopted land, Austria, by pretending to be from an old, noble Austrian family – 'the saddest and most futile gesture of all had been his pretence of a barony'. Felix – who assumes his father's false title to become Baron Volkbein – is the first of the novel's outcasts, nighttime creatures at odds with the world. At a decadent party in Berlin, Felix Volkbein meets Dr Matthew O'Connor, an Irishman who dominates the party with his depraved stories of young men – such as Nikka, who wore nothing at all 'except an ill-concealed loin-cloth all abulge as if with a deep-sea catch, tattooed from head to heel with all the *ameublement* of depravity! Garlanded with rosebuds and the hackwork of the devil' – and the 'savage and refined' American woman, Nora Flood, who is promoting a circus.

The doctor later meets up with Felix in a Paris café, but their drinking session is abandoned when the doctor is called to assist a woman who has fainted in a nearby hotel. The two men discover a dishevelled form on a bed surrounded by exotic plants and flowers:

> About her head there was an effulgence as of phosphorus glowing about the circumference of a body of water – as if her life lay through her in ungainly luminous deteriorations – the troubling structure of the born somnambule, who lives in two worlds – meet of child and desperado.

Barnes's lover Thelma Wood was the original for this portrait of the fluid Robin Vote, with whom Nora Flood soon falls desperately in love. When Robin drifts away into the twilight, impossible to hold, and moves in with the rich American widow Jenny Petherbridge, Nora in her unleashed grief turns to the doctor for comfort. In the fifth fragment of the novel, the beautiful 'Watchman, What of the Night?', Nora asks the doctor to tell her everything about the night. The doctor, dressed in a woman's nightgown and golden wig, responds by talking through Nora's ravaged ravings, telling her stories of the night and those who haunt it – drug addicts, alcoholics, the debauched and 'that most miserable, the lover who watches all night long in fear and anguish'.

Nightwood is remarkable for Barnes's extraordinarily rich language and her intense probing of the darkness of illicit love, jealousy, death, agonised passion and perverse desire. Her vision is prescient in an era – the 1930s – that saw the rise of Nazism intent on eradicating deviance. Barnes's extravagant metaphors and symbols, ferocious and daring, have all the ornate, sensual detail of Surrealist painting, which emerged in Paris in the 1920s and to which Barnes was exposed through her friendship with the Surrealists:

Sometimes one meets a woman who is beast turning into human. Such a person's every movement will reduce to an image of a forgotten experience; a mirage of an eternal wedding cast on the racial memory; as insupportable a joy as would be the vision of an eland coming down an aisle of trees, chapleted with orange blossoms and bridal veil, a hoof raised in the economy of fear.

Djuna Barnes was born into an eccentric household in 1892 in Cornwall-on-Hudson. Her father, a dilettante artist, lived with his wife, mistress, children and his mother, a journalist, who was responsible for Barnes's early education. In 1912, Barnes's mother took her children to New York, where Barnes went to art school, her first experience of formal education, before working as a journalist and artist to help support the family. In 1915 she published *The Book of Repulsive Women: 8 Rhythms and 5 Drawings* in the decadent, depraved mood of Aubrey Beardsley. She soon left New York for Paris, where as a journalist she interviewed expatriate artists and writers. It was in 1921 that she met and fell in love with the artist Thelma Wood, and they set up house together, living a wild and drunken life. Their relationship ended in 1929 when Wood, who had frequent affairs with men and women, began a passionate affair with another woman.

In Paris, Barnes became friends with James Joyce, Gertrude Stein and Ford Madox Ford, who published her stories in his *Transatlantic Review*. In 1928, her first novel, *Ryder*, was published. A semi-autobiographical book which she described as 'a female *Tom Jones*', *Ryder* became a bestseller in the United States. Her second novel, *Nightwood*, was eventually recommended for publication by T.S. Eliot at the prestigious publishing house Faber and Faber, and was published in England in 1936. Barnes's densely written novel influenced writers such as Truman Capote, Dylan Thomas and Anaïs Nin. In 1940, Barnes returned to America, moving to

Greenwich Village in New York, where she lived until she died in 1982, shortly before her ninetieth birthday.

Nightwood's vision of a night-time landscape peopled by social deviants remains a powerful, peculiar and, paradoxically, illuminating testament to human difference.

3 8 . T h e R a d e t z k y M a r c h
by
J O S E P H R O T H
(1 8 9 4 – 1 9 3 9)

❧

IN 1916, JOSEPH ROTH ENLISTED in the Austrian Army and spent
the next two years on the Eastern Front of the First World War.
He would later write of his life: 'My strongest experience was the
War and the destruction of my fatherland, the only one I ever
had, the Dual Monarchy of Austria-Hungary.' Roth lived to see
the destruction of his fatherland, but he never saw, never knew,
his own father, a travelling salesman who disappeared before his
son's birth and later died insane. In its preoccupation with fathers
real and symbolic, *The Radetzky March* articulates Roth's two
tragic losses.

Roth's eighth novel, *The Radetzky March* is a beautiful, poignant
story about fathers and sons, and the inexorable tide of history as it
first elevates then abandons a peasant family, and with it the entire
Austro-Hungarian Empire. Roth writes with wry irony, unfolding

a tragedy from his comic opening, tracing the collapse of an era through three generations of men: the grandfather, Joseph Trotta, a peasant honoured for a freak accident in which he saves the life of the Austrian emperor Franz Joseph; his officious son, the district captain; and his grandson Carl Joseph, a lieutenant unfit for military life. *The Radetzky March* opens in 1859 in the midst of the Battle of Solferino – 'the grandfather's war' – and closes in 1914 with the faltering outbreak of war along the border of Austria and Russia. As the First World War erupts, the grandson, Lieutenant Trotta, futilely dreams. 'Here was the war for which he had prepared himself since the age of seven. It was his war, the grandson's war. The days and the heroes of Solferino were returning.'

The Battle of Solferino was a formative moment in both the nationalist campaign to unite Italy and in the life of Roth's character Joseph Trotta (the grandfather), a Slovenian peasant. Fought in the north of Italy, the battle pitted the troops of Napoleon III of France and Victor Emmanuel II of Piedmont-Sardinia against the Austrian Army under Franz Joseph. Two years later, in 1861, Victor Emmanuel II was proclaimed king of Italy. In *The Radetzky March*, Roth's fictional Joseph Trotta saves the life of the historical Kaiser Franz Joseph at Solferino. In the midst of the battle, Trotta sees the young kaiser lift his field glasses to his eyes and, like any frontline soldier, Trotta knows the gleaming binoculars will attract enemy fire, so he pushes the emperor to the ground and takes a bullet in his left shoulder as he falls. When Trotta recovers, he is awarded the highest military honour in the empire, and for his accidental heroism he is made Captain Joseph Trotta von Sipolje. Trotta is completely disoriented by the honours bestowed upon him. Every night and every morning 'as if his own life had been traded for a new and alien life manufactured in a workshop, he would repeat his new status to himself and walk up to the mirror to confirm that his face was the same . . .' When Trotta, disillusioned and gutted, later requests his discharge from the army, instead of being allowed to sink into longed-for anonymity, he is further elevated: he is made Baron Joseph von Trotta und Sipolje.

The story belongs to the baron's son, the district captain, and grandson, Lieutenant Trotta, who are strangely afflicted by Baron Trotta's noble legacy. Roth's portraits of these two men are astute and agonising in their tragedy. The son, a bureaucrat, knows how to reply tersely to his own son's dutiful letters, how to congratulate him on his promotion to lieutenant, but he is lost when that same son cries out to him in need. 'But how should you behave if your son was drunk, if he cried "Father!" if the cry "Father!" came out of him?' the father helplessly wonders. And when the son tries to thank his father for his help, he finds he cannot: 'And he tried to describe how touched he was. But he found no words for regret, melancholy, and longing in his meagre vocabulary.'

Roth's penetrating psychological insights are matched by his humour and acute understanding of his times. Sent to the eastern border of the empire, Lieutenant Trotta finds himself in a shadowy multicultural world of shifting allegiances and swampland: 'Any stranger coming into this region was doomed to gradual decay. No one was as strong as the swamp.' In this distant outpost dwell Germans, Austrians, Hungarians, Czechs, Russians, Croats, Slovenes, Poles. One of the charismatic locals, Count Chojnicki, observing his dissolute companions, remarks that 'the Poles, of whom he himself was one after all, were skirt chasers, hairdressers, and fashion photographers . . .' Their twilight world is fuelled by alcohol and ruled by merchants who are the crude predecessors of Joseph Heller's machiavellian Milo Minderbinder:

> Always on the move, always on the alert, with glib tongues and quick minds, they might have had the stuff to conquer half the world – had they known what the world was all about. But they did not know. For they lived far from the world, between East and West.

Roth was born in 1894 in Brody, Galacia, now in the Ukraine but then on the far eastern border of the Hapsburg Empire. When he was twenty, Roth transferred from his local university to the University of Vienna and two years later, in 1916, he volunteered for the Austro-Hungarian army. He returned to Vienna in 1918 and moved to Berlin in 1920. In 1923 he began to write for *Frankfurter Zeitung*, travelling widely across Europe and eventually becoming one of the best paid and most respected journalists of the age. Roth also found time to write novels, working in his spare moments in hotel rooms and cafés. It was during these years that he wrote *The Radetzky March*, which was published in 1932.

Roth married in 1922, and in 1928 his wife, Friederike, was diagnosed with schizophrenia and hospitalised. Born a Jew, in the early 1920s Roth was one of the first to become aware of the menace of Hitler and he soon became one of the most outspoken and ardent critics of the Nazi regime. When the Nazis came to power in 1933, Roth severed his ties with Germany and fled from

Berlin by train for exile in Paris, but he was forced to leave Friederike behind in the psychiatric hospital in Berlin. His books were later burnt by Nazi-supporting students in Berlin. Roth's life as an émigré in France was lonely and hard. He struggled to find publishers for his work; lived out of suitcases, moving from hotel to hotel; and drank heavily. In 1939, aged forty-four, Roth died of pneumonia and alcoholism. The following year his wife was killed in the Nazi euthanasia program.

The title of Roth's great novel *The Radetzky March* comes from the music of Johann Strauss the Elder, whose 'Radetzky March' was composed in 1848 to honour the Austrian general Joseph Radetzky, who won decisive battles against Sardinia in the first Italian war of independence. It became one of the most popular pieces of music of the Hapsburg Empire and a symbol of the empire's might – and its refrains haunt the pages of Roth's novel, evoking glory days gone by. Although Roth started out as a communist – he was once known as 'Red' Roth – and always kept his sympathies with the poor, he later grew nostalgic for the old world of the bygone century, before nationalism had torn Europe and the Austro-Hungarian Empire apart. This nostalgia resonates through *The Radetzky March*.

Roth's novels were long neglected and only began to be reissued in Germany in the 1970s. With the translation into English in 2000 of Roth's novel *Rebellion*, the German poet and translator of Roth, Michael Hofmann, ensured that all Roth's novels were at last available in English. The 14th Prague Writers' Festival, in May 2004, at which Hofmann spoke, was dedicated to Joseph Roth.

The Austrian director Axel Corti, passionately committed to adapting Roth's novel for the screen, died in 1993, two weeks before he finished shooting his film of *The Radetzky March*, starring Max von Sydow, Tilman Gunther and Charlotte Rampling. It was first screened posthumously in 1994, as a television miniseries.

THE RED CROSS

The furious violence and bloody destruction of the Battle of Solferino, which opens *The Radetzky March*, prompted the formation of the Red Cross. A Swiss businessman, Henri Dunant, who witnessed the aftermath of the fighting was horrified to see thousands of wounded soldiers left to die on the battlefield. Overwhelmed by the scene and the hopeless cries of agony, he organised the local people to help carry the wounded from the field. Following his shocking experience, he wrote *A Memory of Solferino*, which was published in 1862. In his book, he proposed the idea of an international network of volunteer societies of nurses who would care for the wounded in battle, to be recognised and protected by an international agreement. In 1863, Switzerland sponsored an international conference on the basis of his suggestion, and this ultimately led to the establishment of the International Committee of the Red Cross. The first Geneva Convention (the first treaty of international humanitarian law) dealing with the treatment of battlefield casualties was adopted in 1864 as part of the founding of the Red Cross.

39 . *The Leopard*

by

GIUSEPPE TOMASI DI

LAMPEDUSA

(1 8 9 6 – 1 9 5 7)

❧

THE SICILIAN WRITER GIUSEPPE TOMASI DI LAMPEDUSA, Duke of
Palma and Prince of Lampedusa, wrote only one novel, *The Leopard*,
which he began two years before his death at the age of sixty
in Rome. *The Leopard*, a meditation on the passing of time and
the changing of eras, was rejected as unpublishable during di
Lampedusa's lifetime. Eventually published in 1958, the year after
its author's death, *The Leopard* went on to win the Primo Strega,
Italy's most prestigious literary award. Hailed as a masterpiece, the
novel became an international bestseller. E.M. Forster captured its
essence when he called it 'one of the great lonely books'.

The Leopard opens in May 1860 in Sicily, at the daily recitation
of the rosary in the villa of the Prince of Salina. The Prince, his
wife, son, daughters and the family priest, Father Pirrone, gather in
the drawing room beneath its ceiling painted with the family's blue

shield of the Leopard supported by the deposed gods and goddesses of ancient Rome. Like these ancient deities, the rule of the Prince and his world are doomed. The revolutionary hero Garibaldi is due within days to land in Sicily with his 'Thousand' volunteer troops and within weeks will take the island. Within months, the entire Kingdom of Two Sicilies (the kingdoms of Sicily and Naples jointly ruled by the last Bourbon monarch, Francis II) will be absorbed at the hand of Garibaldi into a unified Italy under the rule of King Victor Emmanuel, crowned king of Italy in 1861.

At the centre of di Lampedusa's novel is the massive, mighty Leopard himself, the Prince of Salina:

> there was constant coming and going between Villa Salina and a silversmith's for the straightening of forks and spoons which, in some fit of controlled rage at table, he had coiled into a hoop. But those fingers could also stroke and knead with the most exquisite delicacy, as his wife Maria Stella knew to her cost; while up in his private observatory at the top of the house the gleaming screws, caps and studs of telescopes, lenses and 'comet-finders' seemed inviolate beneath his gentle manipulations.

The Prince is politically astute yet above politics, he is mathematical, and his sensual appetites are still rampant as he approaches fifty. Like an Olympian god, he watches with a lofty dispassion tinged with regret as the world around him changes forever, as the aristocracy succumbs to the energy of the new liberal bourgeoisie. And yet the Prince's secret knowledge, the irony at the heart of the

novel summarised in his nephew Tancredi's pithy observation – 'If
we want things to stay as they are, things will have to change' – is
that at root nothing really changes, while everything falls apart
and life moves inexorably towards death.

The novel, written while di Lampedusa was dying of lung
cancer, reeks of death and decay. In his most outspoken speech, the
Prince argues that ancient Sicily is too old to understand the new
modern world of factories and progress. In the context of the
industrial world, Sicily is like 'a centenarian being dragged in a
bath-chair round the Great Exhibition in London, understanding
nothing and caring about nothing'. Instead, Sicily is interested
only in death: 'our sensuality is a hankering for oblivion, our
shooting and knifing a hankering for death, our languor, our exotic
ices, a hankering for voluptuous immobility, that is for death again
... novelties attract us only when they are dead, incapable of
arousing vital currents ...' On every page the novel radiates an
almost painful awareness of this passing of time towards oblivion.
Even in a magnificent ballroom, pulsing with the bodies of young
people dancing, destruction lurks: 'from the ceiling the gods,
reclining on gilded couches, gazed down smiling and inexorable as
a summer sky. They thought themselves eternal; but a bomb manufactured in Pittsburgh, Penn., was to prove the contrary in 1943.'

And yet life goes on, through the political ferment, through
change and revolution. The novel is told in eight chapters across
fifty years, from May 1860 to May 1910, driven by the energy of
the Prince's dashing nephew Tancredi, who can read the signs
of the times and positions himself accordingly – first as one of
Garibaldi's Redcoats, then as a member of the regular army

of Victor Emmanuel, His Majesty, King of Sardinia. In his efforts, Tancredi is assisted by the careful manoeuvering of his indulgent uncle, his guardian, who facilitates his ambition and watches over the young man with affection, admiration and some jealousy. When Tancredi falls madly in love with the beautiful daughter of the vulgar, nouveau riche Don Calogero, the Prince gives way to their inevitable union. And yet he sees all: 'The bourgeois revolution climbing his stairs in Don Calogero's tail-coat, Angelica's beauty putting the shy grace of his Concetta in the shade, Tancredi rushing at the inevitable changes.'

Like the Prince, di Lampedusa was born in Palermo, Sicily, into Sicilian aristocracy. Despite his family's disapproval of his literary obsession, di Lampedusa was a passionate reader in Italian, Latin, Greek, German, French and English. He had a particular admiration for another chronicler of the rise of the bourgeoisie, Stendhal, and wrote *Lessons on Stendhal* which was published as a book in 1977. During the First World War, di Lampedusa served in the Italian artillery in Hungary, where he was captured and imprisoned. He later escaped and walked back to Italy. After a nervous breakdown prevented the diplomatic career he desired, di Lampedusa spent his life reading, writing and travelling, and in 1932 he married the Latvian exile Baroness Alessandra Wolff-Stomersee, whom he had met in London. It is said that his cousin, the award-winning poet Lucio Piccolo, inspired him at age fifty-eight to write the novel about which he'd been dreaming for half his life, *The Leopard*.

The Italian filmmaker Luchino Visconti's sumptuous, acclaimed cinema adaptation of *The Leopard* was released in 1963. Perfectly cast, the film starred Burt Lancaster as the Prince of Salina, Alain Delon as Tancredi and Claudia Cardinale as Angelica, and won the Palme d'Or at Cannes. *The Leopard* was re-released in 2004 in a restored, recut version, and its continuing popularity reflects the novel's enduring power as a lush evocation of change and decay.

NIKKI GEMMELL

- *The Lover* by Marguerite Duras
- *Atomised* by Michel Houellebecq
- *The Great Gatsby* by F. Scott Fitzgerald
- *The Man Who Loved Children* by Christina Stead
- *Disgrace* by J.M. Coetzee
- *Beloved* by Toni Morrison
- *Midnight's Children* by Salman Rushdie
- *The Unbearable Lightness of Being* by Milan Kundera
- *All the Pretty Horses* by Cormac McCarthy
- *Lolita* by Vladimir Nabokov

All these novels are marked by an original voice that is coura-geous and fresh — you're often seduced by the boldness of tone from the very first paragraph. Most of these books have a confidence that doesn't falter. (This sense of control is remarkably hard for a writer to sustain. 'For the most part novels do come to grief somewhere,' Virginia Woolf wrote. 'The imagination falters under the enormous strain.') The authors are attempting something new, with a fearless and provocative honesty, and they're taking you along on their journey. They're not afraid to disturb you. They're also moving you — wheedling their way into your consciousness so that these are the books that are held forever in your heart.

London-based Australian writer Nikki Gemmell is the author of four novels, *Shiver* (1997), *Cleave* (1998), *Love Song* (2001) and the bestselling *The Bride Stripped Bare: A Novel* (2004), the last of which was originally published anonymously because of its erotic subject matter.

40. *The Great Gatsby*
by
F. SCOTT FITZGERALD
(1 8 9 6 – 1 9 4 0)

F. SCOTT FITZGERALD, THE HANDSOME GOLDEN BOY of American literature, once said of himself and his glamorous wife Zelda, 'Sometimes I don't know whether Zelda and I are real or whether we are characters in one of my novels.' Fitzgerald's vision, with its blurring of the real and the unreal, may have contributed to his rapid decline into alcoholism – but it was also the source of his genius for evoking in words the ineffable, the radiant dream forever calling us forward, just out of reach, 'a promise that the rock of the world was founded securely on a fairy's wing'. And nowhere is Fitzgerald's genius realised with more focused intensity than in *The Great Gatsby*, his novel of the American dream and its underbelly: violent death.

The Great Gatsby opens in the spring of 1922. The narrator, Nick Carraway, recently returned from fighting the war in Europe and afflicted with the restlessness of his post-war generation, moves east to New York from his Midwestern city to learn the bond business. He rents a cottage in a commuting town on Long Island across the bay from his lovely, breathless cousin Daisy, with her voice full of money and her powerful husband, Tom Buchanan, and is soon drawn into the fantastic life of his neighbour, multi-millionaire Jay Gatsby. No one knows who Gatsby is or where his vast wealth has come from — it could have come from anywhere at a time when speculative fortunes were being made overnight on an American stock market that was rising to dizzying heights following the First World War, or through illegal activities like the sale of alcohol following its prohibition by the Eighteenth Amendment passed in 1919.

Everything about Gatsby glitters, all is light and shimmering surfaces. The whole front of his mansion catches the light, the wind-shields on his monstrous car mirror 'a dozen suns' and Gatsby himself smiles 'like a weatherman, like an ecstatic patron of recurrent light'. He has entered the world of the super rich, a world inhabited by people like the Buchanans, who drift about aimlessly in places where 'people played polo and were rich together'. Over the course of the novel, Gatsby's web of light is smashed apart to reveal the darkness and ashes that lurk beneath it — but what remains, beyond his Olympian wealth, beyond the ashes, is Gatsby's possession of 'an extraordinary gift for hope, a romantic readiness such as I have never found in any other person and which it is not likely I shall ever see again'. *The Great Gatsby* is remarkable for Fitzgerald's tender evocation of this gift for hope, this romantic readiness that drew settlers to the New World and was by Gatsby's day lost in a restless pursuit of wealth and success. Fitzgerald's articulation of Gatsby's dreaming gives rise to some of the most beautiful writing in the novel, such as when he describes the moment Gatsby's dreams are finally given purpose, earthed in the bright-eyed Daisy:

> He knew that when he kissed this girl, and forever wed his unutterable visions to her perishable breath, his mind would never romp again like the mind of God. So he waited, listening for a moment longer to the tuning-fork that had been struck upon a star. Then he kissed her. At his lips' touch she blossomed for him like a flower and the incarnation was complete.

The pages of *The Great Gatsby* resonate with the rhythms and lilt of the Jazz Age, the name Fitzgerald coined for the 1920s. It was an age of feverish change, phenomenal wealth, decadence, loose women, epitomised in Gatsby's extravagant parties by 'a great number of single girls dancing individualistically' with their hair 'bobbed in strange new ways'. Life in this frenzied maelstrom is governed by orchestras that 'set the rhythm of the year, summing up the sadness and suggestiveness of life in new tunes'. It was an era that saw the emergence of sport as a major phenomenon in American cultural life and the worship of its stars like Babe Ruth and amateur golfer Bobby Jones — and two of the novel's central characters, Daisy's husband Tom Buchanan and her best friend, Jordan Baker, are sporting stars: Jordan a golfing champion and Tom a one-time star footballer.

Fitzgerald worshipped football. On his acceptance into Princeton, he telegrammed his mother: 'Admitted, send football pads and shoes immediately.' Born Francis Scott Key Fitzgerald in 1896, Fitzgerald was named for his ancestor Francis Scott Key, who wrote 'The Star-Spangled Banner'. He was the only son of a salesman who eventually settled in St Paul, where Fitzgerald was born. In 1913, he went to Princeton, where he was a brilliant social success, became prominent in the university's literary circles and started to write his first novel, *The Romantic Egoist*, which was rejected for publication but which he later reworked as *This Side of Paradise*. Fitzgerald dropped out of Princeton in November 1917 before graduating to join the army and was posted to Camp Sheridan in Alabama, where he met Zelda Sayre, the daughter of a Supreme Court judge and belle of Alabama. They fell in love, beginning one of the great and tragic public romances of the twentieth century.

When the war ended, Fitzgerald left the army for New York, hoping to make his fortune so he could marry Zelda. He was successful. In 1920, his first novel, *This Side of Paradise*, 'dropped like a bombshell on the American scene', according to Princeton historian J.T. Miller. 'It was questioning the past and giving voice for the first time to the youth of the twentieth century.' The novel became a bestseller and Fitzgerald became famous. He married Zelda and in 1921 their daughter, Frances (Scottie), was born. The following year his second novel, *The Beautiful and the Damned*, was published and in 1924 the Fitzgeralds moved to the French Riviera so Fitzgerald could write in peace. Here he began *The Great Gatsby*, which was published in 1925 to lukewarm reviews. His last finished novel – *Tender is the Night*, published in 1934 – is a tragic evocation of this time in an expatriate community in the South of France, of Fitzgerald's efforts to write *The Great Gatsby*, Zelda's attraction to another man, and her descent into insanity. In 1930, Zelda had her first nervous breakdown and continued to deteriorate until she had to be hospitalised. In despair, the Fitzgeralds returned to America. In 1937, Fitzgerald went to Hollywood, where he found work as a scriptwriter and fell in love with the Hollywood gossip columnist Sheilah Graham. In October 1939, he began *The Last Tycoon*, his novel about Hollywood, but he died of a heart attack aged forty-four before finishing the novel.

The Great Gastby remains one of the all-time enduring classics of American literature, widely loved for its beautiful prose and evocative distillation of the so-called 'American dream'. A Hollywood film of *The Great Gatsby* was released in 1974, starring Robert Redford as Gatsby and Mia Farrow as Daisy.

CHARLOTTE WOOD

What makes a classic? For me it's a book I can't imagine having lived without; a truthful, wholly imagined world, in astonishing language, by a writer unafraid to probe those things that scare us and scar us and make us human. These are my favourites:

- *As I Lay Dying* by William Faulkner
- *Heart of Darkness* by Joseph Conrad
- *The Tree of Man* and *The Solid Mandala* by Patrick White

- *The Great Gatsby* by F. Scott Fitzgerald
- *The Winter of Our Discontent* by John Steinbeck
- *Ulysses* by James Joyce (only got through 200 pages but was dazzled)
- *The Ballad of the Sad Café* by Carson McCullers
- *For Esme – With Love and Squalor, and Other Stories* by J.D. Salinger
- *To Kill a Mockingbird* by Harper Lee
- *The Bone People* by Keri Hulme

Australian writer Charlotte Wood is the author of two novels, *Pieces of a Girl* (1999) and *The Submerged Cathedral* (2004), the last of which was shortlisted for the 2005 Miles Franklin Literary Award.

41. *As I Lay Dying*

by

WILLIAM FAULKNER

(1 8 9 7 – 1 9 6 2)

✤

IN 1929 WILLIAM FAULKNER began writing a novel in the early morning hours while employed as a nightwatchman at the University of Mississippi power plant. He had already published three novels, including *The Sound and the Fury* (1929), but was yet to find widespread success. He staked everything on his new novel: 'I set out deliberately to write a tour-de-force,' he later commented. 'Before I began I said, I am going to write a book by which, at a pinch, I can stand or fall if I never touch ink again.' According to Faulkner, he finished the novel in six weeks. The book he wrote, published the following year, was *As I Lay Dying*. The title comes from Agamemnon's speech from the Underworld in the *Odyssey*, about his ignominious death plotted by his wife on his return home to Greece from the Trojan War. In *As I Lay Dying* it is the wife, Addie Bundren, who dies and her husband, Anse, whose neglect and meanness are implicated in her dying.

As I Lay Dying is composed of fifty-nine fragments spoken by fifteen characters — Addie herself; Anse; their four sons, Cash, Darl, Jewel and Vardaman; their daughter, Dewey Dell; their neighbours; the doctor, Peabody; and various bystanders who are drawn into the outlandish events that follow Addie's death as Anse, for once determined to follow Addie's wishes, transports her corpse from her deathbed to her final resting place in Jefferson. Over the course of the novel, the Budrens' harsh farming life in the backwaters of one of America's most impoverished states, Mississippi, is revealed in beautiful, muscular prose: 'That's the trouble with this country: everything, weather, all, hangs on too long. Like our rivers, our land: opaque, slow, violent; shaping and creating the life of man in its implacable and brooding image.'

Like a Cubist painting, the novel's multiple perspectives are shattered and put back together by Faulkner. Each new view brings to life a character's intimate thoughts sparked by Addie's death, thoughts that are filled with grief, sorrow, incomprehension, selfishness, madness, love. The picture Faulkner paints, never quite seen in its totality, is one of the most bizarre of literature: a straggly group of four men, a girl and a coffin on a cart, accompanied by a fierce, sinewy man on a 'durn circus animal' (Jewel on his piebald horse) trailing across the land through flood and fire under a buzzard-hung sky with a decaying corpse, which, by the time they reach Jefferson, is nine days dead. Two books that filled Faulkner's mind, which he returned to time and again, were the Old Testament and *Don Quixote*, and *As I Lay Dying* is like some surreal incarnation of the spirit of these two books in the soil of Faulkner's 'apocryphal county', the imaginary Yoknapatawpha County where his novel takes place.

As I Lay Dying is rich with profound psychological insights on life, death and madness. The views of death range from the doctor's learned 'I can remember how when I was young I believed death to be a phenomenon of the body; now I know it to be merely a function of the mind — and that of the minds of the ones who suffer the bereavement', to Addie's brutal truth: 'I could just remember how my father used to say that the reason for living was to get ready to stay dead a long time.' Cash's poignant observations on his brother Darl, who is 'touched by God himself and considered queer by us mortals', show his profound understanding of madness: 'Sometimes I aint so sho who's got ere a right to say when a man is crazy and when he aint. Sometimes I think it aint none of us pure crazy and aint none of us pure sane until the balance of us talks him that-a-way.' The novel is also remarkable for Faulkner's vital prose, which captures in a few phrases the life of his characters, such as Anse, who comes alive in all his niggardliness: 'If He'd aimed for man to be always a-moving and going somewheres else, wouldn't He put him longways on his belly, like a snake? It stands to reason he would.'

Faulkner, born the oldest of four sons of Murry and Maud Falkner (Faulkner later added the 'u'), in New Albany, Mississippi, came from an illustrious Southern family whose fortunes had waned. His great-grandfather Colonel William Clark Falkner had fought in the Civil War, made a fortune from railways after the war and bought a plantation. He had also written the bestselling novel *The White Rose of Memphis*. Faulkner's father eventually settled in Oxford, Mississippi, where he became the business manager at the University of Mississippi. Here, Faulkner was able to indulge his passion for riding, shooting and hunting — and reading. Although he left school early, Faulkner was a voracious reader his whole life. He joined the British Royal Air Force in July 1918 and trained in Canada, but the war ended before he flew a plane. When he returned home, he devoted his time to drawing and writing poetry, and by 1925, when he travelled to Europe, had devoted himself to writing. In Europe, Faulkner spent most of his time on the Left Bank in Paris, at the time the centre of Modernism, where he saw the paintings of Cézanne, Picasso and Braque. Faulkner, a talented drawer and painter, brings a Modernist painter's eye to his writing: 'The front, the conical façade with the square orifice of doorway broken only by the square squat shape of the coffin on the sawhorses like a cubistic bug, comes into relief.'

Faulkner's first novel, *Soldier's Pay*, was published in 1926, but it was not until the publication in October 1929 of *The Sound and the Fury* — which Faulkner had written in despair and without regard for its commercial appeal — that he became established as a writer. He found commercial success two years later with the publication in 1931 of the controversial, bestselling *Sanctuary*, about the rape of a college student. In 1929, Faulkner married his childhood sweetheart Estelle Oldham following her divorce from her first husband, and in 1933 they had a daughter, Jill. Like Picasso, Faulkner was extraordinarily productive and innovative in realising his vision — his creative output was enormous (including nineteen novels) and he constantly experimented with form. In 1949, Faulkner won the Nobel Prize for Literature and in his dignified and impassioned acceptance speech he spoke about the numbing post-war preoccupation with physical danger – 'Our tragedy today is a general and universal physical fear' – and the urgent need for writers to engage not with fear but with 'the old verities and truths of the heart, the old universal truths lacking which any story is ephemeral and doomed – love and honor and pity and pride and compassion and sacrifice . . .'

CATHARINE LUMBY

- *Tristram Shandy* by Laurence Sterne. Philosophy or the most prolonged joke in the English language? With *Tristram Shandy*, Laurence Sterne succeeded where many have failed: he wrote an intellectually serious novel that never falls into the trap of taking itself too seriously.
- *Dracula* by Bram Stoker. Quite simply the most compelling erotic love story ever written.
- *Persuasion* by Jane Austen. *Das Kapital* for girls. And, unlike Karl Marx, Jane Austen had a terrific sense of humour.
- *Alice in Wonderland* by Lewis Carroll. The author of *Alice in Wonderland* once sent a young friend another Victorian novel with a warning not to read it because 'it has got a moral in it'. Needless to say, it wasn't by Lewis Carroll.

- *The Picture of Dorian Gray* by Oscar Wilde. A novel of perfect proportions in which Wilde characteristically touches lightly but sharply on the most enduring philosophical conundrums.

- *Ulysses* by James Joyce. My inner feminist says Virginia Woolf is the right answer to Best Modernist Author. But Joyce has so much more life and juice in him. And *Ulysses*, contrary to the myth, is compulsively readable.

- *Lolita* by Vladimir Nabokov. Who needs those other Russians? Nabokov was on to his third country and language, and he still made the locals look illiterate. Brilliant prose aside, the truly impressive thing about this novel is the author's grasp of moral complexity — his sense of the monstrous and the human in us all.

- *Money* by Martin Amis. *Money* is the first novel in which Martin Amis really married the quotidian with the larger literary questions. A writer with an astounding natural ear for prose and dialogue, Amis is the true literary hinge between the modern and postmodern eras.

- *Crash* by J.G. Ballard. Far from being a science-fiction writer, J.G. Ballard is an author who accurately describes, and often anticipates, the best and the worst of modern life. A book which combines sensuality, technology and irony, *Crash* is an object lesson in surviving Western civilisation as we know it.

🌑 *Grand Days* and *Dark Palace* by Frank Moorhouse.
Frank Moorhouse is a writer who truly understands the
virtues of doubt and pleasure. The force and originality
of his work lies in his refusal to shy away from the flux
of identity and the constant dialogue between order and
chaos. His companion novels, *Grand Days* and *Dark
Palace*, are an inquiry into this question on a grand
scale.

Catharine Lumby is an associate professor of media studies
at the University of Sydney. She is the author of *Bad Girls:
The Media, Sex and Feminism in the 90s* (1997), *Gotcha: Life in
a Tabloid World* (1999) and *Tim Storrier: The Art of the
Outsider* (2000), and writes regularly for *The Age*.

4 2 . *L o l i t a*

by

V L A D I M I R   N A B O K O V

(1 8 9 9 – 1 9 7 7)

⁂

IN FEBRUARY 1954, THE RUSSIAN-BORN American writer Vladimir Nabokov wrote to the publishers New Directions, offering them his latest novel: 'Would you be interested in publishing a time bomb that I have just finished putting together? It is a novel of 459 typewritten pages.' New Directions declined to publish his novel but it was eventually published the following year in Paris – and soon after was banned in France. The time bomb was *Lolita*, perhaps the most controversial novel of the twentieth century for its story of 'Humbert Humbert', the pseudonym of a man who at the age of thirty-seven becomes hopelessly obsessed with a twelve-year-old girl, Dolores Haze, whom he renames Lolita: 'She was Lo, plain Lo, in the morning, standing four feet ten in one sock. She was Lola in slacks. She was Dolly at school. She was Dolores on the dotted line. But in my arms she was always Lolita.'

The novel opens with a 'Foreword' by John Ray, Jr, PhD, the cousin of Humbert Humbert's lawyer, into whose care Humbert willed on his death his memoir titled *Lolita, or the Confessions of a White Widowed Male* so it can be prepared for publication. Dr Ray remarks that the manuscript is 'a tragic tale tending unswervingly to nothing less than a moral apotheosis', adding that although the cynic might argue that commercial pornography makes the same claim, the learned would maintain that, unlike the '12 per cent' of American men with his erotic tendencies, Humbert is filled with despair by his urges.

The cynic and the learned reader have been arguing ever since over the content of *Lolita* — is it pornography or art? — a debate that reached new heights in America over Adrian Lyne's 1997 remake of Nabokov's novel starring Jeremy Irons, which faced difficulties getting cinema release in the USA. Nabokov saw his novel as a work of art, containing 'various allusions to the psychological urges of a pervert', in a long tradition of European writing dating from ancient times to the eighteenth century that mixed comedy with lewdness.

Humbert's memoir famously opens with a play on Lolita's name: 'Lolita, light of my life, fire of my loins. My sin, my soul. Lo-lee-ta: the tip of the tongue taking a trip of three steps down the palate to tap, at three, on the teeth.' Humbert then recounts his happy childhood on the Mediterranean, surrounded by golden sand and sea vistas, where one summer he falls 'madly, clumsily, shamelessly, agonizingly' in love with a girl several months younger than him called Annabel. Their passion is so intense that only complete immersion in each other's flesh and souls could have satisfied it —

but Annabel dies four months later of typhoid, leaving her lover with his eternal longing. Humbert, a lucid, bookish European intellectual, conducts a remorseless self-analysis in the pages of the novel. He attributes his passion for Lolita to his ruined love for Annabel:

> We loved each other with a premature love marked by a
> fierceness that so often destroys adult lives. I was a strong
> lad and survived; but the poison was in the wound, and the
> wound remained ever open, and soon I found myself
> maturing amid a civilization which allows a man of twenty-
> five to court a girl of sixteen but not a girl of twelve.

Humbert is torn apart by his illicit desires, which he resists until he moves to America following the Second World War. One day, while looking over a potential lodging, he happens to notice 'Lo': 'from a mat in a pool of sun, half-naked, kneeling, turning about on her knees, there was my Riviera love peering at me over dark glasses . . .'

Lolita is the story of Humbert's love affair with Lolita, which hums across suburban America, along its highways and in its motels. It is a tragic and disturbing novel of possession and desire — and the beauty and erudition and irrepressible playfulness of Nabokov's writing only serve to deepen the tragedy of the story, of which Humbert is only too painfully aware:

> I catch myself thinking today that our long journey had
> only defiled with a sinuous trail of slime the lovely, trustful,

dreamy, enormous country that by then, in retrospect, was no more to us than a collection of dog-eared maps, ruined tour books, old tyres, and her sobs in the night — every night, every night — the moment I feigned sleep.

The novel was eventually published in America by Putnam in 1958, with a note by Nabokov about its genesis. He traces *Lolita* to a story he read in Paris in 1939 or 1940, about an ape who, after great encouragement, eventually produced the first-ever drawing by an animal — a charcoal sketch of the bars of its cage. This poignant report inspired Nabokov to write a short story in Russian, and he returned to the idea years later in America in 1949. 'I was now faced with the task of inventing America,' he wrote. This he did, inventing his own America in words, writing *Lolita* during his many trips in search of butterflies through Arizona, Colorado and Wyoming (Nabokov was a highly regarded, self-taught lepidopterist — a butterfly expert). *Lolita* became a bestseller and its sales enabled Nabokov to retire from teaching and devote himself exclusively to writing.

Nabokov was born in 1899 in St Petersburg, Russia, to an aristocratic family. His father was the head of the pre-revolutionary liberal Constitutional Democratic Party and went into exile when the Revolution broke out, moving with his family to Berlin. Nabokov received a scholarship to Trinity College, Cambridge, where he studied zoology then French and Russian literature, receiving a first-class honours degree in 1923. The previous year, his father was assassinated in Berlin (having rushed to shield the man for whom the bullet was intended), an event that was to haunt Nabokov for the rest of his life. His first novel, *Mary*, written in Russian, was published in 1926, and his first novel in English, *The Real Life of Sebastian Knight*, was published in 1941. In 1925, Nabokov married Vera Evseyevna Slonim, with whom he had one son, Dmitri. In 1940, he moved with his family to America, where he taught at Wellesley College, and then taught Russian and European literature at Cornell University from 1948 until the publication of *Lolita* ten years later.

Lolita has had a widespread impact on contemporary culture, from its coining of the word 'nymphet' to the word 'Lolita' itself, which is defined by the Oxford English Dictionary as 'a sexually precocious schoolgirl'. The first cinema adaptation of the book, for which Nabokov wrote the screenplay, was Stanley Kubrick's 1962 hit film *Lolita*, starring James Mason as Humbert. The Police song 'Don't Stand So Close to Me', released in 1980, refers to a teacher who behaves like Humbert in Nabokov's book. In 2003, a book about a group of Muslim women and one man in Iran who find inspiration in *Lolita* and other literary classics became a bestseller: *Reading Lolita in Tehran: A Memoir in Books* by Azar Nafisi. Nafisi writes: 'no matter how intimidated and frightened we were, like Lolita we tried to escape and to create our own little pockets of freedom . . .'

❋ LOUIS NOWRA ❋

- ❧ *Lolita* by Vladimir Nabokov
- ❧ *In Search of Lost Time* by Marcel Proust

- *Absalom, Absalom!* by William Faulkner
- *Concerning the Eccentricities of Cardinal Pirelli* by Ronald Firbank
- *The Day of the Locust* by Nathanael West
- *The Leopard* by Giuseppe Tomasi di Lampedusa
- *War and Peace* by Leo Tolstoy
- *Huckleberry Finn* by Mark Twain
- *Pale Fire* by Vladimir Nabokov
- *The Great Gatsby* by F. Scott Fitzgerald

Louis Nowra is a prolific, acclaimed playwright, screenwriter, novelist and non-fiction author. His many works include the bestselling memoir *The Twelfth of Never* (1999) and the plays *Cosi* and *Radiance*, which were made into successful films, released in 1995 and 1997 respectively, for which he also wrote the screenplays.

43. The Sun Also Rises
by
ERNEST HEMINGWAY
(1899–1961)

⚘

IN OCTOBER 1926, THE PUBLICATION of a novel by a relatively unknown 27-year-old American writer, Ernest Hemingway, caused a literary sensation. The novel was *The Sun Also Rises*. Its revolutionary approach to prose — unadorned direct sentences, understated dialogue, lean description — and its exotic story of thirty-something bohemian American and British expatriates in Paris and Pamplona captured the disillusion of the post-war times, and the novel was an immediate commercial success. The style of its cool-talking hero Jake Barnes and modern heroine Lady (Brett) Ashley, with her blonde hair cut short and brushed back like a boy, was imitated across America. A review in *The New York Times* enthused:

> No amount of analysis can convey the quality of *The Sun Also Rises*. It is a truly gripping story, told in a lean, hard,

athletic narrative prose that puts more literary English to shame . . . This novel is unquestionably one of the events of an unusually rich year in literature.

Its fortunes were spread by word of mouth — the novel was based on Hemingway's life in Paris and his trip to a fiesta in Spain in the summer of 1925, and the characters were based on real people; the guessing game for discerning their real-life identities helped fuel the novel's popularity.

The Sun Also Rises is narrated by journalist and aspiring writer Jake Barnes, whose injury from the First World War has left him unable to function properly sexually. The novel opens with a story about Robert Cohn, a Jewish writer who travels to Paris after his marriage breaks up. Jake and Robert play tennis together, and in the evenings hang out in cafés and dance clubs with their friends, all writers and artists of some description, getting blind drunk and talking about writing, life, sex and marriage. The novel comes into focus with the appearance one night of the beautiful, English Lady Ashley, Brett, who is waiting for her divorce so she can marry someone else — the Scotsman Mike Campbell. 'Brett was damn good-looking. She wore a slipover jersey sweater and a tweed skirt, and her hair was brushed back like a boy's. She started all that. She was built with curves like the hull of a racing yacht, and you missed none of it with that wool jersey.' Brett trails men in her wake, including Jake. Cohn also falls in love with her, described with classic Hemingway succinctness and macho touch: 'When he fell in love with Brett his tennis game went all to pieces.' An explosive brew is mixed when Jake and his friend, the energetic writer

Bill Gorton, plan a fishing trip to Spain followed by the fiesta in Pamplona — Cohn, still obsessed with Brett, decides to join them. So do Brett and her fiancé, Mike. These fictional events arose from Hemingway's own experience of life in Europe and a trip to Spain.

In 1921, Ernest Hemingway left Chicago with his new wife, Hadley, the first of his four feisty wives, and moved to Paris. The American writer Sherwood Anderson had suggested Paris to Hemingway because it was the centre of a lively expatriate community of artists centred around Gertrude Stein — and Hemingway was a 21-year-old journalist determined to become a writer. Through Anderson, Hemingway met Stein and Ezra Pound, who encouraged his writing. The idea of a story set around bullfighting in Spain came to Hemingway on a trip to Pamplona fraught with sexual tension and innuendo in July 1925 with a group of friends. By September 1925, Hemingway's story had become the first draft of a novel, which he revised in late 1925 and 1926 with the help of F. Scott Fitzgerald (whom he had met in Paris). Fitzgerald recommended Hemingway to his publisher, Charles Scribner's Sons, and the novel — originally *Fiesta*, now renamed *The Sun Also Rises* — was published in 1926.

Hemingway's idiosyncratic spare prose, with its disenchanted tone, still feels fresh and surprisingly modern, despite the fact that it was written over eighty years ago and was one of the most copied styles of the twentieth century. The colloquial, masculine rhythms of Hemingway's prose are cool and funky, the conversations are straight and loose, the drinking is excessive and characterised by numerous frank disclosures about sex and being drunk — such as Brett's 'I must have been blind' (drunk).

The book's two epigraphs evoke the passing and changing of time. The first epigraph, Gertrude Stein's comment about the expatriate writers living in 1920s Paris, 'You are all a lost generation', has been used ever since to describe the entire post-war generation, evoking its feelings of hopelessness and spiritual unease. The second epigraph, from the Old Testament, includes the words 'The sun also ariseth, and the sun goeth down, and hasteth to the place where he arose', which Hemingway hoped would evoke some promise in this sea of despair. The character Jake, based on Hemingway, is irresistibly yet tentatively drawn to the dark cathedrals of Spain – they help him to feel better, the same as he feels good when he walks up a river to fish for trout and is passionate about bullfights.

> I knelt and started to pray and prayed for everybody I
> thought of . . . I was a little ashamed, and regretted that I
> was such a rotten Catholic, but realized there was nothing I
> could do about it, at least for a while, and maybe never, but
> that anyway it was a grand religion, and I only wished I felt
> religious and maybe I would next time.

Hemingway was born in Chicago in 1899, the eldest son of Clarence Hemingway, a doctor, and Grace Hemingway, an accomplished singer. His summer holidays were spent with his family on Lake Walloon in the Upper Michigan, where the vigorous Hemingway became keen on hunting and fishing. He began writing in high school and graduated in 1917. He found a job in Kansas City as a reporter then, during the First World War, drove ambulances for the Red Cross in Italy (he was refused entry to the army because of a bad eye). He was injured just before his nineteenth birthday and sent to hospital in Milan, where he fell in love with his nurse — an experience he immortalised in *A Farewell to Arms*, published in 1929. Hemingway continued all his life to be drawn to war, attracted by its danger and tense living. He worked in Spain as a journalist covering the Civil War, supporting the Republicans against Franco, a period that inspired *For Whom the Bell Tolls* (1940). He later reported on the invasion of China by Japan and covered the Second World War from London, flying missions with the Royal Air Force and crossing the Channel with the American troops on D-Day in June 1944. After the war, Hemingway sojourned at his house in Cuba, then moved to Ketchum, Idaho. Here he was hospitalised for depression and given electro-shock treatment. Two days after his return home from hospital, he fatally shot himself.

Hemingway won the Nobel Prize for Literature in 1954 for his mastery of narrative, notably in *The Old Man and the Sea* (1952), and his influential prose style. He was unable to attend the ceremony, but wrote a brief, typically understated acceptance speech, which included the following poignant observation on the loneliness of the writer: 'For he does his work alone and if he is a good enough writer he must face eternity, or the lack of it, each day.'

44. *For Love Alone*

by

CHRISTINA STEAD

(1 9 0 2 – 1 9 8 3)

THE AUSTRALIAN WRITER CHRISTINA STEAD wrote *For Love Alone*
while living in New York during the Second World War and
this urgent story of the bold, defiant Teresa Hawkins was
published in America in 1945. Teresa is determined to live for
herself and to make something of her life. She will not drift into
spinsterhood or dull marriage, the fate of the poor women she
sees around her in 1930s Sydney. Teresa burns with longing for
love, knowledge, self-definition and financial independence –
'Love, learning, bread – myself – all three, I will get' – and her
desperate needs are fused into one quest when she fixes on
her tutor, Jonathan Crow, who becomes the object of her desire
and, perversely, in so doing becomes her tortured means to a
greater world. 'I only know of one commandment, *Thou shalt
love*,' she declares.

Although *For Love Alone* was Stead's fifth novel, it was only her second novel to be set in Australia (her previous novel, *The Man Who Loved Children* (1940), although based on Stead's childhood in Sydney, was set in America). Writing in the 1940s, Stead was obliged to introduce for her English and American readers the exotic character of Australia: 'In the part of the world Teresa came from, winter is in July, spring brides marry in September, and Christmas is consummated with roast beef, suckling pig, and brandy-laced plum pudding at 100 degrees in the shade.'

Set in Sydney and London during the 1930s, the novel opens with Teresa and her sister, Kitty, sewing roses onto the sleeves of a medieval dress Teresa plans to wear to a wedding, while their self-obsessed, beautiful father, naked to the waist, teases them about marriage and the strange fact they are not lovely. Stead conjures the dynamics of family banter as brilliantly as she evokes the blazing Sydney summer's day: 'a brassy and livid day, come after a year of drought and fierce summer, at the end of February. The air was thick with dust, the smoke of bushfires drifted along the hills and the red glare and combs of flame could be seen even at midday.'

The impoverished Hawkins live by the harbour in Watsons Bay, home to fishermen and to lovers stealing illicit moments under the moonlight, 'the bodies stretched out, contorted, with sounds of the dying under the fierce high moon'. Teresa spends the long summer nights naked in her bedroom, dreaming of her escape from this world, dreaming of the boys in the darkness beyond her window who must long for her as she longs for them. Stead writes with raw intensity about Teresa's urgent longing for sex: 'I am certain that as I lie here now, frenzied with desire and want, all women have lain for centuries.' She finds her escape in her Latin teacher, Jonathan Crow – 'a dark, axe-faced, starved young man with spectacles and a black felt hat cocked' – whose university talk enchants her, and the two drift together. Teresa soon joins his evening discussion group and is thrilled by his unguarded talk of sex: 'What, in fact, is wrong with masturbation? What is wrong with homosexuality? Nothing, perhaps. We won't know until we calmly inquire.' But Jonathan, who is sailing for England to continue his university studies, has loftier things in mind than love.

For Love Alone, about the conflicting demands of love and the call of the road, repeatedly refers to Homer's *Odyssey*. Stead characterises the island continent of Australia as home to voyaging people, who retain the restlessness of all seafarers: 'There is nothing in the interior; so people look toward the water, and above to the fixed stars and constellations which first guided men there.' Australia is Odysseus's Ithaca: 'It is a fruitful island of the sea-world, a great Ithaca ... To this race can be put the famous question: "Oh, Australian, have you just come from the harbour? Is your ship in the roadstead? Men of what nation put you down – for I am sure you did not get here on foot."' Stead's rephrasing of Telemachus's famous question to his father Odysseus, whom he does not recognise, is her moving acknowledgement of the fact that Australia was settled by people travelling across the sea, through the ages, and of the resulting restlessness in the spirit of Australians that Stead felt powerfully in herself.

In pursuit of love and adventure, Teresa follows Jonathan to London, arriving in England in 1936, amid talk of Hitler and war.

Here, Jonathan continues self-centred, misogynistic, perverse and cruel – and Teresa finds him utterly irresistible. Her painful obsession with him takes her out into a world beyond the familiar one she has known; his conversation, charged with sex and his quest for truth, draws her on, alternately electrifying and gutting her: 'Why did he advance and retreat, talking about sordid sexual affairs and then pitying humanity, in one breath?' But through the love of another man, James Quick, in London Teresa eventually discovers that her task is not to love Jonathan but to untangle herself from him, as Odysseus must untangle himself from the snares of Calypso: 'She knew she was taken again, she had nothing to do but work her way out another way, slowly to die, eventually to get away from his mortal fascination.'

Stead was born in Sydney in 1902, and grew up in Watsons Bay. Her father, a self-taught marine biologist, worked in the Department of Fisheries and was a co-founder of the Wildlife Preservation Society of Australia; her mother died when Stead was two. Her father remarried and had six more children, and Stead, the only child of his first marriage, became an outsider. Like Teresa, she escaped as soon as she could. After a brief, agonising career as a teacher, Stead learnt typing and shorthand, tools that would enable her to work anywhere in the world, and in 1928 she sailed for London. Like Teresa, Stead travelled to London in the wake of a tutor: Keith Duncan, a postgraduate scholarship student at the London School of Economics and a free-love advocate like Crow.

In London, Stead worked as a secretary and fell in love with a man in her office, the Marxist writer and economist William Blech (who changed his surname to Blake when they moved to New

York in 1939). Although he was married, Blake and Stead moved together to Paris in 1929. They later returned to London, where Stead's first two books were published in 1934: *The Salzburg Tales*, and her first novel, *Seven Poor Men of Sydney*. In 1939, with the outbreak of war, Stead and Blake moved to New York. Here, Stead taught at New York University and worked as a senior screen-writer at MGM in Hollywood, while writing *For Love Alone*. As Marxists and declared Communists, in 1947 Stead and Blake left America to escape the McCarthy era, eventually settling in England in 1953, having married the previous year. Blake died in 1968 and Stead returned to Australia in 1974. In Australia, she at last found the recognition she had long lacked in the country of her birth, and was awarded the first Patrick White Award, in 1974. Patrick White considered Stead the greatest Australian novelist.

For Love Alone is striking for its brilliant portraits of Teresa, a young girl consumed by longing and with the grit to act on it, and of Jonathan, a young man tormented by his ambitions, crushed and sanctified by his poverty, masochistic and totally consumed by himself. The novel is also remarkable for the electric vitality and bold strokes of Stead's prose: 'Down below flowed a great slaty river, smooth but covered with twisted threads of water, swollen with its great flow and directly under the window was an immense dusk-white flower with drooping petals, surrounded by green and living things.' Stead liked her prose raw and unfinished, with the process of its creation intact, and refused to polish it. She wrote: 'Most of my friends deplore this: they are always telling me what I should leave out in order to have "success". But I know that nothing has more success in the end than an intelligent ferocity.'

Nothing could be truer of the enduring spirit of Stead's writing —
it is charged through and through with an intelligent ferocity.

For Love Alone was made into a film in Sydney in 1986, directed
by Stephen Wallace, with a stellar cast of Helen Buday as Teresa,
Sam Neill as James Quick, and Hugo Weaving as Jonathan Crow.

JILL HICKSON

- *Dombey and Son* by Charles Dickens
- *Emma* by Jane Austen
- *Sons and Lovers* by D.H. Lawrence
- *The Golden Notebook* by Doris Lessing
- *The Tree of Man* by Patrick White
- *The Alexandria Quartet* by Lawrence Durrell
- *Alias Grace* by Margaret Atwood
- *Poppy* by Drusilla Modjeska
- *Desperate Characters* by Paula Fox
- *Waiting for the Barbarians* by J.M. Coetzee

Jill Hickson describes herself as 'sometime agent, editor,
writer and longtime reader'. Regarded as Australia's most
influential agent during the fifteen years she ran Hickson
Associates, Hickson is now the chairman of the Historic
Houses Trust and sits on a number of corporate boards.

45 . *The Twyborn Affair*
by
PATRICK WHITE
(1 9 1 2 – 1 9 9 0)

⚛

WHILE VISITING THE NATIONAL GALLERY of Victoria in Melbourne in 1974, Patrick White was told an intriguing story behind one of the figures in 'The Arbour', painted in Paris in 1910 by Australian artist E. Phillip Fox. The painting depicts a group apparently consisting of two women, a boater-hatted man, and two children – except that the auburn-haired woman dressed in white was, in fact, Herbert Dyce Murphy, a young man who spent much of his youth as a spy for British Intelligence, dressed as a woman, before returning to Australia. Dyce Murphy's deception so captivated White that it sparked his last great novel, *The Twyborn Affair*.

Told in three parts, *The Twyborn Affair* is the story of Eddie Twyborn, whose identity is an uncertain, shifting thing that coalesces into three quite different forms: a faux Byzantine empress, a jackeroo, and the madam of a brothel. Each incarnation contains in various manifestations and degrees the two extremes of Twyborn's psyche — a baroque, voluptuous sensuality and a nun-like purity. White's rich, multifaceted novel opens in February 1914 in the South of France, where a wealthy, middle-aged Australian woman, Joanie Golson, spies by chance an irresistible couple through the windows of their dusty pink villa. Enchanted by the 'long thin brown arms of this girl, the perfection of her jawline, the grace of her body as she turned smiling', Joanie determines to insinuate herself into her life. The girl is 25-year-old Eudoxia Vatatzes, and Part I of the novel interrupts her blissful present and revives her troubled past. Her present Edenic life has been created by her Greek lover, Angelos Vatatzes. As she writes in her diary: 'My thoughts were never a joy — only my body made articulate by this persuasive Greek. Then I do appear consecutive, complete, and can enjoy my reflection in the glass, which he has created.' The arrival of Joanie Golson, and soon after the eruption of the First World War, transform Eudoxia's life irrevocably.

The second part of the novel takes up the story of the beautiful ex-serviceman Lieutenant Eddie Twyborn, returned to Australia from the war in Europe. On a whim, Eddie decides to become a jackeroo on a Monaro sheep station, to lose himself in the Australian landscape and absolve himself from the war. As he explains to his baffled father, Judge Twyborn, who still has hopes that his son will follow him into the law: 'I thought of taking a job, as a labourer more or less — hard physical labour — on the land — and in that way perhaps, getting to know a country I've never belonged to.'

Part III is set in London, where Eadith Trist, resplendent in mauve, amethysts, diamonds and feathers, runs a respected, successful whorehouse. The novel closes in 1940 as the first bombs of the Second World War are dropped over London.

Patrick White's great achievement in *The Twyborn Affair* is his fractured portrait of Eddie Twyborn, protean, bisexual man and/or woman, as he struggles to live with himself and to form relationships with other human beings, almost impossible from such an unreliable, shifting ground. Eddie's passionate affairs with men and women seem ultimately doomed to frustration and misunderstanding. Perhaps only his last, chaste liaison promises the communion he longs for, with a companion who offers him love: '"Love" is an exhausted word, and God has been expelled by those who know better, but I offer you the one as proof that the other still exists.' But, tragically, perhaps the single thing that Eddie most longs for is the most unattainable – the understanding of his mother, Eadie, and his father, the Judge.

White's novel is also notable for its evocation of landscape – the moody sea of the French Mediterranean, the silver-grey Thames, and particularly the Monaro, the high plain country of southern New South Wales: 'The landscape too, was cold, and huge, undulating in white waves towards distant mountains of ink blue. Rocks, not strewn, but arranged in groups of formal sculpture suggesting prehistoric rites, prevented monotony taking over the bleached foothills. These were almost treeless.' Although White never felt at home in Australia, he loved the land. 'I could still grow drunk on visions of its landscape', he wrote, on missing Australia while serving in Europe during the Second World War.

Like Eddie Twyborn, White lived out his life in many arenas. Born in London in 1912, White was the son of a rich pastoral family from the Hunter Valley. His parents returned to Australia soon after his birth, but at the instigation of his energetic, ambitious mother, they moved from the family property to Sydney, to a large house in Potts Point with a garden that ran down to the harbour. At his junior boarding school in Moss Vale, White became a brilliant student, then at age twelve he left Australia to go to school in England, where he began to write poetry and short stories and developed his passion for the theatre. He then worked as a jackeroo in the Monaro, but returned to England to read modern languages at King's College, Cambridge, when it became obvious he was not destined for the land. White loved the novels of Lawrence, Hardy and Tolstoy, but most of all he was passionate about James Joyce, whom he called his god, and his novel *Ulysses*. After university, White moved to London, where, influenced by his friend expatriate Australian painter Roy de Maistre, who introduced him to abstract painting, he reworked the novel he had written in the Monaro. It was published in 1939 as *Happy Valley*.

During the Second World War, White served in the Royal Air Force, and after the war he met his great love and life companion, Manoly Lascaris, in Alexandria, when they were both twenty-nine. White returned to Australia with Lascaris, determined to become a writer. He considered Australia unformed and empty, and wanted to write about it, to contribute to its process of becoming. After he was awarded the Nobel Prize for Literature in 1973, White remarked: 'I don't feel particularly Australian. I live here and work here. A Londoner is what I think I am at heart but my blood is Australian and that's what gets me going.' With his Nobel Prize money, White formed the Patrick White Award, to help fund older Australian writers who had not received due recognition for their work. Christina Stead won the inaugural award.

Published in November 1979, to White's surprise *The Twyborn Affair* became a bestseller and was shortlisted for the 1980 Booker Prize. White, ever thoughtful of other writers and artists, removed himself from the list to make way for younger writers.

The Twyborn Affair inspired former scientist and science teacher Heather Rossiter to pursue Herbert Dyce Murphy's story, which resulted in her 2001 biography of him, *Lady Spy, Gentleman Explorer*. The book was so named because Dyce Murphy had led a life of high adventure, joining Mawson's Antarctic expedition in 1911 before becoming a spy called 'Edith' in pre–First World War Europe.

46 . The Outsider

by

ALBERT CAMUS

(1 9 1 3 — 1 9 6 0)

❧

The trigger gave, and the smooth underbelly of the butt
jogged my palm. And so, with that crisp, whip-crack sound,
it all began. I shook off my sweat and the clinging veil of
light. I knew I had shattered the balance of the day, the
spacious calm of this beach on which I'd been happy.

AND SO THE LIFE OF MEURSAULT, narrator of *The Outsider* (also commonly known as *The Stranger*), is destroyed by his one senseless, sun-
induced act on a beach in Algiers. Meursault kills a man, and he is
arrested and tried for murder. His peculiar indifference to his fate —
or his unwillingness to behave in the manner expected by his
captors — renders him guilty in the eyes of the court, and the events
of his otherwise innocuous life are retold until they form the profile
of the criminal he is deemed to be.

The novel, narrated by Meursault in the lucid, spare prose that is the hallmark of Camus, falls into two parts. In Part One, which opens with the announcement of the death and funeral of Meursault's mother, Meursault is a regular young man who unthinkingly goes about his days, from his mother's funeral to the beach to the movies with a girl who wants to marry him. And then explodes the one random act that crystallises his whole life into something new, an act perhaps brought on by the Mediterranean sun: 'I was conscious only of the cymbals of the sun clashing on my skull, and, less distinctly, of the keen blade of light flashing up from the knife, scarring my eyelashes, and gouging into my eyeballs.' In Part Two, Meursault is imprisoned. His life, taken over by the rule of the court, is no longer his own to dispense with as he pleases: 'Still, there was one thing in those early days that was really irksome: my habit of thinking like a free man.'

The Outsider was Camus' first novel. Published in 1942 in Nazi-occupied Paris in a world at war, the novel captured the spirit of disillusion of its times and was an immediate success. *The Outsider* went on to become France's best-selling novel of the twentieth century and its brooding, handsome, young author (Camus was only twenty-seven when *The Outsider* was published) became a cult figure. When Camus won the Nobel Prize for Literature in 1957 aged forty-four, becoming the second youngest writer ever to do so, in his acceptance speech he characterised his generation as one born in a season of war and revolution – two world wars, the rise of Hitler and Stalin, the Spanish Civil War: 'Heir to a corrupt history, in which are mingled fallen revolutions, technology gone mad, dead gods, and worn-out ideologies'. He spoke passionately about the role of the artist in such an era, when the duty of his generation was like that of none other in history — a duty not just to reform the world, but to prevent the world from destroying itself.

In this new, worn-out world, Meursault drifts with a disaffection that later marks him as 'a criminal at heart'. He unthinkingly abandons himself to the whims of his flesh and to the flow of his life under the hot Algerian sun. *The Outsider* is filled with Camus' fierce passion for the land of his birth, Algeria. In an essay, 'Summer in Algiers', he wrote: 'Men find here throughout all their youth a way of living commensurate with their beauty. After that, decay and oblivion. They've staked all on the body and they know that they must lose.' This worship and indulgence of the body is everywhere apparent in Part One of *The Outsider*: 'While I was helping her to climb on to a raft, I let my hand stray over her breasts . . . I had the sky full in my eyes, all blue and gold, and I could feel Marie's stomach rising and falling gently under my head.' Meursault lives in the present moment, unmoved by ambition or love. When Marie asks him if he loves her, 'I said that sort of question had no meaning, really; but I supposed I didn't.' When his boss asks if he'd like to move to a new branch in Paris, he says he doesn't care: 'As a student I'd had plenty of ambition of the kind he meant. But, when I had to drop my studies, I very soon realized all that was pretty futile.'

Camus was born 1913 in Mondori, a village in the interior of Algeria, into a working-class family. His father's ancestors had settled in Algeria following its conquest by the French Bourbon king Charles X in 1830; his mother was of Spanish descent. Before

Camus turned one, his father was killed in the First World War, and his mother took her two sons, Albert and his elder brother Lucien, to Algiers to live with her mother. They lived a difficult, impoverished life in a small apartment. Camus was a talented student, reserved and focused, excelling in French and mathematics, and his primary-school teacher Louis Germain (to whom he dedicated his Nobel Prize speech) helped him get a scholarship to Algiers High School in 1923. At fifteen, Camus joined a soccer team and it was on the soccer field that he absorbed the basis of the strong moral sense for which he was later famous, the spirit of individual effort as part of a team: '*solitaire et solidaire*' (alone and united). Soccer became a lifelong passion, although an almost fatal bout of tuberculosis forced him to stop playing in 1930. Two years later, he began to write. Camus married twice: his first marriage in 1934 broke up after two years because of his wife's morphine addiction, and he then married Francine Faure in 1940, with whom he had twins in 1945.

Throughout his life, Camus was vigorously engaged in left-wing politics. In Algeria, he worked and wrote for the Théâtre du Travail, which was committed to bringing quality theatre to working people. He admired Dostoyevsky, Malraux, Melville and Faulkner, and wrote stage adaptations of Faulkner's *Requiem for a Nun* and Dostoyevsky's *The Possessed*. As a journalist, Camus reviewed Jean-Paul Sartre's early work, as Sartre did Camus', and the two writers met in Paris in 1943. In Paris, Camus joined the French Resistance and with Sartre edited the Parisian journal *Combat*, whose motto was: 'In war as in peace, the last word is said by those who never surrender.' The friendship between Camus and Sartre was famously broken in 1952 following their disagreement, over the Soviet Union, when Sartre became a Communist and Camus denounced Stalin.

In 1960, aged forty-six, Camus was killed in a car accident with his friend and publisher Michel Gallimard. In the mud by the wrecked car, the manuscript of his last, unfinished novel was found. The novel, *The First Man*, an autobiographical story about his fatherless childhood in Algeria, was published in English in 1995.

Although Camus never wanted *The Outsider* to be adapted for the screen, after Camus' death Luchino Visconti brought it to the cinema in his 1967 film *Lo Straniero*, starring Marcello Mastroianni as Meursault and Anna Karina as Marie. The film was not one of Visconti's more successful screen adaptations – and Mastroianni was considered too old to play Meursault – but the novel that inspired it has remained in print since its first publication in 1942 and continues to be popular among successive generations of students and readers in France and throughout the world.

47 . By Grand Central Station I Sat Down and Wept
by
ELIZABETH SMART
(1 9 1 3 — 1 9 8 6)

WHEN ELIZABETH SMART LEFT her upper-middle-class family home in Ottawa, Canada, aged eighteen to study piano for a year at King's College, University of London, she made a move that would irrevocably alter the course of her life. While in London, Smart picked up a book of poems, read it and fell instantly in love with its author.

Convinced that the only way to live was with passion, guided by the heart and poetic inspiration alone, Smart wrote to the poet, George Barker. They corresponded for almost ten years until after the outbreak of the Second World War, when Smart moved to a writers' colony in Big Sur, California, where she finally met the love of her life. At her instigation and with her financial assistance, George Barker flew to California from Japan, where he had been teaching.

I am standing on a corner in Monterey, waiting for the bus
to come in, and all the muscles of my will are holding my
terror to face the moment I most desire. Apprehension and
the summer afternoon keep drying my lips, prepared at ten-
minute intervals all through the five-hour wait.

But then it is her eyes that come forward out of the
vulgar disembarkers to reassure me that the bus has not
disgorged disaster: her madonna eyes, soft as the newly-
born, trusting as the untempted.

So begins *By Grand Central Station I Sat Down and Wept*, the novel
Smart based on her lifelong love affair with Barker. These opening
lines conjure the narrator's most longed-for desire since first
reading a book of poems in a London bookshop: the moment she
will behold for the first time the man she already loves. But, when
he alights from the bus in July 1940, he is followed by his wife.
Although Smart had arranged for both Barker and his wife to fly
to America from Japan, she had not anticipated the agonising
consequences of her act. The excruciating love triangle that results
from this meeting fuels the narrative of Smart's novel.

With its hypnotic prose, throbbing rhythms and rich metaphors,
By Grand Central Station reads more like a poem than a novel. It is a
lament, composed of tears and blood, earth and sky, as obsessive and
unleashed, as intimate and cosmic, as the paintings of Frida Kahlo.
The story itself is simple – it charts the rise, faltering and unravelling of an intense sexual love affair, perhaps incapable of surviving
ordinary life ('But how can I go through the necessary daily motions,
when such an intense fusion turns the world to water?') – but the

way in which the story is told is so mesmerising, so visceral, that its extravagant emotion is alive. Such intense passion has the power to polarise onlookers and readers, either to transport or offend. When the lovers are arrested on the Arizona border under the Mann Act (for intending to fornicate in Arizona) by two policemen, one remarks: 'We're family men . . . We don't go so much for love.'

The novel is extraordinary for the opulent precision of Smart's prose, which draws freely on myth, the Bible and literature, then cuts these allusions with references to everyday things, such as pots and pans, wilted geraniums and thin children's legs (most likely influenced by Barker's mentor, T.S. Eliot). Frustrated by the limitations of traditional narrative prose, Smart developed a lyrical prose style that she believed could express deep truths in the way that poetry does, by evoking the unspeakable, the inexpressible, through metaphor – 'I am over-run, jungled in my bed, I am infested with a menagerie of desires.'

The rich texture of Smart's language can be heard in the words of her title, taken from the famous opening lines of Psalm 137 (and echoing their use by T.S. Eliot in *The Wasteland*): 'By the rivers of Babylon, there we sat down, yea we wept . . .' The title evokes an intensely traumatic event of Old Testament history – the captivity of the Jews in Babylon following the destruction of the Temple of Solomon in 586 BCE – that produced a great literature expressing the exiled people's desire for revenge, their anguish and longing for God, their wavering repentance. Smart's skill is in her ability to fuse her own intensely personal experience of love and loss with these larger moments of history, to magnify and articulate her own experience of homelessness, her sense of exile, her longing for her own god (Barker). It is hyperbolic. It works beautifully. The devastation and disorientation of Europe during the Second World War, being fought as Smart wrote, are also echoed in her prose, so that what is essentially a love song becomes a haunting chant of loss and longing for an age.

By Grand Central Station is now acknowledged as a masterpiece of poetic prose, but although it received favourable reviews, including one by noted English critic and novelist Cyril Connolly, it did not sell widely when it was first published in England in 1945. Perhaps this is not surprising in a country that was yet to accept publication of *Lady Chatterley's Lover*, D.H. Lawrence's exploration of sexual passion and attack on conservative sexual mores. Smart continued her affair with Barker for many years, and had four children with him, despite the fact that he never left his wife. She lived in England for most of her life, working as a copywriter to support her children – she became the highest paid copywriter in England – and then as the editor of *Queen* magazine.

Michael Ondaatje narrated the film of Smart's life, *Elizabeth Smart: On the Side of the Angels*. He observed of her extraordinary novel that every good reader eventually discovers *By Grand Central Station I Sat Down and Wept*, and finds in it a fundamental and abiding emotional truth.

MANDY SAYER

❧ *One Hundred Years of Solitude* by Gabriel García Márquez

- *As I Lay Dying* by William Faulkner
- *Anna Karenina* by Leo Tolstoy
- *Invisible Man* by Ralph Ellison
- *Madame Bovary* by Gustave Flaubert
- *The Man Who Loved Children* by Christina Stead
- *Love in the Time of Cholera* by Gabriel García Márquez
- *Jane Eyre* by Charlotte Brontë
- *The Good Soldier* by Ford Madox Ford
- *The Collected Short Stories of Ernest Hemingway* by Ernest Hemingway

Mandy Sayer is the author of seven books, including her award-winning autobiographical novel *Dreamtime Alice* (1999) and its sequel *Velocity* (2005), novels *Mood Indigo* (1990) and *The Cross* (1995), and her book of short stories *15 Kinds of Desire* (2001).

48 . *Invisible Man*
by
R ALPH   E LLISON
(1 9 1 4 – 1 9 9 4)
✻

'I AM AN INVISIBLE MAN,' declares the narrator of Ralph Ellison's
only novel. 'I am a man of substance, of flesh and bone, fibre and
liquids – and I might even be said to possess a mind. I am invisible,
understand, simply because people refuse to see me.' The truth of
these disturbing lines is relentlessly revealed in *Invisible Man*, the
story of a young idealistic African-American man in the American
South and Harlem of the 1940s whose early promise and academic
aspirations are confounded at every turn by the very people who
pretend to help him – the white town leaders who invite him to
speak at their gathering, the president of his state college for
Negroes, the socialist Brotherhood by whom he's taken up in New
York. Finally, humiliated, defeated, hounded on every side and yet
with a nascent, defiant sense of himself, he disappears down a
manhole, making official his status as an invisible man.

Invisible Man opens with the unnamed narrator in his bolt-hole recalling the previous twenty years of his troubled life, beginning with the uncharacteristically fierce dying words of his grandfather, who had been a slave. His grandfather's words continue to haunt him and only after the repeated shattering of his hopes and dreams does he begin to make some sense of their cryptic meaning:

> I never told you, but our life is a war and I have been a traitor all my born days, a spy in the enemy's country ever since I give up my gun back in the Reconstruction. Live with your head in the lion's mouth. I want you to overcome 'em with yeses, undermine 'em with grins, agree 'em to death and destruction, let 'em swoller you till they vomit or bust wide open.

The narrator then cuts to one of the most shocking scenes in literature. Having made a brilliant oration at his high-school graduation, in which he successfully demonstrated rhetorically that 'humility was the secret, indeed the very essence, of progress', he is invited to speak at an important town gathering. But, before he can speak, he must take part in a 'battle royal'. In the violent battle that ensues, the narrator learns the depraved depths to which his humility must sink if he is to progress in the world.

Like Stendhal's Julien Sorel, the narrator dreams of furthering himself through his brilliant mind and gift for speech, and, like *The Red and the Black*, the novel is charged with irony and moves with the force of a roller coaster. Along the way, the narrator meets other African-Americans who have found an understanding he cannot yet share, for they are dispossessed and insane – and he distances himself from them in horror, clinging instead to the white world and aspiring to work alongside the duplicitous president of his college. An impoverished African-American farmer, Jim Trueblood, tells a story of how he found the strength to live through disgrace and banishment from home. One night, filled with despair, Trueblood looked up and saw the stars:

> All I know is I *ends up* singin' the blues, I sings me some
> blues that ain't never been sang before, and while I'm singin'
> them blues I makes up my mind that I ain't nobody but
> myself and ain't nothin' I can do but let whatever is gonna
> happen, happen.

This man, despicable in the eyes of the narrator, finds his strength through his own music. Another man, the inmate of a semi-madhouse, sees that the narrator has 'learned to repress not only his emotions but his humanity' – but the narrator, still beholden to his dream, cannot see this until his dream begins to fall apart, which it does with astonishing and devastating rapidity when he is dismissed from his college and sent to New York.

Ralph Waldo Ellison, born in Oklahoma City in 1914, was named after the American poet Ralph Waldo Emerson. His parents, both children of former slaves in Southern USA, moved west to Oklahoma, hoping to bring up their children in a state known for its freedom. When Ellison's father died, his mother found work at an Afro-Methodist Episcopal church, where Ellison could use the

minister's library. He became a passionate reader — of Twain, Stendhal, Dostoyevsky, Faulkner, Hemingway, Joyce, T.S. Eliot — and a
talented trumpeter. He later wrote:

> When I read Stendhal, I would search within the Negro
> communities in which I grew up. I began, in other words,
> quite early to connect the worlds projected in literature and
> poetry and drama and novels with the life in which I found
> myself.

At nineteen, Ellison won a scholarship to study music at the
Booker T. Washington Tuskegee Institute in Alabama, where he
was introduced to the ideas of philosopher Alain Locke
(1886–1954), who had studied at Harvard under William James.
Locke, the first African-American Rhodes scholar at Oxford
University, edited *The New Negro: An Interpretation* (1925), in which
he argued that African-American life in the 1920s was 'not only
establishing new contacts and founding new centers, it is finding a
new soul'.

Ellison then moved to Harlem to study sculpture. From 1938
to 1942, he worked for the Federal Writers' Project (established as
part of Roosevelt's New Deal), interviewing ordinary people and
recording their stories. Between 1937 and 1944, he published
reviews in journals like *Negro Quarterly*, which he briefly edited,
and in 1943 reported on the Harlem race riot, an event that
became the climax of *Invisible Man*. Following the Second World
War — during which he served in the US Merchant Marines —
Ellison married Fanny McConnell and they moved to Vermont.

With the assistance of a Rosenwald Fellowship, he could devote himself to writing, and spent the next seven years working on a novel about black identity and heroism, which was published in 1952 as *The Invisible Man*. His impassioned, surreal novel was on the bestseller list for sixteen weeks and won the 1953 National Book Award for Fiction. Following its publication, Ellison lectured extensively on African-American culture and struggled to write his second novel, which remained unfinished upon his death in 1994.

THE FEDERAL WRITERS' PROJECT

During the Great Depression, the US government invested heavily in cultural development for the first time as part of Roosevelt's New Deal. Programs were established to provide employment for the numerous musicians, artists, actors and writers who faced chronic unemployment not only because of the general economic depression but also because of the advent of new technology (the phonograph, radio and cinema) that was rapidly replacing live entertainment. The idea for an extensive cultural program was suggested by Roosevelt's friend, the artist George Biddle, who had studied painting under the Mexican muralist Diego Rivera and had been inspired by Rivera's vision for public art and his collaborative, collective art projects. The Federal Writers' Project employed thousands of writers during the 1930s and '40s to provide research, writing and editing services to the government. Its most enduring project was the publication of guidebooks to every state and some localities — the American Guide Series — and the recording of oral histories and folklore, including the slave narratives, which remain invaluable sources of American history.

49 . The Member of the Wedding

by
CARSON MCCULLERS
(1 9 1 7 – 1 9 6 7)

CARSON MCCULLERS'S THE MEMBER OF THE WEDDING is the story of
a young girl who suddenly finds herself at sea in the world; she
hates being herself, and she can find no words for the new things
that burst within her:

> It happened that green and crazy summer when Frankie
> was twelve years old. This was the summer when for a long
> time she had not been a member . . . Frankie had become an
> unjoined person who hung around doorways, and she was
> afraid.

McCullers has a genius for evoking the lives of the lonely and
outcast, and for articulating the subtle bonds of affection that
develop between apparently disparate people. In *The Member of the*

Wedding, the lonely is Frankie Addams, caught between the world of her childhood and the uncharted adult world of love and other mysteries; and the companions to whom she resentfully clings one long hot summer are her six-year-old cousin John Henry, as small and fragile as Frankie is big and gangly, and Berenice, who cooks and cleans for Frankie and her widowed father.

The story is simple and most of the action erupts over one weekend, from Frankie's brother's announcement on the last Friday in August that he is getting married that Sunday, to the briefly described wedding and its devastating aftermath. But what McCullers evokes with her lyrical, spare prose and her bare-boned story is one of the most profound portraits in all of literature of the awkward, painful, disorienting metamorphosis from girl-hood into womanhood — a portrait that draws its power from McCullers's ability to capture Frankie's mercurial moods and the whirl of talk around the kitchen table between Frankie, John Henry and Berenice, as Berenice gradually realises what is blossoming in the troubled young girl before her: she is falling in love — with a wedding.

Frankie's urge to belong somewhere suddenly finds an outlet in her brother's wedding, and all her floating dreams of escape from her dull life in a small Southern town into the big exotic world at war that turns without her are focused with an unrelenting intensity on her brother, Jarvis, and his fiancée, Janice. All at once it occurs to Frankie that when she leaves home for her brother's wedding in Winter Hill she will never again return to her old life, and so she prepares to leave home forever. And her preparations must be nothing short of a complete transformation, for her new place in the world as a member of the wedding, far from home and alongside her brother and his fiancée, requires a whole new Frankie, starting with a new name — F. Jasmine Addams, to go with the 'JA names' Jarvis and Janice — and new hair: 'For the wedding I ought to have long, bright yellow hair, don't you think?'

McCullers brilliantly draws the young Frankie in all her seriousness and urgency and sudden need to grow up, crashing against Berenice's straight-talking worldly realism and John Henry's childish play, which was so recently part of Frankie's life: at the game of bridge around the kitchen table, John Henry 'watched all the cards very carefully, because he was in debt; he owed Berenice more than five million dollars'. McCullers can evoke the individual logic of John Henry's childhood and of Frankie's adolescence, in all their full illogic, from within their own experience and without ever once patronising them. In the same way, she can convey Berenice's life as an African-American in the South, with her dream of a world in which 'There would be no coloured people and no white people to make the coloured people feel cheap and sorry through all their lives . . .' When at last Berenice realises the full depth of F. Jasmine's need and emotional turmoil, and takes her in her arms, McCullers, with the lightest, most delicate of strokes, draws one of the most beautiful, heart-rending scenes of the novel.

By the time McCullers came to write *The Member of the Wedding*, she had already published two novels. Her first, *The Heart is a Lonely Hunter*, was published in 1940 when McCullers was only twenty-three years old; it became a bestseller and McCullers became a literary star. Born Lula Carson Smith in Columbus, Georgia, in

1917, McCullers was the eldest child – brilliant and sensitive – of three children. Her father was a watchmaker and jeweller, and her ambitious mother was determined her first-born would be a musical genius. At fifteen, McCullers had the first of many illnesses that were to ruin her health – rheumatic fever. She was later struck by a series of strokes that left her paralysed down one side by the time she was thirty. McCullers became a talented pianist and, at seventeen, she was sent to New York City to study music at the Juilliard, but instead she enrolled in evening classes in creative writing at Columbia University. Her first story, 'Wunderkind', was published in 1936 in Story magazine.

McCullers, passionate, selfish and petulant, met and fell in love with the writer Reeves McCullers, a corporal in the US Army, and they were married in 1937. They moved to Charlotte, North Carolina, where McCullers wrote The Heart is a Lonely Hunter and became the successful writer Reeves would never become. The tension caused by the inequality of their talents, their tempestuous passions, heavy drinking and homosexual affairs led to a traumatic divorce in 1940 and McCullers moved to New York. Here she lived with George Davis, the editor of Harper's Bazaar, and became friends with W.H. Auden, Tennessee Williams (who became her lifelong friend) and Truman Capote. Of his first meeting with her, Capote wrote: 'I remember thinking how beautiful her eyes were: the colour of good clear coffee, or of a dark ale held to the firelight to warm. Her voice had the same quality, the same gentle heat . . .'

After the publication of her second novel, Reflections in a Golden Eye, in 1941, McCullers spent over five agonising years trying to write The Member of the Wedding, struggling with chronic physical pain, unable to type properly — for months she could only type with one finger — and emotional torment, having fallen in love with American writer Katherine Anne Porter (1890–1980), who rejected her obsessive attentions. McCullers married Reeves again in 1945 and the following year *The Member of the Wedding* was published. At the suggestion of Tennessee Williams, McCullers turned her novel into a successful play, which was adapted for the cinema in 1952. The film, which became a classic of American filmmaking, was the director Fred Zinnemann's favourite of all his films.

McCullers spent the last months of her life before her death at fifty dictating her unfinished autobiography, *Illumination and Night Glare* (published posthumously in 1999), in which she wrote: 'I yearned for one particular thing; to get away from Columbus and to make my mark in the world.'

50 . The Catcher in the Rye
by
J . D . SALINGER
(1 9 1 9 –)

❧

HOLDEN CAULFIELD, THE SEVENTEEN-YEAR-OLD narrator of *The Catcher in the Rye*, is one of the most familiar, best loved and most imitated characters in literature. Since his appearance in print over fifty years ago, his distinctive voice and tale of dissolution that leads to a nervous breakdown have inspired millions of teenagers and dozens of writers and filmmakers. *The Catcher in the Rye* is the classic teenage angst story, written with an intimacy and directness – Holden addresses the reader as 'you' as he mulls over life with you – that is irresistibly seductive and remains extraordinarily fresh long after the decade in which it was written. J.D. Salinger's only novel, *The Catcher in the Rye* became a bestseller soon after its publication in 1951 and continues to sell over 250,000 copies a year. Its notoriety has been increased by the famed reclusiveness of its author J.D. Salinger and its association with John Lennon's murderer, Mark David Chapman, who was carrying a copy of Salinger's book when he fatally shot Lennon in December 1980.

The opening lines of *The Catcher in the Rye*, which evoke every novel of growing up ever told while instantly undermining the tradition, are among the most beautiful and arresting in literature:

> If you really want to hear about it, the first thing you'll probably want to know is where I was born, and what my lousy childhood was like, and how my parents were occupied and all before they had me, and all that David Copperfield kind of crap, but I don't feel like going into it, if you want to know the truth. In the first place, that stuff bores me, and in the second place, my parents would have about two hemorrhages apiece if I told anything pretty personal about them.

Holden's edgy voice, filled with slang and attitude, is so authentic that he has become the archetypal alienated teenage boy.

The Catcher in the Rye opens with Holden looking back to the 'madman stuff' that happened over a few days before Christmas the previous year, when he was sixteen. He is expelled from his fourth high school, having failed four of his five subjects (he passed English). He describes Pencey Prep, his exclusive school, with his idiosyncratic, understated humour that undercuts every cliché and truism he turns his eye to. The ads for Pencey refer to the school's reputation for producing 'splendid, clear-thinking young men', but Holden dismisses this claim: 'I didn't know anybody there that was splendid and clear-thinking at all.

Maybe two guys. If that many. And they probably *came* to Pencey that way.'

After a fight with his roommate over a girl, feeling depressed and lonely at school, Holden decides to leave school early and hang out in New York City until the holidays begin, so he can return home 'all rested up and feeling swell'. But his wild time in New York — his drinking in bars and hotels and clubs, his experience with a prostitute, conversations with old friends and his sister, Phoebe, his compromised visit to an old teacher, and his whole run-in with the phony adult world — leaves him utterly broken inside.

The novel's title comes from the lines of the Robert Burns poem that Holden misquotes to his precocious younger sister Phoebe: 'You know that song "If a body catch a body comin' through the rye"?' When Phoebe questions Holden about what he wants to do with his life, he says the only thing he'd really like to be is a catcher in the rye, someone who catches the children playing in the field of rye before they fall over the edge 'of some crazy cliff'. Holden's aimlessness and inability to 'grow up' and become part of the 'phony' adult world have their roots in his younger brother Allie's death, which haunts him throughout the novel. As he begins to lose his hold on the world around him, he calls: 'Allie, don't let me disappear.'

Salinger began writing *The Catcher in the Rye*, his only novel, after serving in the US Army in Europe during the Second World War, an experience that marked him for life. Death and the war, along with sex and books, are Holden's main preoccupations. His older brother, D.B., fought in the Second World War in locations similar to Salinger's own, and hated it. He told Holden that 'the Army was practically as full of bastards as the Nazis were . . .'

The Catcher in the Rye is memorable for Salinger's vital story of a teenage boy lost in the world, unable to settle into adult life that seems to offer him nothing. It is also notable for the brilliant immediacy of Salinger's writing and Holden's flat, wry disenchantment: 'You take somebody that cries their goddam eyes out over that phony stuff in the movies, and nine times out of ten they're mean bastards at heart. I'm not kidding.' And: 'I'm sort of glad they've got the atomic bomb invented. If there's ever another war, I'm going to sit right the hell on top of it. I'll volunteer for it, I swear to God I will.'

Jerome David Salinger was born in New York City on New Year's Day in 1919 to a Jewish father and a Christian mother (who converted to Judaism). Salinger briefly attended New York and Columbia universities before devoting himself to writing, and had several stories published before joining the army in 1942. In the army, he took part in the D-Day landings and worked in the Counter Intelligence Corps. In 1946, he returned to New York, where he continued to write, and he became a regular contributor to *The New Yorker* until 1965.

After the publication of *The Catcher in the Rye* in 1951 and its almost instant rise to the bestseller lists (where it has remained ever since), Salinger continued to publish stories, but in 1965 he retired from public life and publishing because he found celebrity crippling. Salinger still lives in Cornish, New Hampshire, and, according to his daughter Margaret (Peggy) Salinger – who wrote a book about her life and her father, *Dream Catcher*, published in 2001 – he still needs to write every day. Of the enduring appeal of *The Catcher in the Rye*, she says: 'It captures the borderline aspects of adolescence brilliantly, beautifully; how well he writes about what it's like to be on your own and appropriately, adolescently crazy – not having anything sorted out.'

TIM WINTON

- *The Sound and the Fury* by William Faulkner
- *Huckleberry Finn* by Mark Twain
- *Fathers and Sons* by Ivan Turgenev
- *Bleak House* by Charles Dickens
- *The Tree of Man* by Patrick White
- *A Change of Climate* by Hilary Mantel
- *Silence* by Shusako Endo
- *The Moviegoer* by Walker Percy
- *The Man Who Loved Children* by Christina Stead
- *The Sun Also Rises* by Ernest Hemingway

Australian writer Tim Winton is the acclaimed, award-winning author of eight novels, including *Cloudstreet* (1991), *The Riders* (1994) and *Dirt Music* (2001), and the bestselling short-story collection *The Turning*, published in 2004.

5 1 . On the Road
by
JACK KEROUAC
(1 9 2 2 – 1 9 6 9)

✄

JACK KEROUAC SPENT OVER THREE frustrated years searching for a
way to tell the story of his adventures on the road with his friend
Neal Cassady (whom he first met in 1946), struggling to find a new
original voice that would capture the wild and exuberant times
they'd spent travelling across America. Not until he sat down at
his typewriter in April 1951 with a long continuous roll of paper
in place and poured out his story in three weeks, writing thousands of words a day and living on coffee, pea soup and Benzedrine,
did Kerouac find the voice he'd been looking for. The novel that
emerged from his marathon writing spree was published in 1957 as
On the Road, a brilliant, spirited novel, sad and sweet, which made
Kerouac, aged thirty-five, famous overnight. Gilbert Millstein's
review in *The New York Times* called *On the Road* 'the most beautifully executed, the clearest and the most important utterance yet

made by the generation Kerouac himself named years ago as "beat" and whose principal avatar he is'.

On the Road, narrated by aspiring writer Sal Paradise, opens in the winter of 1947 with the arrival of Dean Moriarty in Sal's life: 'With the coming of Dean Moriarty began the part of my life you could call my life on the road.' Sal is living in New Jersey with his aunt, studying and working on his first novel, and Dean is 'a sideburned hero of the snowy West', a sinewy, crazy, enthusiastic dreamer of dreams; Gatsby to Sal's Nick Carraway. Sal and Dean understand each other and they agree to go out West sometime: 'I was a young writer and I wanted to take off. Somewhere along the line I knew there'd be girls, visions, everything; somewhere along the line the pearl would be handed to me.' Sal is drawn to Dean's vitality and 'a kind of holy lightning I saw flashing from his excitement and his visions, which he described so torrentially that people in buses looked around to see the overexcited nut'.

The novel is told in five episodic parts; each narrates a different adventure across America over the course of several years, mostly between New York and San Francisco via Denver, with one great trip to Mexico City. They travel in Greyhound buses, hitch rides in cars and trucks, drive bought, stolen and borrowed cars — with his manic energy, Dean can drive whole nights across the sleeping country, high on drugs and alcohol and jazz, and dreams of the next town and the next girl. Kerouac's beautiful rhythmic prose and portrait of the mad Dean Moriarty are among his novel's most lasting achievements. Sal rejoices in Dean's extraordinary capacity for life and sees it as something sacred:

the only people for me are the mad ones, the ones who are
mad to live, mad to talk, mad to be saved, desirous of everything at the same time, the ones who never yawn or say a
commonplace thing, but burn, burn, burn like fabulous
yellow roman candles exploding like spiders across the stars.

Dean's appetite for life is matched by his longing for sex – 'the one
and only holy and important thing in life' – and by the end of the
novel he has been married three times and has four children.

Kerouac was born Jean-Louis Kerouac in Lowell, Massachusetts,
in 1922 to French-Canadian parents. He grew up in French-
Canadian neighbourhoods and spoke the dialect, so English was his
second language. At seventeen, Kerouac decided to become a
writer. A star athlete at school, he won a football scholarship to
Columbia University but dropped out to become an adventurer.
During the Second World War, he worked as a merchant seaman,
and in 1944 he met many of the characters who would later become
known as part of 'the Beat Generation' and who would appear in On
the Road, including Allen Ginsburg and William Burroughs. They
formed a loose group, looking for new meaning through literature
and experimenting with drugs. Kerouac used the word 'Beat' for his
friends, a word that came from one of Burroughs's drug suppliers,
Herbert Huncke, who used it to describe a 'state of exalted exhaus-
tion' and which the Catholic Kerouac associated with 'beatific', or
blessedness. For Kerouac, who saw himself as a 'strange solitary crazy
Catholic mystic', life was 'holy and every moment is precious'.

In 1946, Kerouac's father died. His death spurred Kerouac to
write his first novel, The Town and the City, which he began in 1948,

aged twenty-six. It was published in 1950 to poor reviews. In the meantime, he had made his first road trip in 1947 and, excited by the new vistas that were opening up to him, began to work on a new prose style, 'spontaneous prose', which would result in *On the Road*. In 1950, Kerouac married Joan Haverty, his second wife (his first marriage, in 1944, had soon ended in divorce). By this time, his idea for his next novel had become clear, as he told his English publisher – he wanted to write 'a novel whose background is the recurrence of the pioneering instinct in American life and its expression in the migration of the present generation; a book provisionally entitled *On the Road*'. He published five more auto-biographical novels, including *The Dharma Bums* (1958) and *Big Sur* (1962), and was working on a long, surrealistic novel about his life when he died in 1969, aged forty-seven, of alcoholism.

❉ CHRISTOS TSIOLKAS ❉

I wonder what it says of the novel that it is easier for me to compile a list of favourite songs or albums or movies than it is to put together a selection of what I consider the best novels I have ever read. Maybe image and melody resonate more strongly than the word – I can immediately think of ten or fifteen of my favourite poems. Or maybe my difficulty says more about me. The following list certainly places me firmly as a child of the last half of the twentieth century, a Western child at that and one influenced greatly by the seduction of the United States. How could it be otherwise?

Wasn't the USA the siren's call, am I not an immigrant's child?

I'm being strict. Just the novel allowed on this list. So no poetry, no plays, no short stories and no non-fiction (though if I was going off to that imaginary desert island I would certainly take with me Raymond Carver, James Agee's *On Film*, Truman Capote's *In Cold Blood*, Pauline Kael's *Deeper into Movies*, Kafka's short stories, Euripides and Suetonius's *The Lives of the Caesars*). Here's the list in no particular order:

- *The Chronicles of Narnia* by C.S. Lewis
- *An American Dream* by Norman Mailer
- *One Hundred Years of Solitude* by Gabriel García Márquez
- *Crime and Punishment* by Fyodor Dostoyevsky
- *The Last Temptation of Christ* by Nikos Kazantzakis
- *Huckleberry Finn* by Mark Twain
- *The Red and the Black* by Stendhal
- *The Heart is a Lonely Hunter* by Carson McCullers
- *A Death in the Family* by James Agee
- *The Prisoner of Love* by Jean Genet

A confession. I have yet to read Proust or to finish *Ulysses*. And an apology that there is only one woman; but, Lord, what a writer she was.

Australian writer Christos Tsiolkas is the author of the widely acclaimed novel *Loaded* (1995), *The Jesus Man* (1999) and *Dead Europe* (2005). *Loaded* was made into the award-winning film *Head On*, which was released in 1998.

5 2 .   *The   Grass   Harp*

by

TRUMAN   CAPOTE

(1 9 2 4 – 1 9 8 4)

✄

LIKE HIS LITERARY IDOL FLAUBERT, Truman Capote was passionately dedicated to his art: 'Flaubert's attitude toward writing, his sense of perfectionism, is what I would like mine to be.' Capote began writing at the age of eight and by the time he was ten realised he wanted to be a writer. Every day he played with his pens and paper, like a musician practising an instrument, and through this rigorous, self-imposed training, he developed one of the most exquisite, true writing styles in the English language. Capote's mastery of the art of writing is everywhere manifest in his second novel, *The Grass Harp* (1951). Harper Lee, his childhood friend, who based the character Dill in her novel *To Kill a Mockingbird* on Capote, aptly described him as 'a pocket Merlin' – and such wonder did this mini magician weave into *The Grass Harp* that, after reading the first five chapters, his publisher Robert Linscott wrote to him that he adored every word 'and had to stop every few paragraphs to hug myself with pleasure. If the last chapter is as good as the preceding ones, this is really going to be a masterpiece.'

Following the commercial and critical success of his first novel, the haunted *Other Voices, Other Rooms* (1948), published when he was only twenty-three years old, Capote was feted across America – as much for the photograph on the novel's back cover of a delicately beautiful Capote reclining seductively, gazing up through a fringe of blond hair, as for his precocious talent and the stylish precision of his prose. Capote, who had long dreamt of fame and fortune, relished his new-found notoriety; but in April 1950, seeking the sun and a quiet place to work, he escaped America to travel to Sicily with his lover, writer Jack Dunphy. They rented an old stone farmhouse in Taormina with views over Mount Etna and the Ionian Sea (the house in which D.H. Lawrence had spent two productive years from March 1920) and here Capote devoted himself to writing each morning with a fierce discipline, 'as calculating as an accountant checking receipts'. He soon tore up the novel he had been working on for some years (*Summer Crossings*, a social comedy set in New York's high society) and turned instead to his early childhood in Monroeville, Alabama, a small town surrounded by fields of corn and cotton where, in the summer of 1930, his parents had abandoned him, aged five, with his mother's cousins: three elderly sisters and a brother.

The story Capote conjured from his Sicilian memories of his childhood in Southern USA was *The Grass Harp*. Dedicated to Miss Sook Faulk, one of the three elderly Monroeville sisters, 'In memory of affections deep and true', the novel shimmers with the fragile power of Capote's childhood memories, of those affections deep and true. *The Grass Harp*, narrated by Collin Fenwick, opens with a question:

> When was it that first I heard of the grass harp? Long
> before the autumn we lived in the China tree; an earlier
> autumn, then; and of course it was Dolly who told me, no
> one else would have known to call it that, a grass harp.

At the age of eleven, Collin is sent to live with his father's unmarried old cousins, Dolly and Verena Talbo, following his mother's death (his father, who had run naked into the yard mad with grief, is unable to care for his son). Unexpectedly, the noisy prying boy finds a place in the reclusive Talbo sisters' large rambling house, in the warm, sweet-smelling kitchen run by Dolly and her friend Catherine Creek: 'Though no honours came my way, those were the lovely years.' The central drama of the story is sparked when the severe, business-minded Verena betrays Dolly's trust, and Dolly, Catherine and Collin take refuge in the only other house they know, a tree house in a China tree. Capote's novel, as gentle as the grass harp that whispers the stories of all the people who ever lived, is remarkable for its beautifully drawn characters, lilting Southern rhythms and lucid prose, more remarkable perhaps because of the explosive personality that produced it.

Capote once said of himself: 'I'm about as tall as a shotgun – and just as noisy.' That is, a shotgun possessed by an extraordinary gift for writing prose of delicate precision and subtle depths. At its best, his prose has a sublime simplicity: 'I prefer to underwrite. Simple, clear as a country creek.' And yet Capote himself was prone to excess and boisterous high spirits; he was a social butterfly who knew everyone, from Tennessee Williams and W.H. Auden to Lee Radziwill, from European princesses and multi-millionaires to Cecil Beaton and Andy Warhol.

Born Truman Streckfus Persons in New Orleans in 1924, Capote was an unwanted child from his conception. His mother was a Southern belle whose dreams of success were dashed soon after her marriage to Archie Persons, a big-talking adventurer who never made good, and she divorced him when Capote was seven and still living with her relatives in Monroeville. In 1932, she married a successful businessman, Joseph Garcia Capote, and decided to have her son back, so young Capote was sent from Monroeville to live with them in New York that same year, which was when he took his stepfather's surname. His mother, now Nina Capote, drank heavily and accused her son of being a 'sissy'. Tormented by Truman's diminutive size (as an adult he was five feet four inches) and feminine appearance, Nina sent him to two psychiatrists in the hope they'd make him a man. In 1939, when the Capotes moved to Greenwich, Capote's English teacher at Greenwich High School, Catherine Wood, recognised her new pupil's extraordinary talent and valued his difference, which she tried to explain to Nina Capote, telling her that unlike the regular boys who would continue doing regular things all their lives, Truman would be famous.

When Capote left school at seventeen, he found a small job on *The New Yorker*, which he left abruptly in 1944 following a perceived insult to the poet Robert Frost. In 1945, after several attempts to get his stories published in *The New Yorker*, Capote finally went to the office of *Mademoiselle* with his story 'Miriam'; and so began a series of lucky meetings, a chain of good fortune that would characterise his life, leading one friend to call him 'a darling of the gods'. 'Miriam', initially read by Rita Smith, was published in 1945 (and won the O. Henry Memorial Award the following year). Enchanted by Capote, Rita Smith introduced him to her sister, the writer Carson McCullers, who recommended Capote to Robert Linscott, a senior editor at Random House. In October 1945, Linscott signed a contract for Capote's unfinished novel *Other Voices, Other Rooms*, telling him: 'Now you're going to be a writer and an artist, we're going to support you, take care of you. You're like a racehorse.' Success and two further novels followed, with the publication of *The Grass Harp* in 1951 and *Breakfast at Tiffany's* in 1958.

Capote then began to consider a new approach to writing a novel, 'something on a large scale that would have the credibility of fact, the immediacy of film, the depth and freedom of prose, and the precision of poetry'. In 1959, he found his subject: an obscure murder in Kansas. For six years he immersed himself in the story, published in 1965 as *In Cold Blood*, which became an international bestseller. This revolutionary journalistic novel was to be the high point of Capote's writing career. His last work, *Answered Prayers*, a non-fiction novel about his rich and famous friends (most of whom saw the few published chapters as an act of betrayal and dropped him), remained unfinished on his death in 1984 from drugs and alcohol.

A film version of *The Grass Harp*, starring Piper Laurie, Sissy Spacek and Walter Matthau, was released in 1995. The producer and director, Charles Matthau, first heard about Capote's novel from the book agent Melanie Ray, who told him it was the best thing she'd read that had not been made into a film. Matthau read the book and agreed. But, like the unsuccessful stage adaptation of *The Grass Harp* written by Capote that premiered in 1952, film cannot capture the truth of this novel, for its essence is contained in Capote's prose, as breathtaking and clear-cut as a diamond. As Capote himself said of *The Grass Harp*: 'It is very real to me, more real than anything I've ever written, probably ever will.' He told his editor while writing it that:

> it keeps me in a painful emotional state: memories are always breaking my heart, I cry – it is very odd, I seem to have no control over myself or what I am doing. But my vision is clear, and if I can half execute that vision it will be a beautiful book.

53 . *The Tin Drum*
by
GÜNTER GRASS
(1 9 2 7 –)

‰

'GRANTED: I AM AN INMATE of a mental hospital; my keeper is watching me, he never lets me out of his sight' – these are the opening words of Günter Grass's wildly imagined, irreverent, fiercely satirical first novel, *The Tin Drum*, which caused an international sensation when it was first published in 1959. The narrator is Oskar Matzerath, and in his hospital cell, on a ream of virgin paper bought for him by his keeper Bruno, he writes the fantastic story of his life. Beginning in 1899 with the story of his maternal grandmother, Oskar then recounts his mother's illicit love for her cousin Jan Bronski, her marriage to Alfred Matzerath, his own birth in their Danzig grocery store on the explosive border between Germany and Poland, and his life in Germany through all its cataclysmic upheaval of the mid twentieth century: the rise of Nazism, the Second World War, and the subsequent division of Germany into East and West.

Oskar is a complex, cheeky, precocious child, even as he turns thirty, boastful and guilt-ridden (he holds himself responsible for the deaths of his beloved mother, Alfred Matzerath and Jan Bronski). He is possessed of an errant vitality and chameleon-like talent for invisibility, which enable him to survive the extraordinary events of his time. His mental development is complete at birth, so as a newborn he is able to understand and judge his parents' first responses to their only child. His presumed father, Alfred Matzerath, sees his new son, Oskar, taking over the grocery store one day. His mother, Agnes, instead sees Oskar on his third birthday with a toy drum. Oskar quickly realises 'that Mama and this Mr Matzerath were not equipped to understand or respect my decisions whether positive or negative' and takes his life into his own hands. Inspired by the drumming wings of a moth against a light bulb, he falls in love with the toy drum his mother promises and when his third birthday arrives, brand-new red-and-white tin drum safe in his arms, he decides 'that I would never under any circumstances be a politician, much less a grocer, that I would stop right there, remain as I was — and so I did; for many years I not only stayed the same size but clung to the same attire.' Vowing never to enter the grownup world, Oskar refuses to grow at all. He practises his drumming, conversing with his drum which beats out the stories of his life, using it to communicate rage and rebellion, and eventually using it purely as a musical instrument, which brings him a recording deal, fame and fortune.

The Tin Drum is remarkable for the vast reach of Grass's vision, the irrepressible energy and wit of his prose, the warm, fully fleshed portraits of his eccentric characters and the bawdy humour he mixes into the tragic history of his country. Grass realised he wanted to be a writer when he was twelve years old, and, following the war, he went to art school, and wrote poetry and drama. All his myriad talents are evident in *The Tin Drum*, in his dazzling, inventive visual and dramatic imagination and the muscular, virtuosic powers of his prose. The novel is like a theatrical monologue that shifts from the first to the third person – Oskar refers to himself alternately as 'I' and 'Oskar' – as Oskar directly addresses the reader, discussing the best way to approach writing a novel, how to begin, where he needs to rewrite, clarify, correct: 'I have just read that last paragraph. I am not too well satisfied, but Oskar's pen ought to be, for writing tersely and succinctly, it has managed, as terse, succinct accounts so often do, to exaggerate and mislead, if not to lie.' This hybrid novel pieced together by the voice of a drum-wielding midget was demanded by the history with which Grass was dealing. The normal conventions of fiction would not do for it, as he made powerfully clear in his Nobel Prize lecture speech: 'Painstaking detail, sensitive psychoanalysis, slice-of-life realism – no such techniques can handle our monstrous raw materials.'

Grass's imagination is boundless and *The Tin Drum* teems with unforgettable scenes and images: Oskar's grandmother's five potato-coloured skirts, four of which she wears at a time and beneath which men, including her grandson Oskar, find comfort; the black horse's head pulled from the Baltic Sea seething with light green and darker eels, an image that recurs and becomes fused with his mother. Then there is a ribald scene in which Oskar seduces a virginal woman by impersonating Satan. As he struggles to come, all the time assuring her that 'Satan is coming', he holds a dialogue with 'the Satan who has dwelt within me since my baptism. I scolded: Don't be a killjoy Satan . . . It's not a bit like you old boy.' But Satan's not in the mood, so virtue triumphs.

Günter Grass was born in 1927 in Danzig-Langfuhr (now Gdansk in Poland), where his parents owned a grocery store (his mother, like Oskar's grandmother, was from Kashubia). Grass served as a soldier in the Second World War and at seventeen was taken prisoner in an American war camp. On his release, he worked in the Rhineland and studied to be a stonemason in Düsseldorf. When the Düsseldorf Art Academy opened in 1948, he studied painting and sculpture, earning his living as a tomb-stone cutter and jazz drummer. In 1956, Grass moved to Paris, where he lived until 1959 and wrote *The Tin Drum*. The novel was successfully adapted for the screen in the 1979 film *The Tin Drum*, directed by Volker Schlöndorff and starring David Bennent as Oskar, which won the 1979 Academy Award for Best Foreign Film and the Palme d'Or at Cannes. The richly realised, surreal film was later banned in Oklahoma, USA, in the 1990s by a judge who ruled it was pornographic.

Grass has been actively involved in German politics, in the 1960s working in the election campaigns of the Social Democrat Party. He is a prolific author of many novels, including *Cat and Mouse* (1961) and *The Dog Years* (1963) – which together with *The Tin Drum* form the Danzig Trilogy – *The Flounder* (1977), *The Call of the Toad* (1992) and *My Century* (1999). In 1999, Grass was awarded the Nobel Prize for Literature. In his moving Nobel lecture, he spoke passionately of the need for controversial storytellers, who challenge the status quo and naturally side with losers. He spoke of the urge to tell stories as 'a form of survival' and traced his own impulse to write to the outbreak of the Second World War and the execution of his mother's favourite cousin who, like Jan Bronski, worked for the Polish post office in the Free City of Danzig. In a response to the ringing words of Theodor Adorno ('It is barbaric to write a poem after Auschwitz'), Grass states that it was the duty of writers in German to 'take the goose step out of German' and to transform writing into memory. 'The only way writing after Auschwitz, poetry or prose, could proceed was by becoming memory and preventing the past from coming to an end.'

TOBSHA LEARNER

- *The Tin Drum* by Günter Grass
- *Orlando* by Virginia Woolf
- *The Vivisector* by Patrick White
- *In the Skin of a Lion* by Michael Ondaatje
- *The End of the Affair* by Graham Greene
- *The Handmaid's Tale* by Margaret Atwood
- *Anna Karenina* by Leo Tolstoy
- *East of Eden* by John Steinbeck
- *The Red and the Black* by Stendhal
- *Love in the Time of Cholera* by Gabriel García Márquez

Born in London, Tobsha Learner is a writer whose best-selling books include *Quiver* (1998), *The Witch of Cologne* (2003) and *Tremble* (2004).

5 4 . One Hundred Years of Solitude

by

GABRIEL GARCÍA MÁRQUEZ

(1 9 2 8 –)

ONE HUNDRED YEARS OF SOLITUDE is the story of Macondo, a Latin-American mountain village, and its founder, José Arcadio Buendía, his wife Ursula, their children and many descendants. Like everything else in Gabriel García Márquez's extraordinary, baroque novel, the very town itself has sprung from love and death: the story of its founding is a romance of passion, violence, ghosts and dreams.

When José Arcadio murders a man who has mocked his virility, the loneliness of the dead man's ghost so torments José Arcadio that he packs up his house and leaves his home town, travelling across the mountains with his wife and friends. In a parody of Exodus, the group heads 'toward the land that no one had promised them' and many months later, camped by a river like a 'torrent of frozen glass', José Arcadio dreams of a city called

Macondo. The following morning, José Arcadio orders the men to clear the land and Macondo is founded.

The story Márquez relates in Macondo embraces seven generations of the Buendía family, all named with the same few names (Aureliano, Arcadio, Remedios, Amaranta, Ursula). It spans well over one hundred years of history, which take in tides of growth and decay, thirty-two armed uprisings organised by Colonel Aureliano Buendía, and the coming of the gringos who wreak havoc with their railway and banana industry, and wantonly massacre 3000 banana plantation workers − an episode that is instantly wiped from Macondo's history. The events of the novel, including this massacre, are drawn from the history of Colombia, from its Spanish colonial days and independence from Spain in 1820, to its civil wars and the coming of American imperialism, fuelled by the introduction of bananas into the United States in 1870 and the rise of the United Fruit Company, which had banana plantations throughout the Caribbean.

One Hundred Years of Solitude is told in circles, weaving backwards and forwards through time like the mysterious parchments of José Arcadio's friend, the gypsy Melquíades, which are not ordered according to conventional, sequential time, but concentrate a century of daily episodes 'in such a way that they coexisted in one instant'. The novel concludes with one of the most haunting and beautiful endings in fiction − and opens with one of fiction's most poignant and arresting sentences: 'Many years later, as he faced the firing squad, Colonel Aureliano Buendía was to remember that distant afternoon when his father took him to discover ice.' The day they discovered ice, preposterously magical in equatorial

Macondo, the world was so young that 'many things lacked names'. Again, Márquez evokes the Old Testament, in this case Genesis and Adam's calling of things by name, which is echoed again in one of the book's more outlandish episodes — an insomnia plague. The people of Macondo are struck down by such profound sleeplessness that they lose their memories and, as their memories fade, they forget the names of things. José Arcadio Buendía solves the problem by marking everything in the town with its name and use: '*This is the cow. She must be milked every morning so that she will produce milk.*'

The naming of things, the finding of language able to describe life in Colombia, was the biggest challenge Márquez faced in writing *One Hundred Years of Solitude*: 'My most important problem was destroying the lines of demarcation that separate what seems real from what seems fantastic.' In his novel, Márquez seamlessly mixes the supernatural and everyday life, as if it were quite usual on a man's death for a 'light rain of tiny yellow flowers' to fall from the sky, or for the most beautiful girl ever born to blithely ascend to heaven while folding sheets in the garden, waving goodbye as she floats heavenward. This blend of the fantastic and the real caused a sensation when the novel was first published in 1967 (in English in 1970). *One Hundred Years of Solitude* became an international bestseller and sparked widespread interest in what was called 'magic realism', a term first used by German art critic Franz Roh in 1925 to describe the revolt against the accepted view of the material world by Expressionist painting, with its fantastic use of colour and distortion of form.

Márquez, the oldest of twelve children, was born in 1928 in

Aracataca, a small town in the Caribbean north of Colombia. He grew up with his maternal grandparents, who had moved to Aracataca following the War of a Thousand Days (1899–1902) in which his grandfather had been a colonel, and lived in a big house filled with ghosts. A trip back to the house when he was twenty-three 'aroused in me such an irresistible longing to write so I would not die'. He studied law at the National University of Colombia in Bogotá, later moving to the University of Cartagena following the April 1948 riots in Bogotá that led to the closure of the university. The same year, he began to work as a journalist and to write stories, inspired by Jorge Luis Borges's translation of Kafka's *The Metamorphosis*: 'I didn't know anyone was allowed to write things like that. If I had known, I would have started writing a long time ago.'

His first book, *Leafstorm and Other Stories* (in which Macondo first appeared), was published in 1955. Márquez travelled to Europe as a correspondent for *El Espectador* and later for the Cuban news agency. In 1958, he married Mercedes Barcha, whom he had loved since she was thirteen. They moved to Mexico, where, after several years of writer's block, Márquez had a vision that told him to tell a story the way his grandmother told her stories, and gave him the opening line of *One Hundred Years of Solitude*. He went straight home and began to write. He has since published many books, including *The Autumn of the Patriarch* (1975), *Chronicle of a Death Foretold* (1981) and *Love in the Time of Cholera* (1985).

In 1982, Márquez was awarded the Nobel Prize for Literature for his work, 'in which the fantastic and the realistic are combined in a richly composed world of imagination, reflecting a continent's life and conflicts'. In a moving speech, Márquez stressed the immeasurable pain and violence suffered by the people of Latin America, and their 'outsized reality':

A reality not of paper, but one that lives within us and determines each instant of our countless daily deaths, and that nourishes a source of insatiable creativity, full of sorrow and beauty, of which this roving and nostalgic Colombian is but one cipher more, singled out by fortune.

NICK EARLS

- *Gulliver's Travels* by Jonathan Swift. It's easy to see *Gulliver's Travels* now as a well-realised piece of speculative fiction – it is this, and, as a work of imagination, it transcends its era. At a deeper level, it relentlessly satirises the politics of early eighteenth-century Britain, while adopting convincingly the style of the time for published journals of voyages. The closer you look at this book, the better it becomes, and the less it is to do with a land of little people and a land of big people.
- *One Hundred Years of Solitude* by Gabriel García Márquez. This was probably the first novel I read by any author from South America. Gabriel García Márquez's writing jolted me with its different perspectives from those of my world – honour and logic and rules work differently; even the leaves have a different way of

falling. Perhaps this was the first story I read that
was bound to a world of heat and humidity, and that
showed them — the heat and humidity — working in
ways that meant something to me. [Nick Earls is based
in Brisbane, Queensland, south of the Tropic of
Capricorn.]

➳ *The Sportswriter* by Richard Ford. *The Sportswriter* is
perhaps the ultimate lesson in building a story around a
character, and in turning a meticulous approach to
detail into compelling fiction. Novels almost never feel
this real.

Australian writer and former GP Nick Earls is the author of
nine books, including the bestselling *Zigzag Street* (1996) and
Bachelor Kisses (1998).

5 5 . *The Quest for Christa T.*
by
C H R I S T A   W O L F
(1 9 2 9 –)

✺

CHRISTA WOLF'S SECOND NOVEL, *The Quest for Christa T.*, is the story of
a long-limbed, dreamy young woman, Christa T., recollected by a
friend who first meets her at school during the dying months of the
Second World War. The unnamed narrator is immediately struck
by the self-contained individuality of the new girl — even her
stockings retain their distinctness, defying absorption into the
larger historical moment: 'and her stockings, darned all the way up
the calf, were ugly and clumsily darned stockings, not the proud
sacrifice of a German woman in the war's fifth year amid a textiles
shortage . . .' Published in East Germany in 1968, *The Quest for
Christa T.* is also the story of historical upheaval. From childhood in
Nazi Germany and westward flight from the advancing Red Army,
through to the birth of the German Democratic Republic (GDR) in
1949, a brief moment of hopefulness in the promise of the new

communist regime, disillusionment, then despair following the brutal Soviet attack on Budapest in 1956: 'Nothing is so difficult as turning one's attention to things as they really are, to events as they really occur, after one has spent a long time not doing so . . .' When it first appeared in English in 1970, *The Quest for Christa T.* was widely acclaimed as one of the best novels in German published since the war. *The Times* reviewer wrote: 'In a desert — and the [East German] literary scene is a desert — you have to look out patiently for any sign of life, but the sight of a beautiful flower may suddenly overwhelm you. Such a book is *The Quest for Christa T.*'

The Quest for Christ T. is a profound, troubled meditation on life and words and identity. 'She was afraid of the imprecision and ineptness of words. She knew that they do harm, the insidious harm of bypassing life, which she fears almost more than the great catastrophes.' Craving meaning, Christa T. has written diaries, notes, letters and scribble on scraps of paper, from which the narrator attempts to put her friend's life into words, first abandoning then drawing on her own and others' memories in order to see Christa more clearly.

Wolf's powers are remarkable. Her writing, possessed of an almost brutal insistence, a penetrating rigour, searching, mistrustful, courageous, conjures scenes and emotions, silences and absences — those fleeting things glimpsed out of the corner of an eye — of such subtle delicacy that their accumulated effect is quite overwhelming. Through a gradual accretion of layers, a stripping away and baring, then a re-collecting, with abrupt shifts between past and present, Wolf recreates a life, a time, leaving the traces of her quest in words: 'You haven't understood a thing if you shrug your shoulders, turn away, turn from her, Christa T., and attend to grander and more useful lives. My concern is to attend to her.'

The narrator's painstaking, determined search for her friend is prompted by her tragic death at too young an age. On the novel's opening page, she tells us: 'I feel she is disappearing. There she lies, in her village cemetery, beneath the two buckthorn bushes, dead among the dead.' From this statement, Wolf tells the story of an apparently ordinary life, of a girl who goes to school, university, drifts along, becomes a teacher, falls in love, marries a country vet – and dies aged thirty-five. Yet through her relentless probing, her starting out and turning back, Wolf's narrator gradually reveals the rare and extraordinary beneath the ordinary, and the inestimable value of a single life. And, while the valuing of this single life is particularly resonant, heretical, in a socialist state whose ideology explicitly values the group over the individual, the story of Christa's quiet refusal to conform to the expectations of society is essentially a celebration of the individual in any society anywhere, whose quest, like Christa's own, is 'To become oneself, with all one's strength. Difficult.' Christa T. is 'trying out the possibilities of life until nothing should be left . . .'

Christa Wolf was born in 1929 in Landsberg an der Warthe (now the Polish town Gorzow Wielkpolski) in Germany. Here she lived until she was sixteen, when her family, fleeing the 1945 post-war invasion of Germany by Soviet troops, escaped to Mecklenburg, which became part of the new German Democratic Republic founded in 1949. Wolf joined the Socialist Unity Party (SED), and became a committed socialist. Although she was critical of the East German regime, it later allowed her the privileges of a successful writer, including the freedom to travel beyond its borders to the West. From 1949, Wolf studied German literature for four years in Jena and Leipzig universities, meeting her husband, Gerhard Wolf, in 1951, with whom she has two daughters. Wolf then worked as a writer and critic for a literary journal, as a research assistant for the German Writers' Union from 1953, and as an editor for the publishing company Neues Leben. In 1959, she moved to Halle, where she worked in a factory for three years before moving to Berlin in 1962.

Wolf's first novel, *The Divided Heaven*, the story of a girl who chooses to remain in East Germany rather than flee to the West with her lover, was published in 1963. It won the Heinrich Mann Prize and in 1963 was made into a successful film directed by Konrad Wolf. Christa Wolf's experience writing the screenplay influenced her approach to her next novel, the fragmented, intercut *The Quest for Christa T.* Published the year of the Prague Spring and its violent suppression of democratic expression, the novel's subjective story of a woman unable to live within the bounds of the GDR was widely criticised in East Germany and attacked the following year at a writers conference. During the 1970s, Wolf was put under surveillance by the Stasi, the East German secret police, and her account of this time, *What Remains*, was published in 1990. Following a trip to Greece, Wolf became fascinated by its ancient myths. Her book *Cassandra: A Novel and Four Essays*, published in 1983, is based on this journey, and she returns to Greek mythology in her 1996 novel *Medea*.

Although critical of the GDR, Wolf argued for its continued existence as a separate state and against its absorption into the

Federal Republic of Germany. Following the reunification of Germany in 1990, Wolf was attacked by West German critics for the support the former GDR had given her as a writer. Her moral authority was further questioned when it was revealed she'd cooperated with the Stasi from 1959 to 1961. Wolf nevertheless continues to be one of Germany's most perceptive and astute commentators. In 2003, she published *One Day a Year: 1960–2000*, a record of her experiences on 27 September over a period of forty years, initially prompted by a request from a Moscow newspaper inspired by Maxim Gorky's 'One Day in the World' project begun in 1936. Of *One Day a Year*, Wolf writes:

> the need to be known, even with our purely problematic features, our errors and mistakes, lies at the heart of all literature and is the motive force of this book. We shall see whether the time for such a venture has come yet.

JAMES BRADLEY

I'm uncomfortable with the idea of the classic, just as I'm uneasy with top tens or best-evers; books are things we make new each time we read them, and that speak to us in different ways at different stages of our lives. And while I think there are works that seem to contain something infinite, something ineffable and mysteriously human, that speaks across time and space, I'd be deeply reluctant to try to reduce them to a mere handful, for any list I could make would necessarily be provisional, a subset of a larger conversation, which we join through the act of reading, one that existed before us and will continue after us. Which is itself an affirmation of a sort, a recognition of the canon not as something fixed, but somehow living.

Australian writer James Bradley is the author of *Wrack* (1997), *The Deep Field* (1999) and *The Resurrectionist* (2006).

5 6 .   The   Words   to   Say   It
by
M A R I E   C A R D I N A L
(1 9 2 9 –)

&

THE WORDS TO SAY IT is the story of a difficult birth, an ultimately triumphant odyssey through near-death and madness. to life. Dedicated to 'the doctor who helped me be born', Marie Cardinal's autobiographical novel recounts her birth and delivery from her mother – but the birth and delivery are not as we commonly understand them, and the doctor who delivers her is not an obstetrician. He is a Freudian analyst and the psychological birth he oversees is as traumatic, bloody and physically demanding as any physical birth. In a seamlessly constructed, compelling narrative, Cardinal writes the rich layers of her character's experience: her three-year unexplained haemorrhaging that no drug nor doctor can cure; the regular visits to her analyst in a Parisian suburb; her growing recognition that he can help her, despite her scepticism; the flow of words that replaces her flow of blood and revives her sun-drenched, jasmine-scented childhood under the blue sky of Algeria. *The Words to Say It* is an extraordinary story about what it means to be a woman born into the constraints of middle-class, twentieth-century western Europe, about mothers, inheritance and madness, and about the alchemical potency of words. The Swedish director Ingmar Bergman, whose films plumb the depths of the psyche, called *The Words to Say It* 'One of the most remarkable books I have ever read'.

Published in France in 1975 and translated into English in 1983, *The Words to Say It* became an international bestseller and a classic of psychoanalytical literature. The novel opens with a description of the damp, poorly lit cul-de-sac in a Parisian suburb that will become the narrator's salvation. For seven years, every Monday, Wednesday and Friday, the cul-de-sac is her life: 'I know how the rain falls here, how the inhabitants protect themselves from the cold. I know how, in summer, a life which is almost rustic establishes itself with geraniums in pots and cats sleeping in the sun.' The narrator has escaped from a sanatorium with a single desperate purpose: to enter one particular house in this street to see the doctor she hopes will save her life. Her psychological collapse so horrendously manifested in physical symptoms – torrents of blood flow almost incessantly from between her legs – that she is forced to realise there are only two paths left for her to travel: analysis with this noted Freudian psychoanalyst or suicide. As a university-educated thirty-something woman with three children, for their sake, she chooses the former.

The rigorous, relentless analysis she undergoes is a strict, traditional Freudian one: she speaks into the silence of her doctor's room while he sits listening behind her. He is not interested in her physical symptoms, her bleeding; he is interested only in her stories, her words: 'Talk, say whatever comes into your head; try not to choose or reflect, or in any way compose your sentences. Everything is important, every word.' Miraculously, without drugs or operations, through words alone the doctor achieves what no other has been able to: her bleeding ceases immediately. But this is only the beginning.

No gynecologist, psychiatrist or neurologist had ever acknowledged that the blood came from the Thing. On the contrary, I was told the Thing came from the blood.
'Women are often "nervous" because their gynecological equilibrium is precarious, very delicate.'

She discovers that she is ashamed not of the blood that had been flooding out of her, but of 'what was going on inside of me, of this uproar, of this disorder, of this agitation; no one should look, no one should know, not even the doctor. I was ashamed of the madness.' This is the Thing, the unknown force inside her, that she must uncover and articulate in order to live — and to do so she must travel back on a wave of words to her troubled childhood in Algeria.

Several months into the analysis, her doctor begins to interrupt her talk. His interventions are infrequent but their effect is mind-opening. 'Such and such a word, what does it make you think of?' he asks. And she discovers that the word he has picked out from the sea of words is 'the key to open a door I had never even seen'.

Through this painstaking process of picking through her words, she returns to life, utterly transformed into herself. *The Words to Say It* is remarkable for the skill with which Cardinal weaves together the two strands of her narrative: the ordinary chronology of her present, chaotic life in the muted light of Paris as she regularly attends her appointments with her doctor, struggling to survive her devastating symptoms while bringing up her three young children (her husband lives in Canada), and the uncontrollable associative chronology of the meandering path of her memories of her Algerian childhood in the 1930s and '40s.

The Words to Say It is astonishing for its story of the extraordinary, healing power of words and the marvel of the 'beautiful, complicated organization of the human mind'. Because her analysis is Freudian, which is so focused on words, the novel is engaged at a profound level with the naming of things – with the finding of words – in order to delineate (and thereby diffuse the terrific power of) the unnamed, which she initially calls the Thing: 'Words were boxes, they contained material that was alive.' And it is words that are her guide through the labyrinth of her past and that become her road to life:

> I began to speak of my mother, never stopping until the end
> of the analysis. Over the years I explored the very depths of
> her being, as though she were a dark cavern. Thus did I
> make the acquaintance of the woman she wanted me to be.

Born in Algeria in 1929, Marie Cardinal studied philosophy in Paris and has taught at the universities of Salonika, Lisbon and

Montreal. Her first novel, *Ecouter la Mer*, was published in 1962 and won the Prix International du Premier Roman. In 1983, a film adaptation of *The Words to Say It* was released in France: *Les Mots Pour Le Dire*. Directed by José Pinheiro, it starred Nicole Garcia as Marie, for which she was nominated for a César Award for best actress in 1984.

ROBYN ARIANRHOD

- *The Power and the Glory* by Graham Greene
- *Anna Karenina* by Leo Tolstoy
- *Portrait of the Artist as a Young Man* by James Joyce
- *Paradise* by Toni Morrison
- *Remembering Babylon* by David Malouf
- *The Waves* by Virginia Woolf
- *The Mayor of Casterbridge* by Thomas Hardy
- *The Glass Bead Game* by Hermann Hesse
- *Briefing for a Descent into Hell* by Doris Lessing
- *Crime and Punishment* by Fyodor Dostoyevsky

Australian mathematician and writer Dr Robyn Arianrhod teaches mathematics at Monash University, Melbourne. She is the author of the acclaimed *Einstein's Heroes: Imagining the World Through the Language of Mathematics*, published in 2003.

5 7 . *B e l o v e d*

by

T O N I   M O R R I S O N

(1 9 3 1 –)

⚘

BELOVED IS THE STORY of love stretched to the furthest bounds of human endurance, of possession and slavery. Toni Morrison's devastating novel opens in 1873 in Cincinnati, and travels back from the haunted present to the agonised past of its central character, Sethe, a one-time slave. The novel's first words are a description of Sethe's haunted house – '124 was spiteful. Full of a baby's venom' – in which she lives with her daughter, Denver. Her two sons, Howard and Buglar, have run off, scared by the ghostly activity, the shattered mirror, the tiny handprints in the cake, and Sethe's mother-in-law, Baby Suggs, dies soon after. When Sethe and ten-year-old Denver decide to call the ghost and it doesn't come, Sethe reminds Denver that it – her dead baby – was not even two years old when she died. ' "For a baby she throws a powerful spell," said Denver. "No more powerful than the way I loved her,"

Sethe answered.' It is this power — of Sethe's love for her dead baby, of the baby's need for her love — that drives the extraordinary events of Morrison's fiercely imagined, superbly executed fifth novel. There is not a word out of place in this book.

Out of the blue, Sethe and Denver's cloistered lives are interrupted by Sethe's old friend Paul D., whom Sethe finds sitting on her porch one day. She has not seen him since her flight from 'Sweet Home', Kentucky, where they were slaves together with Sethe's husband Halle, eighteen years before. Paul D., 'the last of the Sweet Home men', brings the past back to Sethe and slowly the traumatic events of her life begin to well within her steely heart until she can contain them no longer — for Sethe, 'with iron eyes and backbone to match', has long been holding on to terrible secrets. Paul D., with his soulful, abiding presence and own horrors to relieve, brings her a kind of comfort. He has become 'the kind of man who could walk into a house and make the women cry'. The novel, told in three parts and narrated mostly in the third person, is beautifully constructed. Broken into fragments, the stories of Sethe and Paul D. are recollected through conversations, memories and the interweaving of the past with Sethe and Denver's present life in the strange isolated house on the edge of town.

Morrison's novel is exceptional for the emotional depths she plumbs in her characters, whose fierce spirits remain unbroken despite their lives riddled with pain and unutterable degradation. As Baby Suggs says: 'Not a house in the country ain't packed to the rafters with some dead Negro's grief . . .' With her extraordinarily rich, versatile and muscular prose, Morrison seems to have forged a new language of the human heart and soul, one that can encompass untold emotional shades of love and loneliness and need, pride and longing for freedom. Sethe's mother-in-law, Baby Suggs, is a deep presence in the novel. On Saturday afternoons she would go to a clearing, followed by every black man, woman and child, and say a prayer on a large rock before exhorting the children to laugh, the men to dance and the women to cry. Baby Suggs 'decided that, because slave life had "busted her legs, back, head, eyes, hands, kidneys, womb and tongue," she had nothing left to make a living with but her heart – which she put to work at once', becoming an 'unchurched preacher'.

Also remarkable is Morrison's portrayal of her characters' ambivalent ties to the American land. Sethe remembers Sweet Home: 'although there was not a leaf on that farm that did not make her want to scream, it rolled itself out before her in shameless beauty . . .' And Paul D., who after each of his five escapes from captivity, walks across the land, trying to resist its beauty: 'And in all those escapes he could not help being astonished by the beauty of this land that was not his.' Following the Civil War, he walks across the earth relishing his freedom to eat, walk and sleep anywhere, still determined not to let himself be seduced by the beautiful, alien land: 'On nights when the sky was personal, weak with the weight of its own stars, he made himself not love it.'

Published in 1987, *Beloved* won the Pulitzer Prize for Fiction and became a bestseller. Set around the time of the Civil War, it is based on the true story of a runaway slave woman, Margaret Garner, and other slave narratives.

Toni Morrison, born Chloe Anthony Wofford in 1931 in Lorain, Ohio, grew up in the Midwest and went to Howard

University in Washington DC. She graduated with a Bachelor of Arts in 1953 and completed an MA at Cornell University where she wrote a thesis on Virginia Woolf and William Faulkner. Morrison has since taught at universities, including Texas Southern University, Howard University, the State University of New York and Princeton University. She worked as a fiction editor at Random House from 1965, where she established a list of African-American writing. Morrison has published eight novels – her first, *The Bluest Eye*, was published in 1970, her most recent, *Love*, was published in 2003. In 1993, Morrison won the Nobel Prize for Literature.

In her review of *Beloved* in *The Guardian* (16 October 1987), writer and critic A.S. Byatt brilliantly sums up Morrison's achievement, calling it 'an American masterpiece', one that reassesses the novels of writers like Melville and Hawthorne, who:

> wrote riddling allegories about the nature of evil, the
> haunting of unappeased spirits, the inverted opposition of
> blackness and whiteness. Toni Morrison has with plainness
> and grace and terror — and judgment — solved the riddle,
> and showed us the world which haunted theirs.

GABY NAHER

- *Nights at the Circus* by Angela Carter
- *Lillian's Story* by Kate Grenville
- *The Poisonwood Bible* by Barbara Kingsolver

- *The Vintner's Luck* by Elizabeth Knox
- *Fall on Your Knees* by Ann-Marie MacDonald
- *Beloved* by Toni Morrison
- *In the Skin of a Lion* by Michael Ondaatje
- *Anna Karenina* by Leo Tolstoy
- *Nana* by Emile Zola

Australian writer Gaby Naher is the author of four books, including the novel *The Underwharf* (1995), her memoir *The Truth About My Fathers* (2002) and *Wrestling the Dragon: In Search of the Boy Lama Who Defied China* (2004).

5 8 . R a b b i t , R u n
by
J O H N U P D I K E
(1 9 3 2 –)

∞

PUBLISHED IN 1960, RABBIT, RUN is the story of four months in the life of 26-year-old Harry 'Rabbit' Angstrom. Nicknamed Rabbit as a boy, Harry is a six foot three, one-time regional basketball player – 'So tall, he seems an unlikely rabbit, but the breadth of white face, the pallor of his blue irises, and a nervous flutter under his brief nose as he stabs a cigarette into his mouth partially explain the nickname' – which is further explained by the novel's title: Harry has a fleet-footed tendency to flight. In his youth, this flightiness served him well, making him a star athlete, but it does not fit so well with married life in small town Mt. Judge, a suburb of Brewer, Pennsylvania. Rabbit's life peaked on the basketball court and has been winding down ever since into suburban tedium: he is now married with a two-year-old son, Nelson; his wife, Janice, is heavily pregnant with their second child; they live in a shabby rented apartment, and he feels a fraud in his job as a demonstrator of the MagiPeel Peeler at local five-and-dime stores. Like that of the film *American Beauty*, Updike's subject is small-town American suburbia, which he mines to its depths for its moments of wonder: 'the same old middle-class middle that continues to charm me and that I continue to investigate as if it was going to reveal the secret of life', as he called it in a 1980 interview.

Rabbit, Run opens on an evening in early spring. Rabbit, on his way home from work, comes across a group of boys playing basketball in an alley and can't resist joining their game: 'That old stretched-leather feeling makes his whole body go taut, gives his arms wings. It feels like he's reaching down through years to touch this tautness.' Exhilarated, Rabbit continues home, tossing away his cigarettes in a gesture of new beginning. 'The month is March. Love makes the air light. Things start anew.' Rabbit, ever hopeful, returns home to find his wife watching TV, surrounded by the wreckage of domestic life – an empty cocktail glass, choked ashtray, newspapers, broken toys, 'a piece of bent cardboard that went with some break-fast-box cutout'. It all closes around Rabbit like a net. When he goes out to collect their abandoned son (left by Janice with his grand-parents) and car, Janice casually asks him to get some cigarettes for her. Something in the tone of her voice freezes him. He leaves the apartment and runs. Rabbit has no clear idea why he runs – it is an impulse; he just knows there is more to life than this.

Originally subtitled 'A Movie', *Rabbit, Run* is written in the present tense, with the immediacy of cinema – and the novel's seductive, conversational rhythms roll along as if it is not going to unfold the tragedy it does. Updike is obsessed with the visual and his childhood ambition was to be a cartoonist for *The New Yorker*. After graduating cum summa laude as English major from Harvard in 1954, and working briefly in New York, Updike, whose favourite painter is Vermeer, spent a year at the Ruskin School of Drawing and Fine Art in Oxford, England. All this he brings to his writing: a cartoonist's ability to capture an idiosyncratic likeness with a few strokes; a painter's awareness of colour and form – the materiality of things; and Vermeer's fascination with light, his gift for conveying the luminous grace of ordinary stuff ('a junkheap of brown stalks and eroded timber that will in the summer bloom with an unwanted wealth of weeds, waxy green wands and milky pods of silk seeds and airy yellow heads almost liquid with pollen').

Through the beauty of his lucid, fresh-cut prose, sharp yet meditative and wonder-filled, Updike transforms 1950s suburban America into poetry – its TV, ads, household gadgets, dumb marriages, flirtations, sport, banal jobs, cars, cheap restaurants. And, at the centre of this suburban world, Rabbit runs urgently, impulsively seeking the soul of the universe he knows is there but cannot find, that old ecstatic feeling he has lost. He hears the call of the wild but cannot seem to get out of his suburban trap: 'Why was he set down here, why is this town, a dull suburb of a third-rate city, for him the center and index of a universe that contains immense prairies, mountains, deserts, forests, cities, seas?' After Rabbit flees Janice, driving west then circling back to Mt. Judge, he goes out on the town with his old basketball coach, Tothero.

So perfect, so consistent is the freedom into which the
clutter of the world has been vaporized by the simple
trigger of his decision, that all ways seem equally good ...
and not an atom of his happiness would be altered if
Tothero told him they were not going to meet two girls but
two goats, and they were not going to Brewer but to Tibet.

For Updike, writing is a fundamentally religious process: 'Any act
of description is, to some extent, an act of praise ... The Old
Testament God repeatedly says he wants praise, and I translate that to
mean that the world wants describing, the world wants to be observed
and "hymned".' In *Rabbit, Run*, Updike is concerned with sex and
religion and their complex embodiment in Rabbit, whose consuming
preoccupations are naked women and God. And there is something
about the soul in Rabbit that makes everyone love him: his forgiving
wife Janice; his coach Tothero; his lover, Ruth; the Episcopalian
minister Jack Eccles, 'with his throat manacled in white'; and Eccles'
Freud-reading wife, Lucy Eccles. Even Rabbit's parents-in-law, the
Springers, seem to love him more the further he runs from their
daughter. Women try to seduce him and men try to care for him. In
his attempt to explain his irresistible attraction, Rabbit says: 'I'm a
mystic ... I give people faith.' But although he is unable to resist the
love people shower on him, Rabbit quickly feels it as just one more
black bar on the prison of his small-town life. He gets restless – and
'with an effortlessness gathering out of a kind of sweet panic growing
lighter and quicker and quieter, he runs. Ah: runs. Runs.'

Updike was born in 1932 in Reading, Pennsylvania, and grew
up in nearby Shillington. His mother, an aspiring writer, and

father, a maths teacher, brought up their only child in a gentle, Lutheran household. Offered scholarships to two universities, Updike chose Harvard because of its prestigious, satrical *Lampoon* magazine, to which he contributed cartoons, then poems and prose. His childhood dream of contributing to the *New Yorker* was realised in 1954 and, on his return from England in 1955, Updike worked on the staff of the *New Yorker* for two years. Following the publication in 1957 of his first novel, *The Poorhouse Fair*, Updike moved to Massachusetts to become a full-time writer. His second novel, *Rabbit, Run*, was published in 1960 to wide acclaim, and it was made into a film in 1970 starring James Caan as Rabbit. Updike subsequently wrote three more Rabbit books: *Rabbit Redux* (1971), *Rabbit is Rich* (1981) and *Rabbit at Rest* (1990). Updike is a prolific author and has published more than forty books, including the 1984 novel *The Witches of Eastwick*, which was made into the Hollywood blockbuster of the same name, starring Jack Nicholson, Michelle Pfeiffer, Susan Sarandon and Cher.

LUKE DAVIES

The Leopard by Giuseppe Tomasi di Lampedusa. Truly, as everyone says it is, one of the great novels of the twentieth century. An intense study of the passage of time, bathed in the languid Sicilian light and the tragic glow of nostalgia, and capped off by one of the most astonishing and moving final paragraphs in all of literature.

w *Invisible Cities* by Italo Calvino. Marco Polo sits in the
Khan's garden, describing all the places he has visited in
his travels. But are they real? Architectural hallucina-
tions, metaphysical blueprints, and fantasies created of
little more than the shimmering light of mirages.

w *Blood Meridian* by Cormac McCarthy. Possibly a 'boys'
book', but one of the greatest nonetheless. The young
narrator lurches from one violent apocalyptic disaster
to the next beneath the great bowl of the sky in the Old
West in this, literature's most disturbing cowboy novel.
Visceral and brilliant.

w *The Good Soldier* by Ford Madox Ford. The last
Edwardian novel, or the first of the postmodern era? In
any case, this book, published in 1915, is clearly a
fulcrum. The omniscient narrator is gone; the largely
unreliable narrator will henceforth carry the torch.
Deeply moving and, beneath its exquisite veneer, deeply
troubling.

w *Heart of Darkness* by Joseph Conrad. Primal in the
extreme. Word for word, the densest book ever written.
Conrad seems to grasp not just the entire history of
Western imperialism, but the deep insanity of the
human condition.

w *Lolita* by Vladimir Nabokov. It's not just that it's a great
story, or that such eloquence and elegance could emerge
from one character's pathology and delusion.

It's that in the presence of Nabokov's greatness, the reader actually experiences an adrenalin rush; it's that the English language has never been such ruthless fun.

* *All Quiet on the Western Front* by Erich Maria Remarque. Deceptively simple, so pure and unadorned. Because it is so fable-like, it attains the quality of myth, and is perhaps the great war novel.

* The novels of William Faulkner. Where does one begin? *As I Lay Dying* for a bare-bones masterpiece. *Absalom, Absalom!*, say, or *The Sound and the Fury*, for something meaty and challenging. Take a deep breath, don't be overtired or distracted. Focus is everything with Faulkner; you have to submerge, alertly, for the full experience. The pace of modern life is making this experience difficult. (Writer's alert: Remember, read and enjoy Faulkner, but DO NOT try to write like him. It will end in tears.)

* *Nine Stories* by J.D. Salinger. We all know how important *The Catcher in the Rye* is. But *Nine Stories*, the lesser-known cousin, is simply glorious. 'The Laughing Man' is one of the most perfect short stories ever written. (Another contender for this short-story crown is 'Order of Insects' by William Gass, from his sublime collection *In the Heart of the Heart of the Country*.)

* *The Heart of the Matter* by Graham Greene. While Conrad sees the python and the vulture in us all,

Greene gives us greater benefit of the doubt, his starting point being that we are all, in fact, merely deeply flawed humans — going morally mouldy in the tropic heat.

Australian poet and novelist Luke Davies is the author of the bestselling and critically acclaimed novel *Candy* (1997), *Isabelle the Navigator* (2000) and five collections of poetry, including the award-winning *Totem* (2004).

5 9 . *Blood Meridian: or The Evening Redness in the West*

by

C O R M A C   M c C A R T H Y

(1 9 3 3 –)

❧

BLOOD MERIDIAN: OR THE EVENING REDNESS IN THE WEST is a story of violence unleashed by the westward expansion of the United States. Set in the aftermath of the Mexican–American war of 1846, the novel conjures the groups of men who roamed the desert wastelands, some (Americans) out to avenge themselves on the Mexicans, frustrated their war did not end with the conquest of Mexico, others employed by local governors as scalp-hunters, promised so much gold per Indian scalp – and all of them unleashing mayhem.

Into this nightmare world of brutal and lawless American, Mexican and Indian adventurers wanders the kid, a runaway from his motherless Tennessee home (in him, at fourteen, 'broods already a taste for mindless violence'); and above it all rides the massive judge, satanic and lucid, leading 'a pack of vicious looking humans

on unshod indian ponies'. Cormac McCarthy's vision is unrelenting as it erupts across the desert violence upon violence, each
episode more bloody and insane than the last.

The novel opens with the kid crouching by the fire on a winter's
night — outside are fields of snow and forests of a few last wolves —
watching his father who lies drunk. He runs away, across a haunted
landscape, never to return. On his journey south to New Orleans
then westwards, the kid is taken up by a group led by Captain
White, a soldier from the war against Mexico, which (despite the
treaty signed to end the war) he is still fighting with his team of
filibusters so that 'Americans will be able to get to California
without having to pass through our benighted sister republic . . .'
They trail across the desert until they are descended upon by a
troop of Indians, a 'legion of horribles, hundreds in number, half
naked or clad in costumes attic or biblical or wardrobed out of a
fevered dream with the skins of animals and silk finery and pieces
of uniform still tracked with the blood of prior owners'. From the
bloodbath that ensues, in which Captain White's men, living and
dead alike, are scalped (their 'bloody wigs' snatched from their
heads), there is one sole survivor: the kid.

The kid meets up with two renegade men, Toadvine and later
Bathcat, 'a fugitive from vandiemen's land', and the three join the
group of bounty hunters led by John Glanton, who are offered by the
governor in Chihuahua one hundred dollars apiece for Indian scalps
and one thousand for the head of a Mexican rebel. Glanton and his
men ride out of Chihuahua and at Glanton's side rides the judge.
Their scalping expeditions — their unleashed raging across a blood-
drenched and bone-scattered land — make some of the most

harrowing scenes it is possible to imagine. McCarthy's novel is one of the most disturbing and unsettling ever written, and most unsettling of all is the figure of the judge that lies at its black heart.

The judge has been likened to a crazed Captain Ahab of the desert – but the judge, depraved though he might be, is supremely in command of his mental faculties and has no Moby-Dick in his sights on whom he plans to unleash his vengeance for perceived wrongs. In McCarthy's vision, there is no perceived wrong, just evil born of itself in the heart of human beings, incarnate in the judge, under whose controlling gaze even the freedom of birds is an insult. As an old anchorite tells the kid: 'You can find meanness in the least of creatures, but when God made man the devil was at his elbow.' The judge is one of the most extraordinary creatures of literature: 'Towering over them all is the judge and he is naked dancing, his small feet lively and quick and now in doubletime and bowing to the ladies, huge and pale and hairless like an enormous infant.' He has just killed a man.

Over seven feet tall, twenty-four stone and completely hairless, the judge moves like a cat, knows the secrets of rocks, plays the fiddle better than any man, can shoot with his left and right hands ('is eitherhanded as a spider'), can ride and track, and is possessed of an almost supernatural intelligence. His gun is engraved with the Latin words 'Et in Arcadia Ego' (And I am in Arcadia). These words are engraved on a tomb in a painting by seventeenth-century French painter Nicolas Poussin and can be interpreted to mean that death is also in the most peaceful of rural communities (Arcadia) – death is everywhere. The judge, who 'seemed much satisfied with the world, as if his counsel had been sought at its creation', is a master of death. His apocalyptic vision is summed up in his pronouncement: 'War is God'. 'It makes no difference what men think of war, said the judge. War endures. As well ask men what they think of stone.' History, in the form of war, prevails, subverting moral law at every turn. *Blood Meridian* is based on historical events, drawing on the fighting that broke out along the Mexican border in the 1840s, and John Glanton and his 'expedition' are historical figures, recorded in Samuel Chamberlain's book *My Confession: Recollections of a Rogue*, the candid account of Chamberlain's violent adventures as a soldier in the Mexican War and its aftermath (not published until 1956, forty-eight years after his death in 1908).

McCarthy's novel is remarkable for its fully fleshed conjuring of one of the most nightmarish visions ever imagined in words, comparable to the surreal paintings of Bosch and Goya. More extraordinary is the astonishing beauty with which McCarthy evokes this hellish landscape of death, with his hypnotic, rolling rhythms and tormented, supernatural language: 'The thunder moved up from the southwest and lightning lit the desert all about them, blue and barren, great clanging reaches ordered out of the absolute night like some demon kingdom summoned up or changeling land . . .' McCarthy's bats are like 'dark satanic hummingbirds', scalped heads are like 'polyps bluely wet or luminescent melons cooling on some mesa of the moon'. As literary critic Eileen Battersby wrote in *The Irish Times*: 'Cormac McCarthy's violent, lyric masterpiece, *Blood Meridian*, acquires an amoral, apocalyptic dimension through the Miltonic grandeur of the language . . . it is a barbarously poetic odyssey through a hell without purpose.'

Cormac McCarthy was born in Rhode Island in 1933 and grew up near Knoxville, Tennessee. In 1951, he went to the University of Tennessee, where he majored in liberal arts, and in 1953 joined the US Army Air Force, in which he served for four years. He returned to university in 1957, where he twice won an award for creative writing. His first novel, *The Orchard Keeper*, was published in 1965 and won the Faulkner Award for a first novel, which brought him international acclaim. This was followed by three more violent Southern novels – *Outer Dark* (1968), *Child of God* (1973) and *Suttree* (1979), his most autobiographical novel. In 1981, he was given a MacArthur Fellowship (or 'Genius Grant'), awarded by the John D. and Catherine T. MacArthur Foundation, which he used to write *Blood Meridian*, published in 1985. In 1992, *All the Pretty Horses*, the first of the Border Trilogy, became an international bestseller and won the National Book Award. The remaining two books of the trilogy are *The Crossing* (1994) and *Cities of the Plain* (1998).

60. *Underworld*

by

DON DELILLO

(1 9 3 6 –)

࿇

'HE SPEAKS IN YOUR VOICE, American, and there's a shine in his eye that's halfway hopeful.' These are the opening words of *Underworld*, published in 1997, Don DeLillo's massive embrace of America across the last fifty years of the twentieth century. They refer to Cotter Martin, a young boy who's skipping school so he can go to a live-or-die baseball game between the Giants and the Dodgers in New York on 3 October 1951. But the words could equally apply to DeLillo himself and his extraordinary novel. For although his vision is haunted by violence, atomic weapons and waste, murders and the deaths of children from AIDS, drive-by shootings and beatings, *Underworld* sings with the life of its characters and DeLillo's beautiful, edgy prose, which beats out the syncopated rhythms of the American empire. As Michael Ondaatje so poetically put it: 'This book is an aria and a wolf whistle of our half-century. It contains multitudes.'

Underworld opens with a prologue called 'The Triumph of Death', about a baseball match that is won by a last-minute home-run. Up in the stands, Cotter Martin scrambles for the home-run ball, which has just won the game for his team, the Giants, and runs off with it, the raised seams of the ball 'pulsing in his hands'. This baseball is the fixed star of the novel, everything circles back to it on one level or another, and many years later it appears in the hand of the novel's central character, Nick Shay. Only for Nick, a Dodgers supporter, the precious ball is a symbol not of victory but of loss: 'It's about Branca making the pitch. It's all about losing.' If Nick, the ball and 'the mystery of loss' lie at the heart of the novel, then the atomic bomb hovers over it. Also at the game are Frank Sinatra, Jackie Gleason, Toots Shor and J. Edgar Hoover. When the winning run is hit, the crowd erupts in a flurry of flying paper. One glossy page drifts down onto J. Edgar Hoover's shoulder, a reproduction of a painting 'crowded with medieval figures who are dying or dead – a landscape of visionary havoc and ruin'. The painting, Pieter Bruegel's 'The Triumph of Death', reminds Hoover that he's just heard the Soviet Union has conducted an atomic test at a secret location. This news intrigues the conspiratorial FBI chief Hoover, who knows that 'the genius of the bomb is printed not only in its physics of particles and rays but in the occasion it creates for new secrets . . .'

The novel continues to move in this way, in fragments on a large and small scale, that together make up a picture of American life, and DeLillo is as gifted at evoking the big sweeps of history – the atomic bomb, the Cold War, Hoover, Vietnam, Nixon, the rise of the electronic media ('real' death on TV), graffiti art – as he is at conjuring the warmth and minutiae of daily life, conversations, marriages, lonely drives through the desert, sex, rooftop parties, children's play. The novel is composed of six parts with a prologue and an epilogue, and threaded through it is the complex, troubled life of Nick Shay, baseball-obsessed one-time lover of artist Klara Sax, now married to Marian. He first appears at fifty-seven years old, driving a Lexus through the desert – 'Heat shimmer rising on empty flats' – and the novel spirals back into his life to his child-hood in an Italian neighbourhood in the Bronx with his mother, Rosemary, and brother, Matt, once a brilliant chess player who now works underground in a concrete bunker in the desert doing classified weapons work. Nick's father has disappeared; he 'went out to get a pack of cigarettes and never came back'. DeLillo lovingly evokes the lives of Nick, his wife Marian, and brother, Matt, and in one of the novel's highlights ('Cocksucker Blues, Summer 1974', named after the Robert Frank 16mm film of the 1972 Rolling Stones tour of America) he tells of one halcyon New York summer from the point of view of Klara Sax: 'It was the rooftop summer, drinks or dinner, a wedged garden with a wrought iron table . . . This was Klara Sax's summer at the roofline. She found a hidden city above the grid of fever streets.'

DeLillo's world is predominately urban, and he writes about modern life in cities with nervy insight and wry humour: Nick's children are 'grown up people now with a computer after all, with rotating media shelves and a baby on the way and a bumper sticker (this was my son) that read *Going Nowhere Fast*'. Under DeLillo's attentive gaze, the most fleeting of details, the most material of things, can take on an almost soulful resonance:

Waste has a solemn aura now, an aspect of untouchability. White containers of plutonium waste with yellow caution tags. Handle carefully. Even the lowest household trash is closely observed. People look at their garbage differently now, seeing every bottle and crushed carton in a planetary context.

Like his protagonist Nick Shay, who notes that 'The Jesuits taught me to examine things for second meanings and deeper connections', DeLillo had a Catholic upbringing, and its language, rituals and symbols influence his writing (high funeral masses are among his 'warmest childhood memories'). Born in 1936 to Italian parents in New York City, DeLillo grew up in the Fordham section of the Bronx, in a mostly Italian-American neighbourhood filled with family and sport, especially baseball, basketball and football. At eighteen, he got a summer job as a playground attendant and spent his days reading William Faulkner and James Joyce, but as a writer he has been more powerfully influenced by New York City, Abstract Expressionism, filmmakers Godard, Fellini and Howard Hawks, and jazz, than by other writers.

After high school, DeLillo went to Fordham College, majoring in communication arts, and then worked in advertising for five years. In 1966, he began writing his first novel, *Americana*, which was published in 1971 and established him as a writer. In 1975, DeLillo married Barbara Bennett, and they lived in Toronto then travelled through Greece, the Middle East and India for three years, which taught him 'how to see and hear all over again'. On his return to the United States in 1982, DeLillo was struck by a new regular feature on the evening news, 'the daily toxic event' (such as an oil spill or gas leak), and, in response, he wrote his award-winning novel *White Noise* (1984). The author of thirteen novels, DeLillo lives in the Bronx.

The London-based writer William Boyd succinctly summed up the achievement of *Underworld*:

In *Underworld* we have a mature and hugely accomplished novelist firing on all cylinders, at the sophisticated height of his multifarious powers. Reading the book is a charged and thrilling aesthetic experience and one remembers gratefully that this is what the novel can do, and indeed does, better than any other art form – it gets the human condition.

61. Waiting for the Barbarians

by

J.M. Coetzee

(1940–)

❦

'I HAVE NEVER SEEN ANYTHING like it: two little discs of glass suspended in front of his eyes in loops of wire. Is he blind? I could understand it if he wanted to hide blind eyes. But he is not blind.' From its disorienting, unsettling opening, never-before-seen sunglasses described as if they're from an alien world, *Waiting for the Barbarians* tells its unnerving, unpredictable, shocking story with the power and relentlessness of a drill driving towards the outer limits of the dark side of the imagination.

Published in 1980, *Waiting for the Barbarians* is South African writer J.M. Coetzee's courageous, devastating portrait of human relations, history and 'Empire'. As writer Nadine Gordimer so accurately observed: 'J.M. Coetzee's vision goes to the nerve-centre of being. What he finds there is more than most people will ever know about themselves.'

Set in an unnamed empire in a frontier town, originally a fort but now an agricultural settlement of around three thousand people, *Waiting for the Barbarians* is narrated by the town's aging, peace-loving magistrate. In the distance beyond the town live the barbarians, who, in the magistrate's long experience, are 'mainly destitute tribespeople with tiny flocks of their own living along the river'. The people of this little microcosm, barbarian and townsfolk alike, happily coexist; there is little crime, no need for a prison – that is, until the arrival of Colonel Joll, the man with the sunglasses. A member of the Third Bureau, the most important division in the Civil Guard, Joll has been sent from the capital to find out 'the truth' – there have been rumours of unrest among the barbarians and Joll will go to any length to find evidence that they are amassing arms. The Empire must take pre-emptive action, 'precautionary measures, for there would certainly be war', he declares.

Having found two dangerous barbarians – an injured boy and his uncle, an old man – drifting round the settlement, the impatient Joll launches a swift, unprovoked raid and fills the town with barbarian prisoners. The impotent magistrate looks on in astonishment as his town is transformed into a prison, as the granary becomes the holding cell.

And then the magistrate notices a wounded barbarian girl who has been blinded under torture, and a peculiar, tentative love affair unfurls between them – which in Colonel Joll's brutal world becomes the key to the magistrate's undoing. Coetzee is a master of the awkward emotions and errant, flickering passions of aging men:

She undresses and lies down, waiting for my inexplicable
attentions. Perhaps I sit beside her stroking her body,
waiting for a flush of blood that never truly comes . . . I have
not entered her . . . Lodging my dry old man's member in
that blood-hot sheath makes me think of acid in milk, ashes
in honey, chalk in bread.

He is also master of the troubled moral ground on which sexual
affairs between people of unequal power are enacted, old and
young, black and white, men and women. With measured assur-
ance, he spins out his webs of relationships, leaving their ambiguity in the air, provocative and irreducible.

The novel's title comes from the poem 'Waiting for the
Barbarians' by the Greek poet Constantine Cavafy, born in
Alexandria, Egypt, in 1863. The poem opens: 'What are we
waiting for, assembled in the forum? / The barbarians are due here
today.' As the poem continues, the town's leaders gather festively,
decked out in scarlet togas, gold and emeralds, waiting to receive
the barbarians. Then at nightfall, in dismay, they return to their
homes. No barbarians have come; it's even rumoured they are no
more. Cavafy's poem concludes with the lines: 'And now, what's
going to happen to us without barbarians? They were, those
people, a kind of solution.' With a steady, penetrating gaze,
Coetzee's fable-like novel of the same name mines the tragic truth
of Cavafy's words. As the magistrate notes: 'In private I observed
that once in every generation, without fail, there is an episode of
hysteria about the barbarians'; while 'One thought alone preoccu-
pies the submerged mind of Empire: how not to end, how not to

die, how to prolong its era. By day it pursues its enemies . . . By night it feeds on images of disaster.'

John Maxwell Coetzee was born in Cape Town, South Africa, in 1940. His mother was a primary-school teacher and his father worked intermittently as an attorney. Coetzee went to a Marist Brothers school and then to the University of Cape Town, graduating over two years with successive honours degrees in English literature (1960) and mathematics (1961). He then moved to England, where he worked as a computer programmer while researching a thesis on Ford Madox Ford. In 1965, he studied at the University of Texas at Austin, where he wrote a dissertation on Samuel Beckett and graduated with a PhD in English, linguistics and Germanic languages. From 1968 to 1971, he was the assistant professor of English at the State University of New York in Buffalo. He returned to South Africa, and from 1972 worked at the University of Cape Town, which he left in 2000.

In 1969, Coetzee began to write fiction and his first novel, *Dusklands*, was published in South Africa in 1974. His second novel, *In the Heart of the Country*, was published in 1977 and won South Africa's major literary award, the CNA Prize. *Waiting for the Barbarians*, published in 1980, was awarded the Geoffrey Faber Memorial Prize, the James Tait Black Memorial Prize and the CNA Prize. Coetzee has won the Booker Prize twice – with his fourth novel, *Life and Times of Michael K* (1983), and *Disgrace* (1999).

Coetzee moved to Adelaide, Australia, in 2002, and holds an honorary position at the University of Adelaide. His novel *Elizabeth Costello* was published in 2003. That same year, Coetzee won the Nobel Prize for Literature. In his presentation speech, the writer Per Wastberg summed up Coetzee's extraordinary literary achievement: 'With intellectual honesty and density of feeling, in a prose of icy precision, you have unveiled the masks of our civilisation and uncovered the topography of evil.'

J.M. COETZEE

- *Don Quixote* by Miguel de Cervantes
- *Robinson Crusoe* by Daniel Defoe
- *Clarissa Harlowe* by Samuel Richardson
- *Tom Jones* by Henry Fielding
- *Madame Bovary* by Gustave Flaubert
- *War and Peace* by Leo Tolstoy
- *Ulysses* by James Joyce
- *The Castle* by Franz Kafka
- *Absalom, Absalom!* by William Faulkner
- *Molloy* by Samuel Beckett

South African writer J.M. Coetzee is the author of ten novels, including *Waiting for the Barbarians* (1980), *Life and Times of Michael K* (1983), *Disgrace* (1999) and *Elizabeth Costello* (2003).

6 2 . *Midnight's Children*
by
SALMAN RUSHDIE
(1 9 4 7 –)

✣

SALMAN RUSHDIE'S SECOND NOVEL, *Midnight's Children*, is a turbulent,
boisterous tale about modern India unleashed by the loquacious
Saleem Sinai, whose lush, exuberant prose pours forth a tangled
web of stories about his own specially marked life, his eccentric
family and friends, the history of India and Pakistan, their gods,
wars, politicians, cities, geography, food –

such an excess of intertwined lives events miracles places
rumours, so dense a commingling of the improbable and the
mundane! I have been a swallower of lives; and to know me,
just the one of me, you'll have to swallow the lot as well.

Fantastic stories flow from Saleem's pen, as he bullies and
excuses and wheedles, digresses, abruptly addressing the reader

or his sulking listener and would-be lover Padma – who is named after a lotus goddess commonly known as 'The One Who Possesses Dung' and is fed up with all Saleem's 'writing-shiting'. His story, recorded in the pickle factory he runs in his beloved Bombay, is told against the clock, urgently, as his thirty-first birthday approaches and his body begins to crumble: 'I must work fast, faster than Scheherazade, if I am to end up meaning – yes, meaning – something.' And threaded throughout is the fierce political and social commentary of this sometime fool of astute insight, inventive language and unforgettable metaphors: 'India – the new myth – a collective fiction in which anything was possible, a fable rivalled only by the two other mighty fantasies: money and God.'

The novel's opening chapter is called 'The Perforated Sheet', after the sheet that played a key role in the marriage of Saleem's grandparents. His grandfather, a doctor, was allowed to examine the body of a young female patient only through the hole in a sheet. Over the months, he pieces together in his mind her whole body from her various parts, and 'This phantasm of a partitioned woman began to haunt him.' As with most other things in this wildly imagined novel, the perforated sheet has a multitude of resonances. It is a brilliant metaphor for India itself, and of the partial view of the world we all have, as well as being emblematic of Rushdie's method of storytelling, which ranges to and fro over his large canvas, sketching in one chunk of the story and then another, in great generous outbursts from his excitable, argumentative, irresistible narrator.

Midnight's Children opens arrestingly with the words: 'I was born in the city of Bombay ... once upon a time. No, that won't do, there's no getting away from the date: I was born in Doctor Narlikar's Nursing Home on August 15th, 1947', at the stroke of midnight. The time and date are significant because they are the precise moment at which India became independent, making Saleem midnight's child and India's twin, fathered by history: 'I became the chosen child of midnight.' In an extraordinary feat of imagination and verbal magic, Rushdie manages to weave together the life of Saleem with the violent and unpredictable histories of India and Pakistan, from the origins of Bombay as a fishing village, the arrival of India's first Muslims, the Amritsar massacre of 1919, the independence of India and the Partition, wars with China and Pakistan, the rise of Indira Gandhi, the formation of Bangladesh, and the Emergency of 1975, which coincides with the birth of Saleem's son – or not-son.

But Saleem's fantastic life-made-in-prose is not the only thing that holds together this spiralling, over-spiced story, for there are other children of midnight. Saleem Sinai was not the only child to be born in the freakish first hour of India's independence – there were a thousand others, all of them endowed with miraculous gifts.

Using his own gift of telepathy, first discovered in a wash-basket, Saleem mentally makes contact with the surviving 581 children in 1957 and builds a forum of the mind, a 'Midnight's Children's Conference', through which he plans to influence the fortunes of India using the children's special powers. But just as the history of India turns violent, so do the telepathic meetings of midnight's children in Saleem's mind: 'my mind, no longer a parliament chamber, became the battleground on which they annihilated me . . .'

In his digressive mode, Saleem doesn't start his story with anything so obvious as his own birth. He begins where his life really began, in Kashmir in 1915, when his European-educated, Muslim grandfather Dr Adaam Aziz hits his nose while attempting to pray. Dr Aziz is 'knocked forever into that middle place, unable to worship a God in whose existence he could not wholly disbelieve' – this inability to disbelieve and India's irrepressible urge to create gods and mythology are among the continuing preoccupations of Rushdie's teeming novel. Two of the novel's key characters, Shiva and Parvati, are named after Indian gods, and their lives resonate with the gods' stories. Parvati even gives birth to Shiva's elephant-eared son, who resembles the goddess Parvati's son, the elephant-headed Ganesh. India's passion for god-making is multicultural, and Romeo and Juliet, Spencer Tracy and Katharine Hepburn are all embraced among its gods and goddesses of love. And, in an aside typical of the novel's provocative charm, a Christian priest, having been instructed by his bishop to tell his Christian Indian parishioners that Jesus is blue (as 'a sort of bridge between the faiths'), explains the colour of Christ: 'Blue . . . All available evidence, my daughter, suggests that Our Lord Christ Jesus was the most beauteous, crystal shade of pale sky blue.'

Rushdie was born Ahmed Salman Rushdie in Bombay (now Mumbai), India, in 1947. The son of a Muslim businessman, by the time he was ten Rushdie knew he wanted to be a writer. At thirteen, he was sent to school in England and then went to the University of Cambridge, where he received an MA in history in

1968. His family moved to Karachi, Pakistan, in 1964, where Rushdie joined them in 1968, but he soon returned to England and worked in London as a copywriter. His first novel, *Grimus*, was published in 1975. His second, *Midnight's Children*, was published in 1981 and caused a sensation, becoming a critical and popular success and attracting the wrath of the Prime Minister of India, Indira Gandhi. It won the Booker Prize in 1981 and was named 'the Booker of Bookers' in 1993 – the best novel to have won the Booker Prize in the award's first twenty-five years.

In 1988, Rushdie's fourth book, *The Satanic Verses*, famously caused such outrage among Muslims for its perceived blasphemy that Muslim leaders in Britain denounced it, there were public demonstrations in Pakistan, and the Ayatollah Ruhollah Khomeini of Iran issued a fatwa, calling for the execution of Rushdie and everyone involved in the book's publication. Rushdie immediately went into hiding, protected by Scotland Yard. He continued to write and publish books, including a book of essays, *Imaginary Homelands* (1991). The fatwa was eventually lifted by the Iranian government in 1998. Rushdie, who has become a celebrity writer, appeared as himself in the book-launch scene of the 2001 film *Bridget Jones's Diary*.

Bibliography

Primary sources

Austen, Jane, *Persuasion*, Penguin, London, 2003

Balzac, Honoré de, *Old Goriot*, trans. Marion Ayton Crawford, Penguin, Harmondsworth, UK, 1983

Barnes, Djuna, *Selected Works of Djuna Barnes*, Faber & Faber, London, 1998

Brontë, Charlotte, *Jane Eyre*, Wordsworth Editions, Ware, UK, 1999

Brontë, Emily, *Wuthering Heights*, Penguin, London, 1985

Bulgakov, Mikhail, *The Master and Margarita*, trans. Michael Glenny, Harvill Press, London, 1996

Camus, Albert, *The Outsider*, trans. Stuart Gilbert, Penguin, London, 1977

Capote, Truman, *A Capote Reader*, Penguin, London, 2002

Cardinal, Marie, *The Words to Say It*, trans. Pat Goodheart, Allen & Unwin, Sydney, 1993

Cervantes, Miguel de, *Don Quixote*, trans. Tobias Smollett, Modern Library, New York, 2001

Chopin, Kate, *The Awakening and Selected Stories*, Penguin, New York, 1984

Coetzee, J.M., *Waiting for the Barbarians*, Vintage, London, 1997

Conrad, Joseph, *Youth/Heart of Darkness/The End of the Tether*, Penguin, London, 1995

Defoe, Daniel, *Robinson Crusoe*, Penguin, Harmondsworth, UK, 1985

DeLillo, Don, *Underworld*, Picador, London, 1998

Dickens, Charles, *Bleak House*, Penguin, Harmondsworth, UK, 1987

Dostoyevsky, Fyodor, *The Idiot*, trans. David Magarshack, Penguin, London, 1986

Eliot, George, *Daniel Deronda*, Penguin, London, 1995

Ellison, Ralph, *Invisible Man*, Penguin, London, 1965

Faulkner, William, *As I Lay Dying*, Vintage, New York, 1990

Fielding, Henry, *Tom Jones*, Penguin, London, 1985

Fitzgerald, F. Scott, *The Great Gatsby*, Penguin, Melbourne, 1974

Flaubert, Gustave, *Madame Bovary*, trans. Alan Russell, Penguin, Harmondsworth, UK, 1981

Forster, E.M., *Howards End*, Penguin, London, 2000

Grass, Günter, *The Tin Drum*, trans. Ralph Manheim, Vintage, London, 1988

Hamsun, Knut, *Pan*, trans. James W. McFarlane, Souvenir Press, London, 1985

Hardy, Thomas, *Jude the Obscure*, Modern Library, New York, 2001

Hawthorne, Nathaniel, *The Marble Faun*, Everyman, London, 1995

Hemingway, Ernest, *The Sun Also Rises*, Scribner, New York, 1954

Hesse, Hermann, *Narcissus and Goldmund*, trans. Ursule Molinaro, Bantam, New York, 1971

Homer, *Iliad*, trans. Robert Fagles, Penguin, New York, 1998

Homer, *Odyssey*, trans. Robert Fagles, Penguin, New York, 1997

James, Henry, *The Wings of the Dove*, Penguin, London, 1980

Joyce, James, *Ulysses*, Penguin, London, 2000

Kafka, Franz, *The Trial*, trans. Idris Parry, Penguin, London, 2000

Kerouac, Jack, *On the Road*, Penguin, London, 2000

Lampedusa, Giuseppe Tomasi di, *The Leopard*, trans. Archibald Colquhoun, Harvill Press, London, 1996

Lawrence, D.H., *Women in Love*, Penguin, Harmondsworth, UK, 1984

Mann, Thomas, *Death in Venice and Other Stories*, trans. David Luke, Vintage, London, 2003

Mansfield, Katherine, *Selected Stories*, Oxford University Press, Oxford, UK, 2002

Márquez, Gabriel García, *One Hundred Years of Solitude*, trans. Gregory Rabassa, Penguin, London, 2000

McCarthy, Cormac, *Blood Meridian: or The Evening Redness in the West*, Picador, London, 1990

McCullers, Carson, *The Member of the Wedding*, Penguin, London, 2001

Melville, Herman, *Moby-Dick*, Barnes & Noble Classics, New York, 2003

Morrison, Toni, *Beloved*, Vintage, London, 1997

Nabokov, Vladimir, *Lolita*, Penguin, London, 1984

Richardson, Henry Handel, *Maurice Guest*, Sun, Melbourne, 1965

Rhys, Jean, *Wide Sargasso Sea*, Penguin, London, 1997

Roth, Joseph, *The Radetzky March*, trans. Joachim Neugroschel, Penguin, London, 1995

Rushdie, Salman, *Midnight's Children*, Vintage, London, 1995

Salinger, J.D., *The Catcher in the Rye*, Penguin, London, 1994

Smart, Elizabeth, *By Grand Central Station I Sat Down and Wept*, Flamingo, London, 1992

Stead, Christina, *For Love Alone*, Imprint, Sydney, 1999

Stendhal, *The Red and the Black*, trans. Catherine Slater, Oxford University Press, Oxford, UK, 1998

Tolstoy, Leo, *War and Peace*, trans. Rosemary Edmonds, Penguin, Harmondsworth, UK, 1985

Undset, Sigrid, *Kristin Lavransdatter*, trans. Charles Archer (Volume I with J.S. Scott), Abacus, London, 1995

Updike, John, *Rabbit, Run*, Andre Deutsch, London, 1972

Virgil, *The Eclogues, Georgics and Aeneid of Virgil*, trans. C. Day Lewis, Oxford University Press, Oxford, UK, 1977

Wharton, Edith, *The Age of Innocence*, Virago, London, 1988

White, Patrick, *The Twyborn Affair*, Vintage, London, 1995

Wolf, Christa, *The Quest for Christa T.*, trans. Christopher Middleton, Virago, London, 1988

Woolf, Virginia, *The Waves*, Penguin, London, London, 2000

Secondary sources

Author's note: In addition to the secondary sources listed below, I have drawn on several of the fine introductions by scholars and noted writers that accompany many of the recent editions of the classic texts featured in this book.

Ackland, Michael, *Henry Handel Richardson: A Life*, Cambridge University Press, Melbourne, 2004

Bowen, Stella, *Drawn from Life: A Memoir*, Pan Macmillan, Sydney, 1999

Caldwell, Wallace Everett & Gyles, Mary Francis, *The Ancient World*, Dryden Press, Hinsdale, IL, 1966

Calvino, Italo, *Why Read the Classics?*, Vintage, London, 2000

Clarke, Gerald, *Capote: A Biography*, Hamilton, London, 1988

Davies, Norman, *Europe: A History*, Pimlico, London, 1997

Dunn, Jane, *Virginia Woolf and Vanessa Bell: A Very Close Conspiracy*, Virago, London, 2000

Gribbin, John, *Science: A History 1543–2001*, Penguin, London, 2003

Incorporated Brontë Society, *Brontë Parsonage Museum*, Brontë Parsonage Museum, Keighley, UK, 1989

Kermode, Frank, *Lawrence*, Fontana, Bungay, UK, 1973

King James Version, Authorized, *Holy Bible*, World Bible Publisher, Iowa Falls, IA

Koval, Ramona, *Tasting Life Twice: Conversations with Remarkable Writers*, ABC Books, Sydney, 2005

Lanahan, Eleanor, *Zelda, An Illustrated Life: The Private World of Zelda Fitzgerald*, Harry N. Abrams, New York, 1996

Lawrence, D.H., *Phoenix I: The Posthumous Papers of D.H. Lawrence*, Penguin, Harmondsworth, UK, 1972

Maddox, Brenda, *Nora: A Biography of Nora Joyce*, Hamish Hamilton, London, 1988

Marr, David, *Patrick White: A Life*, Random House, Sydney, 1991

Moore, Harry T., *The Priest of Love: A Life of D.H. Lawrence*, Penguin, London, 1974

Nafisi, Azar, *Reading Lolita in Tehran: A Memoir in Books*, Hodder Headline, Sydney, 2004

Plath, James (ed.), *Conversations with John Updike*, University Press of Mississippi, Jackson, MS, 1994

Savigneau, Josyane, *Carson McCullers: A Life*, Women's Press, London, 2002

Souhami, Diana, *Selkirk's Island*, Weidenfeld & Nicolson, London, 2001

Taylor-Guthrie, Danille (ed.), *Conversations with Toni Morrison*, University Press of Mississippi, Jackson, MS, 1994

Troyat, Henri, *Tolstoy*, Penguin, Harmondsworth, UK, 1980

Woolf, Virginia, *A Room of One's Own*, Penguin, Harmondsworth, UK, 1945

Electronic texts

'Advice to a Young Writer, Given and Taken: Robert Southey and Charlotte Bronte', www.wmich.edu

Allen, Brooke, 'A Real Inferno: The Life of Christina Stead', www.newcriterion.com

'America in the Gilded Age', http://members.aol.com/profd avidmont/gilded.htm

Athill, Diana, 'For the Love of Jean', http://books.guradian.co.uk

'Beyond Lolita: Rediscovering Nabokov on his Birth Centennial', www.cnn.com

Blackwell, Tom, '1920: Fitzgerald's Own "Paradise"', www.capitalcentury.com

Borger, Julian, 'Sins of the Fathers', http://books.guardian.co.uk

'Conrad in the Congo', http://caxton.stockton.edu

Defoe, Daniel, 'On the Education of Women', http://classiclit. about.com

Encyclopedia Britannica CDRom, International Version, 1999

Gaskell, Elizabeth, *The Life of Charlotte Bronte*, http://classiclit. about. com

Grenier, Cynthia, 'Reading Sigrid Undset', www.catholiceducation .org

Gussow, Mel, 'Master's Apprentices', www.theage.com.au

Harrison, Norman, 'House of Words: Of Lemon Groves, Lawrence and Capote – Fontana Vecchia as Silent Muse', www.pif magazine. com

http://academic.brooklyn.cuny.edu

http://bookfinder4u.com

http://members.tripod.com

http://nobelprize.org

http.pers-www.wlv.ac.uk

James, Henry, 'Preface to *The Wings of the Dove*', www.online-literature.com

Jong, Erica, 'Fiction Victim', www.salon.com/sept97

Kapp, Isa, 'Toujours Normandy – and Gustave Flaubert', www.worldandi.com

Keim, Albert & Lumet, Louis, *Honore de Balzac*, http://etext. library.adelaide.edu.au

Larsen, Lars Frode, 'Knut Hamsun', http://odin.dep.no

Locke, Alain, 'Forward [sic] to *The New Negro: An Interpretation*', www.yale.edu

'Marital Tragedy' (review of *The Sun Also Rises*, 31 October 1926), www.nytimes.com

Paton Walsh, Nick, 'Devil to Pay Over Film of Bulgakov's Novel', http://books.guardian.co.uk

Prague Writers' Festival, 14th, www.pwf.pragonet.cz

'Ralph Waldo Ellison: Biographical Sketch (1914–1968)', nathanielturner.com/ralphellison2.htm

The Victorian Web, www.victorianweb.org

Watson, Philip, 'Bloom or Bust', http://film.guardian.co.uk

Whitman, Alden, 'Vladimir Nabokov, Author of *Lolita* and *Ada* is Dead', www.nytimes.com

Wolf, Christa, *Ein Tag im Jahr* [*One Day a Year*]: 1960–2000, www.randomhouse.de

www.biblion.com/litweb/biogs

www.classicreader.com

www.dublintourist.com

www.gardenvisit.com

www.kafka-franz.com

www.mahatma.org.in

www.melville.com

www.meta-religion.com

www.newyorker.com/critics/books

www.nzedge.com/heroes/mansfield

www.pemberley.com/janeinfo

www.turnerclassicmovies.com

www.yale.edu/hardysoc

ACKNOWLEDGEMENTS

My thanks go to the following people:

To Michael Hill, for everything.

To my friend Kathy Mossop, who first asked me to write about classics for *Good Reading* magazine.

To Jane Palfreyman, a great friend and truly inspiring publisher.

To Jo Butler, for her attentive and thoughtful editing; and to Jon Gibbs and all at Random House.

To all those writers and others who so generously responded to my invitation to contribute lists of up to ten of their favourite classic novels for this book.

To the friends whose talk about books has stimulated me over the years, especially Felicity Howell, Luke Davies, Georgia Blain, Gaby Naher, Sophie Cunningham, Jane Messer, James Bradley, Laura Paterson and Mandy Sayer.

And to Jackson and Scarlet Hill, who make my days.